Digital Government at Work

Digital Government at Work

A Social Informatics Perspective

Ian McLoughlin and Rob Wilson
with Mike Martin

OXFORD
UNIVERSITY PRESS

OXFORD
UNIVERSITY PRESS

Great Clarendon Street, Oxford, OX2 6DP,
United Kingdom

Oxford University Press is a department of the University of Oxford.
It furthers the University's objective of excellence in research, scholarship,
and education by publishing worldwide. Oxford is a registered trade mark of
Oxford University Press in the Uk and in certain other countries

© Ian McLoughlin and Rob Wilson 2013

The moral rights of the authors have been asserted

First Edition published in 2013

Impression: 1

British Library Cataloguing in Publication Data
Data available

Library of Congress Cataloging in Publication Data
Data available

ISBN 978-0-19-955772-1

Printed and bound in Great Britain by
CPI Group (UK) Ltd, Croydon, CR0 4YY

Links to third party websites are provided by Oxford in good faith and for
information only. Oxford disclaims any responsibility for the materials
contained in any third party website referenced in this work.

For our Spouses and Families

Preface

This book takes an essentially social scientific stance as befits the expertise of the principal authors and its target audience. However, the story it presents and analyses has been the outcome of a truly multi-disciplinary engagement beyond the normal boundaries of social science. For me, trained as a hardware designer in electronics, the work on which this book is based was the culmination of a long journey. I spent my early career developing speech technologies and tools for the analysis of human factors in the ICL Systems Strategy Centre at Stevenage. I was then privileged to be associated with a long series of national and European collaborative research projects that contributed to the invention and development of, amongst other things, distributed systems architectures.

Next, by chance, I was parachuted into the world of telecommunications. This was a deeply shocking experience. They seemed to use the same technologies and terminologies as we IT folk did but they were completely different, to the point of alienation, in both the detail of their engineering practice and the business environment in which they operated. It took me quite a time to begin to understand and appreciate the differences between our applications and their services and to learn to work with them, at a time when the technological world was changing profoundly with deregulation and the emergence of the internet and these very distinctions were undergoing a complete transformation.

In the next phase of my career, in the Centre for Software Reliability at Newcastle University, I seemed to spend most of my time in 'forensic' work, trying to understand why things go so horribly wrong so often in the world of big ICT projects, in particular in the public sector. It was at this stage that seeds sown in the distributed systems architecture projects of the 1980s started to develop. I began to recognize the need to be as serious and rigorous about the intentional or 'conversational' aspects of systems as we were about the physical aspects of function, capability, and capacity. Roles and responsibilities had to become first-class concepts in the architectural discourse or we would continue to make the same mistakes.

Two things then happened in close succession which profoundly changed things. The first was being appointed the technical director of the regional health record development project mentioned in Chapter 3, having had no previous contact with clinical informatics or the public sector. The second was the funding of the AMASE project (outlined in the Appendix) and the fortuitous option of it being hosted at Newcastle University in a social science oriented business school rather than in a school of computing science. From this the collaboration with Ian, Rob, and colleagues, and the struggle to make sense of each other and of the world of public service practice, began.

Usually, the presenting problem involved partnership formation and the building of trust and understanding in the context of the creation of 'systems of care'—a term which is, ultimately, an oxymoron. And faced with these problems, and attempting to adopt the role of honest, disinterested, and informed technologist and systems architect, I was forced to come to the conclusion that the marvellous edifice of rational systems design, which had been the core of my career and interests all my professional life, was a significant part of the problem rather than the source of the solution. This conclusion was, of course, strongly reinforced by my critical social science colleagues! This challenge and dilemma has forced me to delve deeper and deeper into a wide range of literatures in the search for useful meta-theory but I remain an engineer who wants to make better things and to make things better. In social informatics, being critical is not enough. The aim of this book is to make a better mistake than this.

Mike Martin

Acknowledgements

This book has its origins in an over-a-decade-long journey that started at the University of Newcastle upon Tyne in the late 1990s. The genesis of this enterprise lay in what later became known as 'the full Mike'. This was a lengthy, interesting, and seemingly never to be comprehended mother of all power point presentations on the nature of things socio-technical by Mike Martin—whose contribution to the research and many of the ideas behind this book we gratefully acknowledge.

For much of the time the main vehicle for our endeavours has been the Newcastle University Centre for Social and Business Informatics (SBI). Formed in 1999, this grew into a fully fledged University research centre and in later life has become part of what is now KITE, the Centre for Knowledge, Innovation, Technology and Enterprise. Over the years, research grants, projects, and colleagues have come and gone. Given the collective efforts involved, it is more than appropriate to recognize the numerous other colleagues and research partners who have also contributed to both the development of our ideas and the research findings that we report.

First and foremost, we are hugely indebted to John Dobson, James Cornford, and, last but not least, Roger Vaughan. We owe a special debt to many others as well including, in no particular order, Ros Strens, Sue Baines, Bridgette Wessels, Elaine Adam, Sarah Walsh, Neil Pollock, Sarah Skerratt, Paul Richter, Con Crawford, David Wright, Bob Malcolm, Greg Maniatopoulos, Giampaulo 'Monty' Montilletti, James Carr, Pat Gannon-Leary, Lynne Humphrey, Helen Limon, Bob Sugden, Ranald Richardson, Andy Gillespie, Judy Richards, Vicki Belt, Dave Preece, Linda McGuire, Karin Garrety, Richard Badham, Larry Stillman, Mario Bonatti, Nick Booth, and Neil Jenkings.

Thanks are also due to the UK Engineering and Physical Sciences Research Council (EPSRC), UK Office of the Deputy Prime Minister (ODPM)—now Department of Local Government and Communities—and European Commission (EC) and the many other sponsoring and partner organizations, managers, technology suppliers, professionals,

and services users who worked with us on various parts of the research programme. Ultimately, of course, the views presented are our own take on a long collective experience and we exonerate all of the above from any blame with regard to mistakes, misinterpretations, and any other failings of the text.

The writing of this book has been undertaken at opposite ends of the globe as Ian relishes the Melbourne lifestyle and Rob and Mike continue to live out the 'Geordie dream'. Our interactions in completing the text have been aided in various ways by both Monash and Newcastle Universities for which we express our gratitude. Finally, of course, we would like to acknowledge the help and support of our nearest and dearest—Jane, Ellen, Marie, Patrick, Lou, James, Alistair, Fleur and Bernadette, Marie-Louise and Paul—none of whom has been neglected during the writing of this book. This in part explains why it has taken rather longer than expected to complete! A very final thanks then to our Commissioning Editors, especially Emma Booth, for their patience and forbearance.

Ian McLoughlin, Rob Wilson, and Mike Martin

We are grateful for permission to reproduce the following:

Cambridge University Press for:
Figures 0.1, 0.2, and 8.4 from R. G. Wilson, M. J. Martin, S. Walsh, and P. Richter, 'Re-Mixing the Digital Economies of Care in the Voluntary and Community Sector (VCS): Governing Identity and Information Sharing in the Mixed Economy of Care for Children and Young People', *Social Policy and Society*, 10/3 (2011): 379–91.

Figure 1.2 from J. Hartley, 'The Innovation Landscape the Public Service Organizations', in J. Hartley, C. Donaldson, C. Skelcher, and M. Wallace (eds), *Managing to Improve Public Services* (Cambridge University Press, 2008), 197–216.

Figure 5.3 from P. Richter and J. R. Cornford, 'Customer Relationship Management and Citizenship: Technologies and Identities in Public Services', *Social Policy and Society*, 7/2 (2008), 211–20.

Elsevier for:
Figure 1.1 from K. Layne and J. Lee, 'Developing Fully Functional e-Government: A Four Stage Model', *Government Information Quarterly*, 18 (2001), 122–36.

Oxford University Press for:
Figures 2.1, 2.2, and 2.3 from R. Badham, 'Technology and the Transformation of Work', in S. Ackroyd, R. Batt, P. Thompson, and P. Tolbert (eds), *The Oxford Handbook of Work and Organization* (Oxford: Oxford University Press, 2005), 115–37.

Taylor & Francis for:
Figures 4.1 and 4.2 from S. Walsh, R. Wilson, S. Baines, and M. Martin, '"You're Just Treating us as Informants!" Roles, Responsibilities and Relationships in the Production of Children's Services Directories', *Local Government Studies*, 38/6 (2012), 1–20.

Contents

Contents

List of Tables

List of Figures

List of Boxes

Abbreviations

AGIMO	Australian Government Information Management Office
AMA	Australian Medical Association
AMASE	Advanced Multi-Agency Service Environment
ANAO	Australian National Audit Office
APC	Australian Productivity Commission
ATO	Australian Tax Office
B2B	Business to Business
CAF	Common Assessment Framework
COAG	Council of Australian Governments
CSIR	Council for Scientific and Industrial Research (South Africa)
EC	Commission of the European Community
EU	European Union
EHR	Electronic Health Record
ERDIP	Electronic Record Development And Implementation Program
ERP	Enterprise Resource Planning
FAME	FrAmework for Multi-agency Environments
G2B	Government to Business
G2C	Government to Citizen
G2G	Government to Government
GFC	Global Financial Crisis
IfSC	Information for Social Care
IG	Infomation Government
IRT	Information, Referral, and Tracking
JUG	Joined-Up Government
LSP	Local Service Provider
NAO	National Audit Office
NBN	National Broadband Network (Australia)
NEHTA	National e-Health Transition Authority
NHIMAC	National Health Information Management Advisory Council
NHS	National Health Service
NESTA	National Endowment for Science, Technology and the Arts
NPfIT	National Programme for Information Technology

Abbreviations

ODPM	Office of the Deputy Prime Minister
OECD	Organization for Economic Cooperation and Development
OLDES	Older Peoples E-Services @ Home
PCEHR	Personally Controlled Electronic Health Record
PD	Participatory Design
PwC	Pricewaterhouse Coopers
RFA	Requirements for Accreditation
RSCC	Regional Smart Card Consortium
SAP	Single Assessment Process
SEHR	Shareable Electronic Health Records
SPOT	Single Point of Truth
UN	United Nations
VESCR	Virtual Electronic Social Care Record
WHO	World Health Organization

Introduction

Mrs Cannybody's Dilemma[1]

'Mary' is 17 years old and is a single mother with a six-month-old baby. She has been attending her local Sure Start centre located in a provincial region of England. The UK Government established Sure Start in 1998 with the aim of 'giving children the best possible start in life' and assisting in reducing child poverty. The centres are places where the parents of babies and toddlers in particular can find support, advice, and a range of health, social, educational, and other services. Local government authorities in the UK have a statutory responsibility to provide services for children, along with many other public services, in their locality. In the region where Mary lives, the authority has commissioned a national charity concerned with the interests of children and young people—*The Charity*—to manage and deliver the Sure Start project. The commissioning of organizations from the voluntary and community sector to deliver services in this way has been a growing trend in the UK, not least because of the perceived 'special relationship' that organizations like *The Charity* have with their clients compared to statutory public agencies. The centre which Mary is attending is located in a city in the north of the region and is being managed, on a temporary basis, by a Mrs Cannybody.

In the same region, *The Charity* also delivers counselling, therapy, and support services to children and young people who have suffered sexual abuse or exploitation. This is a specialized service, whose availability is not widely publicized and to which professional practitioners refer clients. *The Charity* also works with the police, probation service, courts, and social services. For example, in another city in the south of the region, *The Charity* is involved in a programme of initiatives to control prostitution—seen as a particular problem in that locality. Here, a year previously, a police-led action closed down a prostitution

---

1 This case is based on real events. It is drawn from Martin (2007) and Wilson *et al.* (2010).

ring. The pimp, 'Derek', who ran the ring, was prosecuted and sent to prison. Mary was one of Derek's prostitutes. As part of a 'Prostitution Response Programme', initiatives were taken by *The Charity* to support the then-pregnant Mary. She was relocated from the southern city to the northern city in the region and a number of services were activated to help her rehabilitate herself and build a new life. Mary had made it clear that she wanted to put her previous experiences behind her but that she was only prepared to discuss these with her individual counsellor at *The Charity*'s specialist support service.

Mrs Cannybody is not a qualified social worker but is highly experienced, having been involved in voluntary and contract social work for *The Charity* for many years. Recently she has noticed that Mary has become withdrawn and unhappy. She cannot, however, get Mary to discuss her problems and, as a result, is concerned about her wellbeing. Of course neither Mrs Cannybody nor anybody else in the *Sure Start* centre is aware that Mary is also attending sessions at *The Charity*'s counselling service. Meanwhile, Derek had been released on parole, after serving twelve months, on condition that he attended one-on-one and group counselling sessions for ex-abusers. *The Charity*'s office in the city where the prostitution ring was based also runs these sessions. The relationship between Derek and his ex-abuser counsellor is intended to be therapeutic and supportive and not one of supervision and control. Whilst in prison, Derek had told his counsellor that he had become a 'born-again Christian'. He also claimed to be the father of Mary's child and said that he now wants to 'do the right thing by her' and support both her and the child.

Digital Technology in Public Services

Until relatively recently information and communication technologies (ICTs) have rarely figured in discussions and literature concerning the nature and development of public organizations and the delivery of public services (Dunleavy *et al.*, 2006: 2–3). Whilst computers have been a core part of government operation since the 1950s, their impact was largely internal (Margetts, 2006). However, the development of the internet and related digital technologies has profoundly changed this. Over the past ten or so years the core operations of government and public service agencies have become increasingly dependent upon the efficient operation of networked digital technologies and the effective functioning of associated management and organizational arrangements (Dunleavy *et al.*, 2006: 10). Governments are now able, for example, to distribute information to the wider society in new ways and also to capture and store much more information about citizens and the effectiveness of the services they receive (Margetts, 2006: 262). In keeping with such developments, organizations like *The Charity* has been under increasing pressure to provide detailed reporting to both local and central government to conform to policy requirements for better information on the services that are funded. This has included, for example, providing information to local government on the services delivered, their activities, costs, and outcomes to enable more 'joined-up' delivery between different levels of government. In addition (during the early 2000s) the UK Government proposed a new national database of all children under the age of 18 in England (see Chapter 4). This required that voluntary organizations report information to it as well. The implications of these requirements for service providers were significant, often raising issues of how to gather and provide aggregate data across their local, regional, and national operations to meet these and other reporting requirements.

In the case of *The Charity* the response to this issue was a proposal by the head of the information technology department to procure and deploy a 'data warehouse'—a concept common in the private sector—as part of a new 'enterprise information architecture'. This would replace existing computerized but fragmented local case management and record systems. All information pertaining to Mary and Derek's cases, and all other cases with which *The Charity* was involved, would instead be captured, cleansed, and integrated into a warehouse where data could then be accessed by all of the different support services. The warehouse would therefore provide the basis for the interrogation and analysis required to satisfy the new external reporting requirements and a more effective means of sharing information across *The Charity*'s many service operations and projects. The basic outline of the proposed scheme, along with the various envisaged relationships between front-line practitioners and their clients, is illustrated schematically in Figure 0.1.

Mrs Cannybody's dilemma is born of an all too common 'wicked problem' of providing care services in situations of complex need on the front line of public service delivery. It revolves around her concern for Mary's well-being and the question of whether anyone else in *The Charity* might have information that they could share and which might have a bearing on this concern? The relationships in which Mary's case is embedded are complex. Of the three case workers within *The Charity*, two have a relationship with Mary—Mrs Cannybody herself and Mary's specialist support counsellor. A third case worker, the

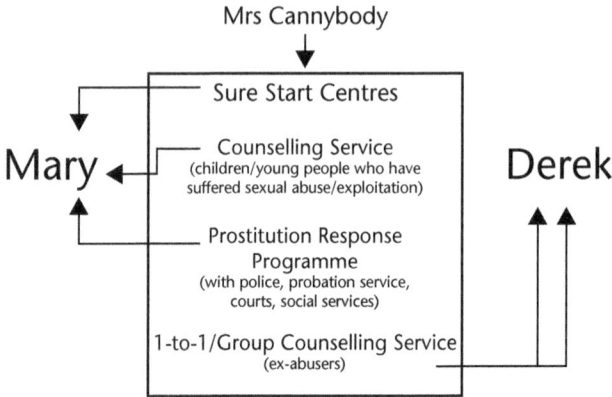

Figure 0.1 The Data Warehouse Proposal

Source: Wilson *et al.* (2011). Reprinted with permission of Cambridge University Press.

counsellor for ex-abusers, has a relationship with Derek. In addition, Derek's record may have a historical, indirect link to Mary, for example via police records concerning the prostitution ring or through the birth record of Mary's child.

Mrs Cannybody, of course, does not know any of this and neither do any of the other participants have the full picture or 'view' of the client and their situation. As it happens, some information is available to her via existing case management and record systems. However, it is very difficult to match cases using the systems because the unique identifiers of each individual client are specific to the service or project within which the case has arisen (indicated by the horizontal lines between the different services in Figure 0.2). Therefore, unless Mrs Cannybody knows people in that other service or works across services within the organization, joining up this information is very difficult. This of course has some significant merits, in that these internal barriers to sharing information do serve by default to protect the wishes of clients such as Mary where they wish to keep certain matters confidential. It is in this context, given her concerns over Mary's well-being, that Mrs Cannybody had to work out how best to seek more information.

In principle the proposed data warehouse could provide Mrs Cannybody with a more systematic way of exploring these concerns. However, a move towards a more integrated information system solution of this type also poses new issues concerning the sharing of

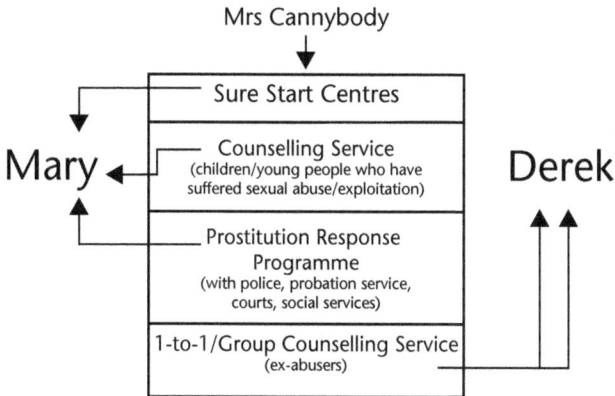

Figure 0.2 Existing Case Management and Record System

Source: Wilson *et al.* (2011). Reprinted with permission of Cambridge University Press..

information in complex circumstances such as those in Mary's case. In particular, the barriers that may have by default offered some protection to clients like Mary in the past would be removed. How, in a more 'disintermediated' and digitalized environment, would the necessary information—whatever that may be—get shared at the right time, with the right consents, with the right people for the right reasons? In a digitalized world, we would suggest, Mrs Cannybody's dilemma takes on a further and more profound dimension. How for example, could she be sure that the acts of accessing information in the data warehouse and sharing it with other colleagues and agencies, and their subsequent use of it, would be consistent with the wishes of the client?

The Digital Government Phenomenon

It is issues such as these and the interlocking informational and organizational challenges that lie behind them that provide the focus for this book. The point of the data warehouse for *The Charity* was to respond, as many public service providers have been challenged to do, to the need to modernize the way they gather and report information on the one hand and to share information in the practice of front-line service delivery on the other—in both instances, with the aim of providing a more customized and effective service for clients. For some observers, such developments are seen positively and as being at the heart of attempts to transform the delivery of public services through e-enabling their delivery and the digitalization of information. Others take an opposite and negative view and see the 'disintermediation' that this implies—that is, the substitution of digital means for traditional face-to-face and paper-based service delivery—as posing a threat to privacy and civil liberties and as breaking the essential 'subjective relationship' between service providers and those for whom services are being provided. In this book we argue that both of these views are ultimately limiting.

Governments across the globe increasingly view digital technologies as the primary means through which public services and other core activities of government can be transformed. Terms such as 'electronic' or 'e-government', 'the virtual state', and 'digital government' have emerged as ways in which these developments might be captured, and the claimed improvement they offer over bureaucratic, paper-based, and face-to-face organizational forms and practices inferred. We will use the term digital government to refer to the phenomenon in general, although from time to time, to save repetition in the text, we shall also use the terms e-government and e-enabled services.

The idea of the e-enablement of government and public service delivery has its origins in the Clinton–Gore Administration (1993–2001) in the USA (Lips, 2008). In one of the first uses of the term 'electronic government' (Hughes, 2008), the Clinton–Gore vision was of a 're-invention' of government as a 'virtual state' in which 'smart cards' loaded with information about the citizen holder and other technologies would be used to replace paper-based systems and be 'fairer, more secure' and 'more responsive to the customer' (Gore, 1993: 114). Such virtual systems would operate in parallel to what Vice-President Gore referred to as the emerging 'information super-highway' constituted by the networking of computers that we now commonly refer to as the world wide web and the internet. As a result of this super-highway, 'the interaction between government and citizens would be transformed with the goal to provide better access to government services' (Lips, 2001: 76).

The metaphor of the 'super-highway' has long since been surpassed and in the ensuing twenty years the meanings and possibilities associated with 'the internet' have both expanded and been enhanced. For example, the idea of the internet as both an interactive and open medium, through which users can share information and knowledge and collaborate to develop new technological, social, and cultural innovations, is currently the focus of much attention. In the arena of digital government this is claimed to be supporting a 'second wave' (Dunleavy and Margetts, 2010) of transformation. Innovations cited here include the much-vaunted 'Web 2.0 Government' (where citizens use social net-working and related technologies to participate in the design of their own digital content); open data and 'citizen sourcing' (where governments make available data through websites for citizens and others to use, for example to develop new social innovations); and 'the internet of things' (enabled by ambient computer and so-called 'media-info-com' devices which permit material objects to have a virtual presence and communicate and share information about their status and use on the internet with 'zero touch' by humans). All of the above can be supported, it is claimed, by 'government in the cloud' (the use of flexible third-party-provided shared computing resources and services) and the spread of super-fast broadband networks. Indeed, some claim that innovations in virtual and networked forms of service delivery will finally signal the end of public bureaucracies and their monopoly on the delivery of public services (see e.g. Benkler, 2006; Comode and Krishanmurthy, 2008; Eggers and Goldsmith, 2008; Lukensmeyer and Torres, 2008; Codagnone and Osimo, 2010; Deloitte, 2011).

However, in one of the earliest and most influential in-depth academic studies of initial attempts in the USA to 'build the virtual state', Jane Fountain (2001) found that such developments were in no way inevitable. In fundamental ways, she argued, the outcomes of the adoption of digital technologies in public services are conditioned by the way public managers 'enact' these possibilities in particular organizational and institutional circumstances. In countries such as the UK, for example, it has been noted that attempts to use new digital technologies and the internet to 'e-enable' services have been conducted in the wider context of the management and institutional paradigm of so-called New Public Management (NPM). NPM places a strong emphasis on the marketization of public services, reducing the size of the state, and improving the efficiency of public agencies and service delivery. Some have argued that NPM has been a major constraint on the development of the 'virtual state' (see e.g. Pollitt, 2003; Alford and Hughes, 2008; Harris *et al.*, 2011). Whether entirely down to NPM or not, typically it seems digital government projects exhibit relatively high rates of project cancellation, whilst a significant proportion are completed over budget, late, or are not fully functional (Heeks, 2006; Foley and Alfonso, 2009; Margetts, 2006). One UK Government report concurred in the following fashion, 'Government IT projects have too often missed delivery dates, run over budget or failed to fulfil requirements' (Cabinet Office, 2000*b*: 4). Many commentators also point to the high levels of investment involved but the low take-up by their intended users and the emergence of new risks and costs such as data breaches and the threat to citizen privacy and civil liberties (see e.g. Heeks, 2005, 2006; Margetts, 2006; *The Economist*, 2008; Lips, 2008).

Such critiques notwithstanding, other researchers have remained optimistic concerning the possible emergence of what they term a 'new era of digital governance' (Dunleavy *et al.*, 2006; Dunleavy and Margetts, 2010). They claim an emerging fragmentation, erosion, and at least partial collapse of the existing dominant NPM reform paradigm. Indeed, it is argued that this is now sufficiently established to permit the emergence of new and alternative paradigms. These are more facilitative of the requirements for 'a range of information technology-centered changes, involving the reintegration of functions into the governmental sphere, adopting holistic and needs-oriented structures and progressive digitalization of administrative processes' (Margetts, 2006: 255).

Digital Government: A Social Informatics Perspective

How, in the light of a decade and half of experience of digital government are we to explore, make sense of, and evaluate such competing claims? Two of the most influential scholars in the field of public management have recently suggested that 'joining-up' the hitherto disparate disciplinary worlds of public management and information technology is a 'key challenge for contemporary study' in addressing such questions (Hood and Margetts, 2007: 177). In a similar vein, our own starting point rests on the assumption that technology-related organizational change must be understood as a socio-technical process through which context-specific outcomes are shaped (Clark *et al.*, 1988; McLoughlin and Clark, 1994; McLoughlin, 1999; McLoughlin and Badham, 2005). When applied specifically to the relationship between information technology and organizational change this perspective is strongly related to the field of organizational and social informatics (henceforth 'social informatics' for short).

The late Robert Kling, one of the founders of this approach, defined social informatics as 'the interdisciplinary study of the design, uses and consequences of ICTs that takes into account their interaction with institutional and cultural contexts' (Kling *et al.*, 2000: 15). One consequence is a specific focus on the users of new technologies and the context in which that use takes place. A second is that the development of digital technologies is not dictated solely by a technological logic. Rather this is inevitably entwined with a social one or, as Brown and Duguid (2000) put it, despite often being portrayed and thought of differently, information has a 'social life'. A third is that, whatever the creative possibilities enabled by digital technology, these are frequently denied or limited by existing ways of making sense of things, be these dominant technological, managerial, or cultural paradigms or a combination of all three (McLoughlin, 1999). Finally, a prerequisite to a social informatics perspective is an 'analytical scepticism' (Woolgar, 2002) towards grand narratives and taken-for-granted assumptions about the capabilities of digital technologies and 'definitive accounts' about their likely impact or effects on the social world.

We suggest that the phenomenon of digital government provides a new and highly fruitful arena in which to apply a social informatics perspective and to develop new insights. First, digital government projects represent one of the largest and most significant areas of public investment in information technologies at the organizational, sectoral, or even national level. These investments are based on a sometimes extreme faith in, if not 'pathological enthusiasm' about, the capacity and capability of digital technologies and their capacity to transform government (Gauld and Goldfinch, 2006). Second, many of the technological solutions being applied have been developed in the private sector, and whilst in many instances successful in transforming both the business world and the customer experience (see e.g. Li, 2007), their seamless translation into the rather different social organizational and institutional context of public service and government presents a new and fundamental challenge.

Third, in contrast to the private realm, the nature of innovation in public service is not well understood or researched (Hartley, 2008). This suggests that e-commerce 'products' (and their associated system architectures, business models and processes, project and change management methods), which may work well in a private sector context, may not be so relevant or effective in the public realm where innovation will also need to embrace changes in roles, relationships, and responsibilities both within and across a range of service providing agencies (Martin, 2013). Finally, and following from this, the consequences of the large-scale deployment and adoption of digital technologies and their interaction with the institutional and cultural context of public service and administration are likely to highlight in fundamental ways new and novel relationships between technology and organization. In turn this calls for new concepts and approaches for understanding and influencing the unfolding events, trends, and developments as public agencies, managers, professionals, and others grapple with what Fountain (2001) terms the 'puzzles' posed by the digital age.

In this book we argue that a social informatics perspective provides the basis for such a new conceptualization of the relationship between technological and organizational change in the context of digital government. This is necessary both for our understanding of the fate of existing attempts through policy and practice to transform the delivery of public services using digital technologies and, most importantly, the identification of new ways in which digital government might be made to work better. We suggest that our approach has the potential to move both theory and practice beyond the polarized positions of optimism/pessimism and opportunity/threat that follow from adopting, without due analysis, simple dichotomies such as 'virtual versus real' and 'digital versus paper'. Critically, it also places the 'denizens of communities' (Lefevre, 1991) in the realm of public service delivery—be they engaged in commissioning, delivery, or service use (collectively 'the users')—and their needs and requirements at the centre of innovation in both technology and services.

Research Focus and Book Outline

This book reflects the findings of a substantial programme of original public-funded research conducted by the authors and colleagues since the late 1990s. The research programme embraced a wide variety of digital government projects concerned with innovation and improvement in the delivery of services. As such, we were not concerned with digital government as a means of directly improving the democratic or policy-making processes (e.g. through e-voting or on-line petitioning, and the like). Important though these dimensions are, services and their delivery are the most 'visible' aspect of government and the aspect citizens 'care about the most' (6 et al., 2002: 140). Arguably, there are even more opportunities to strengthen the democratic process by deploying digital technology to empower both service providers and users. Equally, of course, digital technology might be deployed in ways which pose a threat to democracy by threatening the autonomy and discretion of service providers, and the privacy and civil liberties of citizens as service users.

In exploring such issues, the services we examined covered attempts to 'join up' or integrate health and social services for children and young people, adults, and older people. In many instances the services concerned addressed complex care needs within these broader populations, such as children with disabilities or 'vulnerable' older people living alone at home. Our studies also focused on collaborative partnerships with the private sector in the provision of a mix of integrated services such as the procurement of software systems, the application of 'smart cards', and the design and development of 'virtual' tele-care platforms. Our studies focused on the specific issues of service delivery at the local level and on local government authorities, in particular, as the pivotal agency in managing the processes of technological and organizational change required to coordinate and join up service delivery. The research was conducted mainly in the UK, but has also involved projects in Europe and Australia and was informed by parallel developments in comparable national settings. Further details can be found in the Appendix.

In Chapter 1 we explore digital government and its potential to transform public services. We examine the policy context as it has evolved over the past two decades with a focus on the policy origins of key objectives such as 'joined-up working', 'information sharing', and the 'transformation' of service delivery through greater information system integration. In Chapter 2 we examine what we term the 'three dimensions' (Badham, 2005) of the analysis of 'digital government' and develop an understanding of both the 'user' and 'technology' as co-constructed (Oudshoorn and Pinch, 2003). In Chapter 3 we turn to what many see as the central problematic of digital government— the nature of integration. In information systems terms, integration is typically represented as the linking together of disparate computer systems and databases in some way. In public management, integration has been understood in organizational terms as the means through which more coordinated services and joined-up delivery can be achieved. Chapter 4 focuses on the arena in which these two notions of integration come together, attempts to join up government through information sharing and multi-agency working. In Chapter 5 we explore the issues of information governance and the management of identity that come to the fore when attempts are made to record and share information by digital means. Chapter 6 considers the central role of service providers at the local level—the so-called 'street level bureaucrats'—who are in the 'front line' of attempts to bring about service transformation. Chapter 7 returns to the designer/user issues and considers more closely one of the key arguments of the book. That is, that users—be they citizens or other 'end-users' and front-line service providers—can be a key source for the co-production of innovation in public service delivery.

Chapter 8 draws all of these arguments together and seeks to identify key insights into how digital government can be made to work more effectively in practice.

In keeping with our social informatics perspective, the scope and possibilities for public managers, professionals, and the users and clients of services to configure and shape both services and systems through their own practice are once again stressed. If there is to be a new era of digital government, it is not technology that will drive such innovation but rather the co-production of new configurations, meanings, and actions—what we term a new form of 'architectural discourse'. It is through such a discourse that any new technological and organizational possibilities will be co-constructed and realized. As we will try to show through our original research, the ability to embed this kind of discourse and practice in the trajectory taken by the future evolution of 'digital era governance' is the core issue in the emergence and sustainable development of the digital government phenomenon. Moreover, this is vital if we are to avoid the many mistakes of the past and present.

1

Digital Government and Public Service Innovation

Introduction

Digital technology provides what some see as the basis for transformational change in the way the state operates and public services are delivered and experienced. For some this is leading to a 'virtual state' (Fountain, 2001) and a new 'era of digital governance' (Dunleavy *et al.*, 2006) where public services are e-enabled and available on-line to citizens and other users on a '24/7' basis (Kraemer and King, 2006). Digital technologies have also been seen as the basis of radical or 'disruptive innovation' in public service delivery, overturning existing business and service models and radically changing how services are provided and who provides them (Christensen and Raynor, 2003; Christensen *et al.*, 2009). We begin this chapter by considering what is meant by digital government in more detail. We then turn to identifying the key policy agendas driving digital government and examine some of the key trends in the development and take-up of e-enabled service delivery in the UK and comparable cases elsewhere. Finally, we examine the nature of innovation and digital disruption of public services and the different forms it may take.

What is 'Digital Government'?

Defining social phenomenon is always a fraught business. The fluid and interpretative nature of the social world inevitably means that any attempt to fix the meaning of something runs the risk of bringing clarity at the expense of the exclusion of other aspects. By the same token, prior assumptions can be allowed to shape the perception of something in a particular way that again excludes, wittingly or otherwise, alternative views and interpretations. The debate over the definition of

13

digital or e-government—or to be more precise, the very naming of the phenomenon—is illustrative of this problem.

For example, 'digital' or 'e-' government are examples of a range of terms, 'virtual', 'cyber', 'network', 'tele-', and the like, which appear as an 'epithet applied to various existing activities and social institutions' if not society as a whole (Woolgar, 2002: 3). The 'epithetized phenomenon' is typically used to 'conjure a future consequent upon the effects of electronic technologies':

> While it is often unclear from these labels exactly how the application of the epithet actually modifies the activity/institution in question, a claim to novelty is usually central, especially at the hands of those promoting the new entity. The implication is that something new, different, and (usually) better is happening. (Woolgar, 2002: 3)

We can observe, for example, that the attachment of the e-prefix—e.g. 'e-business' or 'e-commerce'—is now widespread in the private sector and has passed into everyday usage. For proponents, the deployment of similar digital technologies in the public sector is a logical corollary and integral part of the 'modernization' of public agencies in much the same way that the world of commerce is assumed to have been transformed. 'E-government' and associated terms such as 'e-enabled public services', 'e-democracy', provide a means through which new 'virtual' forms of service delivery can be contrasted, to use Woolgar's (2002) terms, with the 'ordinary' or 'real' world of existing bureaucratic forms, and indeed to support claims of improvement upon them.

However, critics would suggest that such epithets place too much emphasis on the way in which, in this instance the 'e-', that is, the technologies of digital government, are autonomously shaping state and public organizations. As Lips and Schuppan note, this albeit dominant view, focuses on the impact of digital technologies on public organizations and institutions rather than on how these technologies are, or perhaps could, be used by such entities (Lips and Schuppan, 2009: 740–1). Other writers, mindful of the problems with the 'e-' prefix, have preferred to use the term 'digital' or 'virtual' in an effort to leave open the idea that the outcomes of technological change are in some way shaped by organizational and other choices and decisions (e.g. Dunleavy *et al.*, 2006; Fountain, 2001). However, these attempted solutions can still be said to retain a seemingly unquestioned notion of the contrast between the virtual and the real or the digital and the paper-based forms of public organizations and the institutions of the state.

At the same time, the use of the term 'government' has also been called into question. The suggestion is that this places too much focus on the existing organizational and institutional arrangements for exercising governance and not enough on emergent forms—such as multi-agency working, partnerships, and other 'network' forms of organizing—which many see as prerequisites of the development of new service models (see e.g. 6 *et al.*, 2002; Klijn, 2002). Taken together, therefore, 'e-' and 'government' could be seen to suggest a definition that refers to the manner in which a given set of technologies with assumed characteristics and capabilities are being used to e-enable an existing set of services and associated organizational and institutional arrangements. In short, not a 'disruptive innovation' at all!

Given these issues, others have sought to place more emphasis on the development of new organizational and institutional arrangements and associated innovations in service provision. It is argued that these should be the starting point for any definition that in turn emphasizes improved forms of governance rather than just the technological improvement of existing service delivery. For example:

> Beyond e-government, the notion of e-governance evokes a tantalizing promise: that fully applying 'e' tools to our institutions and processes of governance will be a transformative process. E-governance holds out possibilities for applying new modes of information exchange, providing integrated and distributive approaches to operations and service delivery and leading democracies to open and participatory systems of policy-making. (Oliver and Sanders, 2004: p. viii)

This also points to a problem with the relationship between e-government and transformation. O'Neill (2009), for example, distinguishes between what she terms 'instrumental' and 'systemic' transformation. The former refers to 'doing the same things differently' whilst the latter points to changes in relationships and behaviours which result in 'doing different things' (O'Neill, 2009: 755).

The Stages of Digital Government

A further feature of attempts to define e-government has been a variety of schemata which purport to show the stages of e-government through which progress to more 'mature' or 'sophisticated' arrangements may be mapped, measured, or evaluated. One approach has been to focus on enabling technological capabilities and capacities such as those embodied in the design and functionality of websites (see e.g. EC, 2001; OECD, 2003). Another has been to examine user needs, government provision of e-services and infrastructure, and user take-up, in order to assess the readiness of global regions or nations to move through different stages of e-government development (e.g. UN, 2008). Whilst varying in their detail, most of these definitions map out a trajectory for evolution through a number of stages—typically four or more. These usually assume an increasing degree of disintermediation of service delivery and integration of underlying technological and organizational arrangements (see e.g. West, 2005: Dunleavy *et al.*, 2006: Layne and Lee, 2001).

In a typical example Layne and Lee (2001) provide a four-stage model (see Figure 1.1). This maps the anticipated evolutionary development of digital government along two dimensions. The first refers to the degree of technological and organizational complexity in modes of service delivery. The second to the degree of integration involved between, on the one hand, vertical (state, regional local levels) and the other horizontal layers (lateral relations between levels) of government. Four developmental stages are identified. First, 'cataloging', where much in the same way that notices are posted on conventional notice boards, digitized information is posted on-line to websites where the supply is essentially one-way with little opportunity for two-way communication with citizens. Second, 'transactions', where some services are made available on-line and citizens and others can begin to interact with government and public agencies, in particular in relation to more transactional relationships such as paying taxes and so forth.

The third and fourth stages are 'vertical integration' and 'horizontal integration'. Here the emphasis is on transforming service delivery rather than just 'automating' and 'digitizing' existing services. Accordingly these stages involve deeper changes in the way government and public service delivery is organized to permit greater coordination between different levels of government on the one hand and different functions on the other. The net effect of greater coordination between agencies at different levels and functions is that citizens see 'government as an integrated information base' (Layne and Lee, 2001: 125). There are also implications for front-line practitioners who, instead of being routine processors of information on bureaucratic 'assembly-lines', become 'overseers' of a fully integrated and automated process (Layne and Lee, 2001: 131).

Similarly, West (2005) identifies a much-cited model of four stages of development: billboard, partial service delivery, portal, and interactive democracy. This schema gives more prominence to the evolving functionality of website interfaces between government and citizens (see West, 2005: 8–12). In the billboard stage—as in the 'catalogue' stage—government websites are deployed to post information about government services. In the second partial service delivery stage

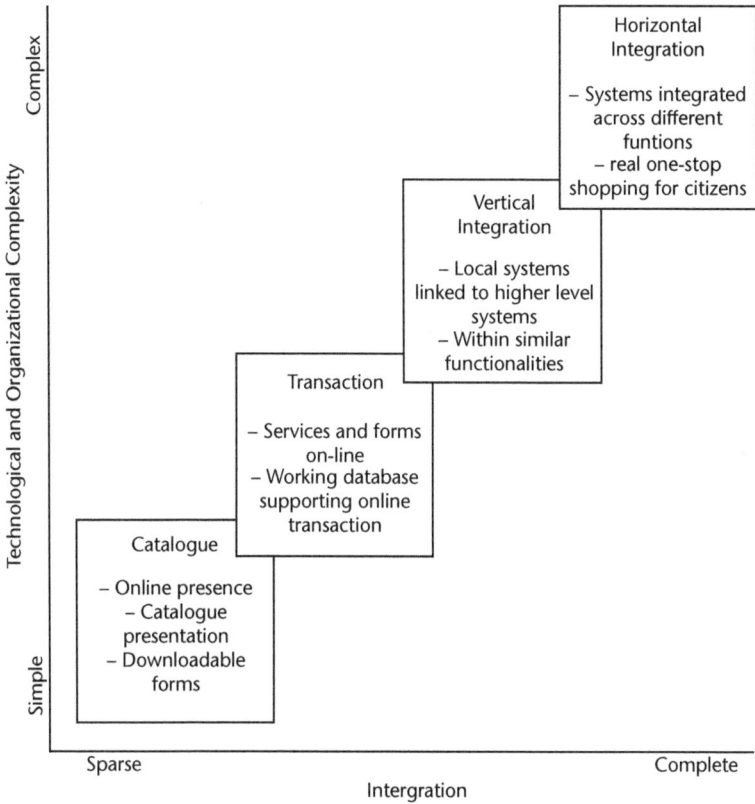

Figure 1.1 Digital Government Maturity Model
Source: Layne and Lee (2001). Reprinted with permission from Elsevier.

more transactional functionality is developed. In the third 'portal' stage, instead of each government department and agency or divisions and departments within agencies, having their own website, a single 'one-stop' point of entry is provided. The fourth stage seeks to move further in this direction by trying to make government and public agencies more responsive to user needs and requirements and also public officials and professionals more accountable to citizens for service delivery.

Of course, passage along such developmental pathways is not necessarily linear and unproblematic and can be expected to vary in different contexts. For example, West (2005) suggests that in some circumstances innovation and change might take place at sufficient pace and with the kind of breadth and depth that it might be regarded as transformational, bringing about forms of 'interactive democracy'. On the other hand, in other cases, progress might occur at a slower pace and in a less sophisticated manner to the portal stage, in what amounts to more 'secular change'. Finally, even more modest developments involving a shift from 'billboard' to 'partial service delivery' would be indicative of more 'incremental change' (West, 2005: 8–11).

Whilst useful in providing a potential way of assessing the progress of digital government we should note at the outset that such schemata have a major flaw. That is, they start from a set of assumptions about technological capability and then define e-government, or its progression, in terms of the capacity and extent to which government and public agencies are able to adopt and to realize these capabilities in practice. In short, they suffer from the 'e-' problem identified above. In particular, models of the evolution of digital government tend to assume innovation follows a linear sequence, that movement through this sequence is indicative of progress in terms of performance and ultimately transformation, and that the determinants are the capacity of public organizations to adopt and use the technologies of e-government in the way that they were intended by designers and developers and now demanded by citizens and other users (Mayer-Schonbergger and Lazer, 2007: 1). It has also been suggested that such models tend to be overly reflective of those thought to signify progress towards e-commerce in the private sector. For example, they place too much stress on the transactional element of citizen interactions with government and on the achievement of efficiency gains. The nature and evolution of innovation and improvement in more complex areas of social need such as social and health care are not fully considered (Codagnone and Osimo, 2010).

The Transformation Agenda: The UK in Comparative Perspective

The building of the 'virtual state' is a global project. Governments in both the developed and developing world have turned their attention to the manner in which digital technologies might assist in achieving policy objectives to reform, modernize, and bring about improvements in government and public services (Foley and Aflonso, 2009). For the governments of developed nations at least, 'the issue is no longer whether government is on-line, but in what form and with what consequences' (Chadwick and May, 2003: 271). Since the onset of the global financial crisis in late 2008, some observers have identified an added impetus to use digital government as a means of cutting public expenditure whilst at the same time improving the provision of public services, thereby offsetting the effects of financial crisis on the public purse (UN, 2010: 44). The most significant example of this is provided by President Obama's 2009 stimulus legislation in the USA (see below).

As such initiatives serve to illustrate, behind the policy rhetoric there 'is a general presumption that the use of ICT in government is beneficial' (Foley and Aflonso, 2009: 372). However, there is also a growing realization that the process of transformational change required to realize such benefits involves more than just the adoption of new digital technologies by public agencies and then making available e-enabled services to users. It is also clear that organizational changes, embracing structures, behaviours, and cultures, are required in adopting agencies in order to provide public services in a more user-, rather than producer-, centred way (Lau, 2005). At the same time, the take-up of new services by users does not appear to be related to the sophistication of the services on offer (OECD, 2009) and, as a result, there is a risk that much investment in the supply of e-enabled services may be misplaced or even wasted.

We can illustrate these points through a brief review of the policy goals and progress being made in relation to digital government in three English-speaking countries: the UK, USA, and Australia. Each nation is typically seen as either at, or near the forefront of, the development of the digital transformation of government and public service delivery (see e.g. UN, 2010).

In the UK, digital government emerged in the late 1990s as one element within a broader objective of the then governing Labour Party to modernize the workings of government and the delivery of public services (Cabinet Office, 2000a). According to Organ (2003), Labour's reform agenda had 'e-government at its heart, playing an instrumental role in joining-up organizations to create citizen focused public services' (Organ, 2003: 21). As a result, initiated in the 1990s and continuing into the new millennium, a major investment to 'transform' national and local government took place (Cornford et al., 2003). This commitment was initially symbolized by Tony Blair's pledge as Prime Minister in March 2000 that 100 per cent of all public services would, where possible, be made available electronically by 2005—a deadline brought forward from 2008 (Silcock, 2001). Whilst such targets were somewhat vague in their detail and the definition of electronic 'judiciously broad', by the mid-2000s it was estimated that some £14 billion per annum was being spent on digital government projects, even if 'on-line' included the provision of services over a device invented in the late 19th century—the telephone (Hudson, 2002: 519; Margetts, 2006: 250).

From the mid-2000s, concerned that these investments were not being translated into more tangible and observable benefits, the government placed much greater emphasis on the need to realize efficiency gains through both technological and organizational transformation. Modernization and transformation were now proclaimed as new goals. For example, a key national policy statement—*Transformational Government, Enabled by Technology* (Cabinet Office, 2005)—set out a vision for 21st-century government involving:

- Broadening and deepening of government's professionalism in terms of the planning, delivery, management, skills, and governance of IT enabled change.

- The adoption of a shared services culture in both the front and back office, involving information infrastructure, and enabling efficiency gains through 'standardization, simplification and sharing' (Cabinet Office, 2005: 7).

- The design of services around the citizen or business and not the provider, involving 'coordinated delivery channels' (Cabinet Office, 2005: 7).

A series of reports and strategy statements subsequently emerged detailing elements of this vision and associated implementation plans (see e.g. Cabinet Office, 2005, 2006; Gershon, 2004; Lyons, 2007; Varney, 2006). These documents highlighted, to varying degrees, the problems of bringing about multi-agency working and information sharing across agency boundaries. Notably, the reviews identified this area as the major area where progress was still required in order to achieve productivity and service performance improvements (Varney, 2006).

This assessment seemed to be endorsed by other observers. For example, Accenture, the management consultants, has since the turn of the century carried out a series of annual surveys of the impact of e-government. In their 2007 survey they suggested that, in the previous three years, reform in the UK had 'lost momentum' (Accenture, 2007: 120). In part, this was a consequence of a decline in confidence in the government outwith of the transformation agenda, however, it also reflected the fact that the UK still lagged behind in developing more 'citizen-centric' services relative to others (Accenture 2007: 120–1). Such concerns were fuelled by a seemingly endless run of reports of either project failures or significant data security breaches (Margetts, 2006: 256).

When it came to the actual take-up of e-enabled services by UK citizens, available evidence seemed to suggest that the use of such services was lower than by their European counterparts and the populace of many other countries outside of Europe (Margetts, 2006). Such findings were the more striking when compared to the relative enthusiasm shown for the use of the internet to access other types of information such as on new consumer products, arranging travel, or dealing with financial institutions. British citizens, a relatively small minority of core users aside, were it seems much less likely to interact electronically with their government or public agencies than their bank or on-line retailers (Margetts, 2006: 259). To add insult to injury, despite the levels of investment made, these efforts were not apparently appreciated by those they were intended to benefit. For example, in one national survey only 19 per cent of UK citizens 'considered their government to be doing either a "good" or "excellent" job in this area' (cited by OECD, 2009: 3). Since the election of a Conservative-Liberal coalition government in May 2010, policy towards digital government has been framed within the broader context of austerity measures to combat the impact of the GFC. For example, the government has abandoned costly and controversial projects to create centralized databases containing citizen information, most notably in the National Health Service (see Chapter 4); promoted investment in tele-care in an effort to reduce health and social care costs (see Chapter 7); and most recently declared that transactions between central government and citizens should be 'digital by default' to reduce the costs of service provision (Cabinet Office, 2012).

United States of America

As already noted, the term 'e-government' is generally taken to have originated in the United States. In fact, US Governments and public agencies have historically been leaders in the use of information technologies, in particular at the Federal level where the state is typically 'the largest user of such technologies in the world', often in projects which are the largest attempted (Cortada, 2008: 33). However, the nature of the United States federal system, combined with its 'size and scale', means that the uptake of e-government has resulted in outcomes 'more heterogeneous, fragmented and variable than perhaps any other country' (Fountain, 2009: 19).

Consistent with this legacy, the Clinton–Gore administration commenced a trend that involved digital government being a key element of Federal reform programmes (Fountain, 2009: 102). This entailed public agencies putting information on laws, rules, regulations, policy, and practical advice on-line for citizens, whilst also developing transactional services in areas such as tax, licensing, registration, and permits. At the same time, these web-based innovations were intended to drive a 're-engineering' of public organizations. The aim was to make them more accessible and responsive to citizen requirements through 'one-stop shops' and the like, whilst cutting out the middle layers of the bureaucratic workforce; as Al Gore put it, to make public agencies that worked 'better and cost less' (cited by Fountain, 2009: 8).

As Fountain notes, by the late 1990s, what had become the 'National Partnership for Re-inventing Government' initiative had resulted in the creation of thirty Federal 'virtual agencies' (providing services in areas such as tax, international trade, and law enforcement), and a Federal government website (www.firstgov.com) which eight or so years into the new century remained 'one of the largest repositories of web pages in existence' (Fountain, 2009: 103). However, according to Fountain, these and many other initiatives tended to be decentralized and not the subject of any 'overarching co-ordination and control' (Fountain, 2009: 103). Thus, whilst fostering grassroots innovation in the provision of public services, e-government-driven innovation in the Clinton–Gore era lacked oversight and formal arrangements for its regulation and coordination (Fountain, 2009: 103).

The Bush administration (2001–9) continued to see e-government as a means of state and public sector reform but placed more emphasis on cost reduction in the context of worsening budgetary conditions. Despite the massive investment in digital government by the previous administration, the Bush White House observed that little improvement in public sector productivity and overall performance had taken place. The administration saw this as a consequence of a lack of strategic use of information technology to coordinate, join up, and integrate government. It sought to exert more control and coordination over a 'fragmented e-government landscape' through stronger business-like methods of control and accountability and, after the events of 9/11, to develop a renewed focus upon homeland security (Fountain, 2009: 104).

One response was the development of twenty-five projects, overseen by an Office of e-Government established by an e-Government Act (2002), and funded to the tune of US$345 million over four years. A further set of seven 'Lines of Business' projects were funded from 2004. All these projects focused on the development of lateral relationships between agencies through the sharing of services and more general 'cross-agency initiatives' (Fountain, 2001: 105–9). The projects were 'led largely by IT professionals' without significant involvement of 'seasoned civil servants' (Fountain, 2009: 108). The projects were focused at the Federal level with a consequent lack of integration with state- and local-level development. By the same token, at the state level, the extent of innovation varied 'dramatically', whilst at local level within states, the use of digital government as a tool of reform typically 'lagged' (Fountain, 2009: 109; see also West, 2005).

The first administration of President Obama (dubbed 'President 2.0' by *Newsweek*) came into office in November 2009. During the President's election campaign pioneering and extremely effective use of the internet was made through social networking sites (Davis *et al.*, 2009). Subsequently the Obama White House declared its intention to continue in this innovative vein with a likely emphasis, according to some observers, on using web-based technologies to provide more 'transparency' and 'connectedness', allowing users to have more say over decisions (Lyons and Stone, 2008). President Obama's stimulus legislation (The American Recovery and Reinvestment Act—ARRA—of 2009) was intended to restart the economy through investment in science-based innovation. A total of US$19 million was voted to support the introduction of new information technologies for health care, with the goal of making the health records of the entire population electronic by 2014 (Hoffman and Podgursky, 2009). The White House also made the business of the Obama administration available to mobile devices, to supplement other web-based channels already being used such as Facebook, MySpace, and Twitter. At the time of writing, the administration is again exploiting the enabling power of the internet to mount its campaign for the 2012 Presidential Elections.

Australia

As in the UK, initial impetus to developing digital government in Australia was given by a Prime Ministerial commitment made in 1997 to place 'all appropriate' services on-line, in this instance by a target date of 2001 (Teicher and Dow, 2002: 233). According to one academic review, this and other developments placed Australia amongst the 'early leaders' in the development of e-government (Dunleavy *et al.*, 2008: 14). In the first years of the new century, the Federal Government produced a strategy for on-line government and cross-agency working and a customer-facing attempt to develop a one-stop portal through which citizens could access public services. Subsequently, strategic policy statements set out a 'transformational' agenda based on using digital technologies to provide more responsive public services (AGIMO, 2006). This strategy built on earlier policy statements concerning the modernization of government and the development of the infrastructure of the information economy (AGMIO, 2004). It set out a vision for e-government that identified four strategic priorities and associated high-level implementation plans. These were defined in terms of 'meeting user needs', 'connected services', 'value for money', and 'enhanced capability', and took the form of policy measures to address skills gaps in meeting these priorities (AGIMO, 2006).

Within this framework a number of major e-government projects were initiated by the Federal Government, along with a number of specific state-level initiatives. At the Federal level, for example, the Australian Tax Office (ATO) established itself as a leader in the development of on-line lodgement facilities for tax returns, a service that was made available to all taxpayers in 2001. Subsequently these facilities were progressively enhanced and the ATO website (www.ATO. gov.au) won international recognition for its usability and accessibility (Teicher and Dow, 2002: 241). At state and local government levels other examples of 'best practice' were identified with regard to the innovative use of portal and web technologies to make government services available on-line or enable public participation in government decisions (Hughes, 2008; Teicher and Dow, 2002: 189). For example, in the context of government response to the global financial crisis, the United Nations draws attention to the use of the internet to enable citizen engagement in the budgeting process at Heathcote in regional Victoria. Here, 20,000 citizens took the opportunity provided by the local government website to prioritize the deployment of stimulus funds provided by the State Government (UN, 2010: 15).

However, whilst there are notable examples of progress in getting the services of single government departments and agencies on-line and in making these services available through portals and the like in a more citizen-centric way, there is still much evidence that digital government in Australia remains, as was observed ten years ago, a 'work in progress' (Teicher and Dow, 2002: 233). For example, progress towards multi-agency working and more joined-up delivery of services, to 'do new things' rather than the 'same things' differently, proved more difficult than anticipated. Similarly, large-scale and sometimes over-ambitious projects—such as in health care or smart card technology—have become subject to long and unanticipated delays, revision, and in some cases have been abandoned. This seems to have been the case especially where a number of agencies have been involved or where partnerships with private sector suppliers or operators have been attempted.

Hughes makes the valid point that, in countries such as Australia, early progress in relation to digital government is more apparent in so-called government to business (G2B) interactions (e.g. in relation to the procurement of goods and the like from private sector suppliers) than between government and citizens (GtoC) (Hughes, 2008). This is due in large part to the need to connect the majority of citizens to high-speed internet access and provide them with electronic identities which would enable them to access e-enabled services. At the time of writing the Federal Government has taken major steps towards the implementation of a world-leading high-speed 'National Broadband Network' (NBN), the aim of which is to connect nearly all Australian homes and businesses. However, the scheme remains a matter of political dispute and controversy concerning its feasibility and benefits.

It is also noteworthy that, since the early 2000s, even in areas previously seen as at the leading edge of developments such as the ATO, further progress has been plagued by problems (Dunleavy et al., 2008). In early 2009, for example, a new $824 million computer system upgrade caused major problems and delays in processing and issuing tax refunds, prompting threats of legal action from the accountancy profession due to the effects on their business (Johnson, 2010). The Australian National Audit Office (ANAO) investigated the problems and noted a number of areas where the management of change in the ATO might be improved, including more effective involvement of end-users in system development and implementation (ANAO, 2009).

Looking back on developments in Australia since the turn of the century, Dunleavy et al. (2008: 24) concluded that 'Australia's e-government is characterized by a supportive environment but a variable record, with early success in e-government being superseded by a lack of central initiatives or "joined-up" strategy'. In large part, this may well reflect the federal structure of Australian government and the difficulties of joining up services both within constituent states and between them (Gershon, 2008). Since 2005, the Federal Government has conducted annual citizen satisfaction surveys. The most recent, sixth survey in the series (which is now to be discontinued) reveals a picture in which the internet has stabilized as the preferred channel of communication (compared to telephone and personal face-to-face) with government. Interestingly, it was those who contacted government face-to-face who had the highest level of satisfaction with the service they received, although admittedly this was only slightly higher than for those who used the internet (AGIMO, 2011).

Digital Government in Global Perspective

National-level portraits give some impression of the overall development of e-government in arguably exemplary cases. However, these examples also need to be seen in the broader context of overall trends in digital government at the global level. In this respect non-governmental organizations (NGOs), management consultants, and a host of others keen to influence and inform policy and practice have been active in attempting to capture these trends (see e.g. Accenture, 2007; EC, 2001; OECD, 2003, 2009; UN, 2008, 2010, 2012). At the same time, we should sound a note of caution. Whilst useful and informative, these kinds of studies have a tendency to overstate and 'talk up' progress compared to more academically rigorous and in-depth research which, typically, tends to be 'more modest' in its assessments (Teicher and Dow, 2002: 243). Indeed, some have gone further and suggested that, rather than providing a realistic picture of take-up, these studies in fact reflect a distortion of the behaviour of public agencies as they seek to do the things that enable them to score well in the surveys and rankings that are involved (Lips, 2008).

This said, the United Nations (UN) has developed an influential and what it claims to be authoritative 'e-government readiness index' (UN, 2008). The index is based upon a number of measures. These seek to assess such things as the extent of infrastructural development, the provision of on-line services, and the presence and development of human capital requirements to support the take-up of e-enabled services, all of which are seen as prerequisites of what the UN defines as 'connected e-government'. In this high-level phase of evolution, analogous to the maturity models discussed above, the emphasis shifts definitively from the 'provision of services' to one of 'increasing the value of services' to their users (UN, 2008: 4).

Since 2002, the index has been updated by the UN through a number of surveys of national trends within the 190 plus member states (UN, 2008, 2010, 2012). At the time of writing, the latest available survey shows the three countries considered above—the UK, USA, and Australia—in 3rd, 5th, and 12th places respectively in e-government development (UN, 2012). As one might expect, the top twenty places are consistently dominated by the most developed and high-income nations and the UN report paints an optimistic picture about the transformative potential of digital government in such nations. In the case of non-developed countries, however, it is concluded that digital government remains 'a distant hope' (UN, 2010: 4).

Whilst providing some indication of global trends, the UN surveys, as with nearly all such studies, are exclusively based on evaluations of changes in the supply-side of e-enabled services (in most such studies this is often seen exclusively in terms of web presence) rather than changes on the demand-side. That is, the actual use being made of new e-enabled services by citizens and others is not addressed or, as in the UN surveys, only assessed indirectly. In general there is little evidence collected, let alone methods developed, to assess the 'shape, structure and quality' of e-enables services such as government websites, from a user viewpoint. This includes, for example, questions of how easy websites are for users to find on the internet in the first place and then how easy it is for the user to find their way around when they do get there (Margetts, 2006: 258).

The Nature of Innovation in Public Services

All of the above highlights the complexities of bringing about innovation in public service delivery (Mulgan and Albury, 2003). Hartley (2005) argues that innovation in the public sector differs in fundamental ways to innovation in the private sector. Whereas in the latter an innovation is more or less readily understood in terms of a new product, system, or other artefact, this is not so straightforward in public services. Of course the long-term implications and effects of a new consumer product or suchlike may not be known or knowable but the innovative nature of the normally material object or thing is still, Hartley suggests, evident. However, innovations in public services and systems of governance are less easy to distill and identify. Here, 'innovation is usually not a physical artifact at all, but a change in the relationships between service providers and their users. In such changes judgements have to be made about processes, impacts and outcomes, as well as product' (Hartley, 2005: 27).

Public service innovation encompasses development of new services and the application of technologies to service improvement as well as new market relations and changes in the mix of service providers and associated service innovations—e.g. which might arise from an enhanced role for the private or voluntary or community sector in service delivery. We would underline that this distinction between innovation in products and relationships does not only apply to purely administrative processes. Indeed, as we will see, it is particularly relevant to the more complex relationships found in the care and development services, such as services for children and health.

Not only can innovation be said to be different in the public sector, but so is the nature of the drivers of change too. In the private sector the search for competitive advantage means that innovation tends to be a protected activity, with the sharing of knowledge being limited to close collaborators and partners. In the case of public service innovation, however, the driver is increasingly a desire to increase public value and this is best accomplished through the widespread dissemination and diffusion of 'good practice' in order to 'achieve widespread improvements in governance and service performance, including efficiencies' (Hartley, 2005: 27). The increased emphasis on innovation and improvement is partly related to shifting managerial regimes within public organizations. Traditional models of public organization give a low emphasis to both innovation and improvement. The regimes of 'new public management' (NPM) increased the emphasis on innovation in managerial processes and improvements in the quality of service through increased customer focus. The future challenge is to secure innovation at all levels that is both transformational and supportive of continuous improvement in the delivery of front-line services (Hartley, 2005: 29–30).

In the public services, the non-technical dimensions of innovation embrace a wide variety of processes and outcomes that go beyond innovations in technology itself. This serves to highlight the distinction between innovation and improvement, which Hartley contends in the public services are quite distinct. For example, a change in the technology of government or the delivery of a service might be considered an innovation in itself. However, the fact of their design, development, and adoption or procurement and implementation of a technology does not mean an improvement in organizational terms has been achieved. Rather, suggests Hartley, 'innovation' can only be said to have occurred, 'where it increases public value in the quality, efficiency or fitness for purpose of governance or services' (Hartley, 2005: 30). In order to secure improvements innovation may well require, not just new technological means of service delivery, but also changes in what services are delivered, the processes required to deliver them, the places in which they are delivered in the case of virtual services, the strategies behind service commissioning and resourcing, and in governance arrangements themselves. This latter requirement arises because the sources of innovation can no longer be assumed to be 'top–down' but rather to occur in multiple ways and more often than not involve a significant engagement with and involvement of service users themselves.

Some of these ideas are summarized in Figure 1.2. This distinguishes between high and low levels of innovation and improvement

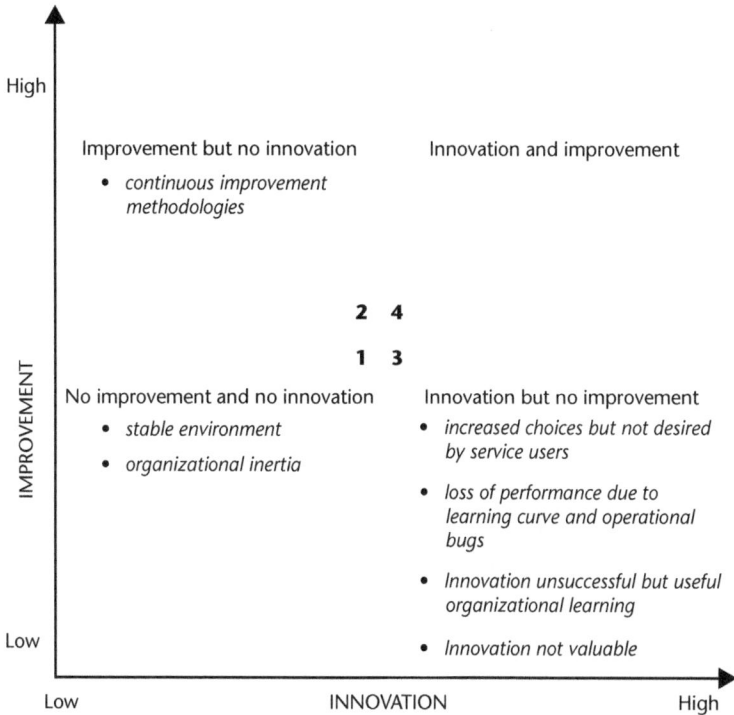

Figure 1.2 Innovation and Improvement in Public Service Delivery
Source: Hartley (2005: 31). Reprinted with permission of Cambridge University Press.

respectively. Given the evidence we have reviewed in this chapter it is interesting to speculate where most digital government projects might be placed in this figure. It would seem reasonable to suggest that few digital government projects have led to both innovation and improvement in service delivery along the lines Hartley defines. Equally, given evidence of high investment in the supply-side of e-enabled services but less obvious take-up by services users on the demand-side, one might form a view that if there really has been significant innovation as a result of digital disruption in the technology of service delivery, this has not led to significant overall improvement, at least as recognized by service users.

Hartley's framework encompasses the development of new services and the application of technologies to service improvement as well as new market relations and change in the welfare mix. Importantly, it can accommodate social innovation, defined as 'new ideas that meet unmet needs' (Mulgan, 2006: 4) and 'innovations in governance', which refers to innovations that 'burst the boundary of an organization's hold on a given (and complex) problem' (Moore and Hartley 2008: 15). We would underline that this distinction between product and relationship applies to all administrative processes in public service delivery but is particularly relevant to the more complex needs and relationships found in areas such as health and social care.

Conclusion

Attempts at the e-enabled transformation of public services by government have to date, more often than not, fallen short of their stated goals and objectives. As Lips has recently noted, 'governments are struggling to bring about the fundamental changes required to achieve transformation' (Lips, 2008). According to Margetts, whilst on the 'supply-side' sufficient changes are afoot in the e-enabling of services to suggest a fundamental transformation of government and public organizations is possible, on the 'demand-side', policy 'rhetoric is still running ahead of results', with 'some of the potential for e-government' remaining 'unused' (Margetts, 2006: 262). Most commentators tend to point to 'people-related' issues rather than technical ones as the key problem. The enabling technology is available and proven, it is often suggested. The issue is in getting people to adapt and organizations to change in order to exploit these opportunities—a problem that appears more acute in the public sector than elsewhere. However, as we will show in the following chapters, the issues involved in embracing digital government are more fundamental than just a mismatch between an increase in 'technology supply' held back by 'barriers' to increased 'user demand'. In order to explore this further, however, we first need to understand in some depth the precise relationships and dynamics at work in the relationship between technological change, on the one hand, and changes in public service organizations, on the other. This is the task of the next chapter.

2

A Social Informatics Perspective

Introduction

The objective of this chapter is to analyse in more detail the different ways in which the relationship between technological, organizational, and institutional change that is at the heart of digital government can be conceptualized and better understood. Central to this concern is the issue of how we understand the relationship between those who design and develop digital technology on the one hand, and those who deploy, implement, and use it on the other. This is a key relationship through which any socio-technical arrangement is shaped. Our intention, therefore, is to start to develop our social informatics perspective and move away from the 'e' view of e-government, referred to in the previous chapter (Lips and Schuppan, 2009). Thus we will question in analytical terms the uncritical acceptance of technology as the 'driver' of organizational change and that technical capabilities and characteristics have immutable impacts upon organizational outcomes. Instead, we will explore various analytical insights that have contributed to the social informatics approach. In their different ways these provide an 'analytical lens' that can both 'open the black box' of the technologies of digital government and enable the exploration of the socio-technical nature of their development, deployment, and use in and by public service organizations. We begin, however, by setting out the case for a social informatics approach in a little more detail.

Why a Social Informatics Perspective?

As we noted in the Introduction to this book, research on public service organizations has largely ignored the social analysis of information and communications technology. This is despite the growing and significant body of academic studies emanating from Scandinavia, the UK, and wider Northern Europe (in fields as diverse as participatory design, socio-technical systems, science and technology studies, and computer-shared cooperative work) and, of course, the growing centrality of such technologies to the operations of public service organizations themselves. In fact, similar arguments have recently been made with respect to the contemporary study of technology and organization as a whole (Orlikowski and Scott, 2008). It has been suggested that the analysis of technology has typically been 'passed over' entirely; ignored because of a disciplinary bias towards social aspects of change; been downplayed because of a tendency to treat the technical as 'taken for granted' and part of the 'institutional infrastructure'; or simply been seen as too difficult to analyse, for example because of the rapidity and complexity of technological development (Orlikowski and Scott, 2008: 435–6). In short, in analytical terms, technology has been 'missing in action' (Orlikowski and Scott, 2008: 434).

It should already be evident that the technologies of digital government raise key issues concerning the nature of public organizations, the nature of the services that they provide, the work of front-line service providers, and the implications of all of this for those who use those services. The effects of these technologies cannot be safely assumed to lie outside of the analytical frames used to examine contemporary changes in public service organizations. As Orlikowski and Scott (2008) note more generally:

> Such technological entailments are far from simple, straightforward, certain, or predictable, and they are associated with a range of organizational outcomes, many of which are emergent and unanticipated. What do such technological entailments imply for organizations, their norms and forms of structuring, their capabilities to act and interact, their performance of current and future strategies, and their possibilities for innovation and learning? Who decides what technologies get deployed in organizations, how are these designed, who gets to use and change them, and with what consequences? Given increasing reliance on technologies to get work done within and across organizations, these questions are highly salient and their answers profoundly affect the kinds of organizational realities that are produced. (Orlikowski and Scott, 2008: 436)

A social informatics perspective offers one approach to the challenge of how to bring technology more squarely back into the analysis of change in public (and other) organizations. In particular it promises to do so in a way that brings together both technical and social analysis in a practical as well as theoretical attempt to address core issues of how technologies might be shaped more effectively in their design and use.

As Kling and his colleagues have noted, social informatics is *empirical* in that it 'helps interpret the vexing issues people face when they work and live with systems in which advanced ICTs are important and increasingly pervasive components' (Kling *et al.*, 2000: 15); it is *analytical* in that it develops 'concepts and theories on the basis of empirical research'; it is *critical* since it 'seeks to find voice for a multiple of stakeholders and not just take as given the view of those who sponsor, finance or otherwise support technological change'; and it is *normative*, 'in so far as it seeks to specify alternative ways in which ICTs might be designed, implemented and used' (Kling *et al.*, 2000: 15–18).

The Three Dimensions of Digital Government

The emergence of digital government has given new emphasis to the interdependence between technological and organizational change in public organizations. In this section we explore various analytical approaches that have sought to better understand this interdependence. We differentiate these approaches in terms of what Badham (2005) refers to as 'one-', 'two-', and 'three-' dimensional views of the relationship between technology and organization (see also McLoughlin, 2009). Our reason for doing this is to make explicit different models of the social dynamics of contemporary technological and organizational change in public services. Each dimension involves specific assumptions about this dynamic and the nature of the relationship between technology and organization. As a result, each has different things to say about the scope for choice and decisions that face those who commission, resource, deliver, and of course use public services. They also provide important analytical insights and elements for the further development of a social informatics perspective on digital government.

One-Dimensional Views

In one-dimensional approaches a causal relationship is assumed between changes in technology and changes in organization. 'Technology' and 'organization' are seen as separate analytical entities. In this 'one-dimensional' view the relationship between them takes one of two forms. In the first, technology is seen as having an independent external impact on organizations. In the second, the direction of causation is reversed and technology itself is seen as 'socially shaped' by the economic, cultural, policy, and institutional context governing

STRUCTURAL IMPACT

T ────▶ S

SOCIAL AGENCY

T ◀──── S

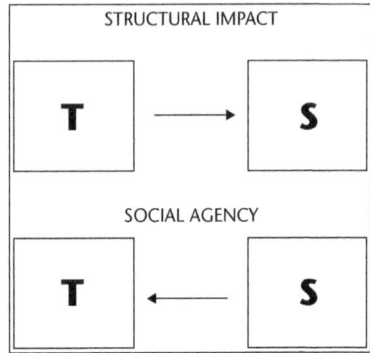

Figure 2.1 One-Dimensional
Approaches
Source: Badham (2005: 132).

its development and deployment within organizations (see Figure 2.1). Here technology has a mediating but not determining effect on organizational outcomes. Strictly speaking, the first view provides a starting point for social informatics insights rather than being a perspective from within the social informatics frame itself. This is because, in this first one-dimensional view, technology is seen as not open to social influence. Instead it is regarded as an exogenous variable impacting on but not shaped by human, organizational, or other social factors. This kind of approach is often referred to as a 'technological determinist' or a 'techno-centric' view.

An example of this is of course the 'e' view of 'e-government'. Here the focus is upon the increasing potential for the transformation of public organizations offered by digital technologies. A progressive movement through distinct stages of maturity or sophistication in the use made of technology is often predicted. It is assumed that the adoption and implementation of digital technologies will enable public organizations to progressively adopt a more 'customer-focused' orientation. This entails innovations in organization as well as technology in order to provide more integrated or 'joined-up' services. Progress to these more 'mature' and 'transformational' uses of the technologies of digital government involve, *inter alia,* increased electronic mediation of the interactions between the citizen and the state that, at the same time, reduce the need for direct citizen interaction with public organizations and public servants, especially for more routine information provision and transactional events.

This particular 'technological effect' has been referred to as the 'dis-intermediation' of service delivery—i.e. 'the stripping out or slimming down or simplification of intermediaries in the process of delivering public services' (Dunleavy, 2010: 7). It is also the basis for the concept of the 'virtual agency' (Fountain, 2001), where the most significant inter-actions between service users—and between service providers engaged in delivery to users—take place through e-enabled means. Significantly, the barriers to achieving such change tend not to be seen as techno-logical. Instead, 'the social', in the form of human, organizational, or institutional factors, is often cited as the source of constraints upon technological progress and evolution. It is worth again noting that this view does not distinguish between simple, administrative interactions that can, at least in principle, be safely and appropriately reduced to a process and implemented in a more or less simple protocol, and the more complex ones of care and development. 'Disintermediation', we will suggest later, implies quite different meanings and values in these two types of service interaction.

The socio-economic shaping of digital government

The second example of a one-dimensional view draws more directly on the fundamental assumptions of the social informatics approach—that is, that technology is itself a product of social, economic, and polit-ical forces and dynamics. This therefore reverses the line of causality. Rather than the technology of digital government being seen as inde-pendent of and as acting on the 'social', it is itself recognized as 'socially shaped' (Bellamy and Taylor, 1998). This stands in direct opposition to the 'techno-centric' view that technology determines organizational change. Such insights have particular implications in terms of the crit-ical phases of development and deployment of technologies where key choices and conditions can shape future technological effects.

For example, much of the technology of digital government has pri-marily been developed by and for the private sector using system devel-opment methods more or less appropriate to that context. Such systems embody the inscriptions—assumptions, values, and models—of their designers and the designers' views of user requirements. However, it has been argued that the temporal, spatial, and organizational separa-tion between designers and users can result in a 'design–use mismatch' and 'contextual collision' (Heeks, 2005: 61). This is most likely when the world of the user that is inscribed in the system supplied by the designer—inevitably only a reflection of such group's understandings of the user gained at some distance and normally located in an entirely different context—contradicts the situated realities of the context of use (Heeks, 2005: 58–61).

Heeks (2005) explores this phenomenon in the context of the pursuit of digital government in developing nations. Typically, the technologies involved are procured from suppliers who have designed them to meet organizational requirements within advanced Western societies. His research suggested that nearly all such projects in developing countries ended in either outright or partial failure and that only a small minority have enjoyed success in the sense that, on the whole, stakeholders achieved their goals and that project outcomes were in the main positive. The major reason for such high rates of failure were, he argues, the nature of the assumptions and requirements inscribed and embodied by their designers in the systems supplied. These assumptions concerned such things as how hardware, software, and data would be configured; what users would or could do with systems and their objectives and values, skills, and competences; and the structures and resources available to manage both implementation and operation in the adopting context. In the vast majority of instances of the deployment and use of the digital technologies studied, it seems that what made sense in the developed world context of the designer did not hold when the same systems and the assumptions inscribed within them were 'carried' to the developing world for their deployment and use.

For example, a project in a poor, rural area in India planned to use a chain of internet kiosks located in villages to provide access to cost-effective public services. However, it floundered because the designers had assumed that both reliable electrical supplies and telecommunications infrastructure were present, as they would have been in a developed country. Another case, also in India, concerned a networked information system intended to provide a more transparent way of dealing with criminal cases by a state police force. Here designers made a key assumption about the users, namely that police officers were 'honest, efficient and rational' in the way they worked. In practice the local culture was political and corrupt and the system was used to serve other ends. Another instance illustrates how designers frequently take no account of how users may appropriate systems for their own purposes. Here a project to improve information for citizens by making data from departments in a particular ministry available through websites assumed the intended users had the necessary motivations, skills, and resources to access this information. Project sponsors were aware that this was not the case but proceeded anyway and encouraged intermediaries in the form of consultants to work with end-users. This resulted in users being supported to develop personal uses for the web technology outwith those intended by the project (e.g. creation of personal web pages, on-line chats, etc.). Whilst possibly diverting the project away from its intended objective, the effect that emerged over time was the development of the very motivations, skills, and resources required by the end-users that were lacking when the web technology was initially deployed.

In some instances attempts were made to rework designs to try and close the gap between the assumptions embedded in the systems and the needs of users in a developing world context. For example, a national welfare agency in South Africa deployed a new computer system to integrate two pension funds. Particular skill requirements for users were inscribed in the system design but these turned out not to be matched by the skills present within the agency that was to implement and use the system. When this was realized, changes to the design were made which would permit the required skills to be brought in from outside the agency. It then emerged that the outsourced solution was not adequate either, even where additional training relevant to the user context was provided. Further changes to the system design were made to reduce complexity and eliminate the need for the skills requirements that were proving so difficult to satisfy.

The Digital Doorway

We can give some further illustration of these points through recent research by colleagues at Monash University which one of the authors (McLoughlin) has been associated with. The Digital Doorway is a social inclusion initiative developed in response to South African President Mbeki's statement in 2002 that 'technological literacy' was the 'key to the country's future in an increasingly globalized world'. The project was first developed by the Meraka Institute of the South African Department of Science and Technology and the Council for Scientific and Industrial Research (CSIR). The aim was to improve technological literacy in deprived, rural, and remote regions (a major issue in a country where up to 50 per cent of the population is living in poverty). In response a robust single or multi-user 'Digital Doorway Terminal' was designed and developed. The design was adapted specifically for the conditions to be found in the context of the use and the nature of the users.

The terminals are essentially standard computers encased in bespoke high security enclosures with strengthened screens and keyboard peripherals (see Figure 2.2). They are able to provide both cached and direct internet experiences in public locations to the communities in which they are installed. In South Africa, the Digital Doorways have proven extremely popular and have diffused to well over 150 locations. Whilst there is an absence of systematic evidence, it appears that use by schoolchildren in the deprived communities in which the

Figure 2.2 Digital Doorway Terminal
Source: With thanks to Larry Stillman for advice on location.

technology has been deployed is high and improvement to learning outcomes is apparent. Overall, though, use seems to be dominated by males aged 10–14 years.

At first sight, the Digital Doorway would appear to be an example of how contextual collision can be overcome. Here the technical requirements inscribed into systems by designers seem to have been strongly related and relevant to the context of use, encouraging significant take-up by at least some segments of user communities. By the same token, subsequent development of the designs appears also to be related to the evolving needs of the communities (e.g. detail design changes have been made over time and upgraded and new lighter portable versions developed, as well as other supporting initiatives such as mobile classrooms in which the terminals can be used).

However, a further proposed project intended to deploy the Digital Doorway in what on the face of it might be regarded as similar circumstances in remote, rural, and deprived indigenous communities in Australia (communities who, notwithstanding the wealth of the nation around them, typically 'enjoy' social, economic, and health conditions more akin to communities in the 'third world') illustrates how the collision of contexts carried by technologies is not limited to technology transfer between developed and developing countries. In the Australian context, despite the apparent similarities in the problem the Digital Doorway is intended to address, the project has found it difficult to gain similar momentum. Even though there has been government recognition that providing access to the internet and digital technology is a key element in supporting the development of indigenous communities, strong support from the leadership of one Aboriginal community in East Kimberley for acquiring the system, and the willingness of an Australian university to assist in transferring the technology from South Africa, progress has been slow and the resources needed to take the project forward have not been forthcoming. Despite what appear to be obvious parallels with the context in which the Digital Doorway was designed and developed, it appears that appropriation and take-up in the context of indigenous communities in Australia have been much more difficult than might have been imagined (see Stillman *et al.*, 2010).

Two-Dimensional Views

Two-dimensional views move beyond the simple cause and effect models implicit in the impact of technology and social-shaping approaches. They question the key assumption that there is a clear conceptual distinction between technology (albeit with the embodied inscriptions of its designers) and the social world that it either impacts upon or is shaped by (Badham, 2005: 126). The emphasis is instead on the mutual shaping of the technical and organizational through 'the dynamic interactions between people (or organizations) and technology over time', where outcomes are the result of a process that is 'mutually dependent, integrative and co-evolving' (Orlikowski and Scott, 2008: 446). The aim is to analyse the 'mutual interaction' or 'duality' between technology on the one hand and the interplay with the management, organizational, and institutional frameworks

INTERACTIVE SOCIAL AGENCY

Figure 2.3 Two-Dimensional
Approaches
Source: Badham (2005: 132).

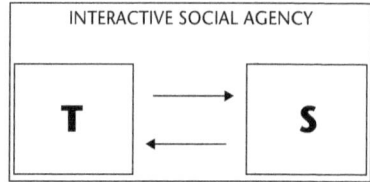

around its development, deployment, implementation, and use on the other (see e.g. Barley, 1986; Orlikowski, 1992). Figure 2.3 illustrates this 'mutual shaping' (McLoughlin, 1999) perspective.

One of the most developed examples of this kind of approach in the realm of digital government is provided by Jane Fountain's (2001) theory of 'technology enactment'. She argues that 'objective' technologies such as the internet, networked computer systems and telecommunications, hardware, software, and digital devices do not in themselves 'transform' the institutions of the state. Rather, it is the manner in which these 'objective technologies' are understood, configured, selectively developed, operated, and improved that shapes outcomes. In turn, all this is dependent upon specific governmental agencies and inter-agency relations that themselves shape the actual form of technology in particular contexts. Fountain terms this process 'technology enactment' (Fountain, 2001: 98).

In Fountain's terms such 'enactments', by reasserting the key role played by the 'social' in understanding the dynamics and effects of technology, constitute a 'reverse arrow' or an 'inverted response' to the 'technology-determines-society' model. In so doing, the effects of technology and 'organizational/institutional arrangements are connected reciprocally' and, analytically, 'both function' as 'dependent and independent variables' with each having 'causal effects on the other' (Fountain, 2001: 12–13).

> Institutions and organizations shape the enactment of information technology. Technology, in turn, may reshape organizations and institutions to better conform to its logic. New information technologies are enacted—made sense of, designed, and used (when they are used)—through the mediation of existing organizational and institutional arrangements with their own internal logics or tendencies. These multiple logics are embedded in operating routines, performance programs, bureaucratic politics, norms, cultural beliefs and social networks. (Fountain, 2001: 12)

As such, 'information technologies are not so much adopted or implemented', as often portrayed in the one-dimensional perspective, but rather are 'enacted by decision-makers' (Fountain, 2001: 12).

Technology enactment takes place through the ongoing decisions made by public managers, professionals, and others when deciding what, how, and where these technologies should be deployed and used. However, whilst in principle the outcomes of the application of the technologies of digital government are unpredictable, variable, and often unexpected, in practice choices over its use may in fact reinforce existing 'organizational, political and institutional logics' (Fountain, 2001: 12). In this way 'enactment' can be seen to be based on two notions. First, this involves a process where environmental stimuli are selectively perceived by actors with 'bounded rationality' who then create their own subjective 'definitions of the situation'. Second, a tendency is also involved for such subjective perceptions to become routine, taken-for-granted views as part of 'the propensity to represent, act out, or enact institutionalized (or routinized) performance processes and standardized organizational arrangements' (Fountain, 2001: 89).

What this means is that, whilst 'entrepreneurial or visionary professionals might use the internet to develop new networked organizational forms or new capacity' (Fountain, 2001: 90), it is more likely that such enactments will be constrained by conservative and stability-oriented sets of institutional structures, norms, and practices, which then become inscribed in enacted technology (Fountain, 2001: 88). Fountain's 'two-dimensional' view can therefore help us understand in a more sophisticated way why 'transformational' e-government is often more a matter of rhetoric than actual accomplishment and why the outcomes, as in previous generations of information-technology-based change, tend to reinforce the organizational status quo rather than change it.

Indeed, as some of the evidence reviewed in Chapter 1 would indicate, the enactment of the technology of e-government, whilst improving services in some respects, has tended to do so largely within a framework of reinforcing 'siloed', 'aggregated', and 'centralized' forms of public service delivery. For example, Fountain studied three examples of digital government in the USA during the 1990s—the early days of the internet. Two were projects which sought to integrate the work of several Federal agencies, one in relation to the production of international trade data and the other in the provision of services to the small business sector, a forerunner of many such portals and eventually of FirstGov, the 'one-stop shop' for Federal government services (see Chapter 1). The third case was a battlefield-control system developed by the US army. This was the basis for a virtual form of military organization, in distinct contrast to the archetypal form of command and control normally found in battlefield settings.

In each case, prevailing organizational logics and institutional arrangements appeared to act as a constraint on the full development of e-enabled integrated organizational outcomes. In attempting to integrate trade data the most powerful actor—US Customs—was effectively able to veto a project it saw as threatening its vital interests; combining information of use to small businesses held on different agency websites proved far more complex and difficult than first imagined, as individual agencies failed to see value for themselves in such an endeavour; and rather than transform battlefield decision-making new technology was enacted to fit in with the existing roles, relationships, and routines of command and control. Ultimately, in each case, the integrating potential of digital technology 'was forced to succumb to the status quo', and the enacted results fell far short of the transformative potential of the 'objective technology' concerned (Fountain, 2001: 89).

Of course, such findings can lead ultimately to rather pessimistic conclusions. They would seem to suggest that the extent to which public service delivery can ever be fundamentally transformed to the benefit of service users them will, in most instances, be severely circumscribed by the institutional constraints of the 'status quo'. However, as Yang observes, Fountain's approach may best be regarded as a 'start rather than destination' for analysis (Yang, 2003: 432). In particular, whilst clear on the nature of the constraints, it does not address the core issue of how 'elected officials, public managers, technology providers and citizens can work together to overcome institutional obstacles' (Yang, 2003: 432). Indeed, in Fountain's analysis these actors are inevitably trapped in what we might view as a 'virtual cage of digital bureaucracy', where institutional and organization norms are inscribed in and sustained by the technologies of digital government.

Beyond One- and Two-Dimensional Views

One-dimensional views see technology as having effects on organizations, either directly or in a form where they mediate the broader social, economic, and political forces that shape them. According to Orlikowski and Scott, such views are based on

> an ontological commitment to a world of discrete entities that have some inherent and relatively stable characteristics. This is a focus on individual actors and things that are seen to be largely independent, but linked

through uni-directional causal relationships, and having largely determinant effects. (Orlikowski and Scott, 2008: 7)

This points to a 'determinist' problem that has bedevilled both one- and two-dimensional analysis. One-dimensional views see 'technology', albeit to varying degrees, as an 'external social fact' that 'enables or constrains structural change and action' (Badham, 2005: 117). Even when 'socially shaped', 'technology' is still represented as an 'embodied structure' since, through its design and development, rules and resources are inscribed within it. In analytical terms, technology is still portrayed as having particular effects that are independent and separate from any social basis.

Two-dimensional views seek to avoid this problem by seeing 'actors and things' as 'related through reciprocal and emergent processes of interaction' that result eventually in 'co-evolved or interdependent systems' (Orlikowski and Scott, 2008: 8). However, by adhering to a view that at some point 'technology' does become 'stabilized', 'frozen', or 'congealed' sufficiently to have both 'enabling' and 'constraining' effects, the ontological commitment to the separate independent existence of 'technology' is still maintained. Indeed, in examples such as Fountain's enactment model, the exogenous status attributed to 'objective technology' means that it appears uninfluenced by the enactment process in any way; yet at some point, imbued with dominant institutional norms, enacted technology assumes a similar immutable character, resulting in the entrapment of social actors.

Whilst offering many insights, therefore, it can be suggested that both one- and two-dimensional perspectives conceal important aspects of the relationship between technology and organization. In particular, both tend to draw attention to the nature of this relationship at particular points—such as in the design phase of technology development—and place less stress on the way 'all organizational practices and relations *always* entail some sort of technological (or material) mediation' (Orlikowski and Scott, 2008: 19; original emphasis). At the same time, the view of technology as having impacts or as being mutually shaped assumes, without question, that the social is always clearly separable from the technical, whether when being designed and developed or when being implemented and used (Orlikowski and Scott, 2008: 20).

Three-Dimensional Views

According to Badham, a three-dimensional view seeks to take the insights of one- and two-dimensional views and add the insight that the distinction between 'technology' and 'organization' is itself an emergent, malleable, and contingent socio-technical entity (Badham, 2005: 133). Orlikowski has recently taken a similar position and referred to this kind of thinking as a 'sociomaterial' or 'practice-based' approach (Orlikowski, 2007, 2010). This is founded on a 'relational ontology' where 'people and things only exist in relationship to each other' and have no 'inherent properties, but acquire form, attributes, and capabilities through their interpenetration' (Orlikowski and Scott, 2008: 21). Leonardi and Barley (2008) offer further insight by suggesting that there has tended to be a confusion in organization studies between seeing technology as a determining variable in organizational change, and the notion of the materiality of technology having an inseparable and entangled bearing on the nature of work and organizing. In other words, to focus on the materiality of work and organizations is not to say that the nature of work and organization is determined by technology but rather to recognize the entanglement in practice of the social and technical (see Figure 2.4). A similar point was made by one of the authors and colleagues some years ago—the 'technology baby' should not be thrown out with the 'determinist bathwater' (Clark et al., 1988: 11).

The socio-material view, to date and in our knowledge at least, has not been used to analyse technologically related organizational change in public services. However, we believe it may provide an important part of the analytical toolkit for the further development of a social informatics perspective on digital government. For example, one implication of this line of thought is that it is not technologies as 'embodied structures', and 'constructed with particular materials and inscribed with developers' assumptions and knowledge about the world at a point in time', that people and organizations interact with. Rather, these interactions occur through the everyday 'use of the technology'. In practice this 'involves a repeatedly experienced, personally ordered and edited version of the technological artifact, being experienced differently by different individuals and differently by the same individuals depending on the time or circumstance' (Orlikowski, 2000: 408). In

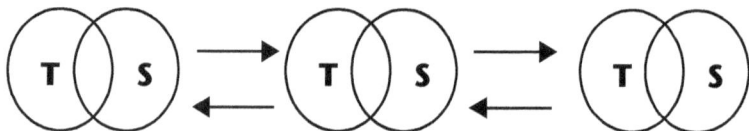

Figure 2.4 Three-Dimensional Approaches
Source: Badham (2005: 133).

other words, not only is the use of technology 'enacted', but also so is what we take to be 'technology' itself through use.

Critically, it is this constantly 'enacted' dual characteristic that defines the structural component of technology and not capacities and capabilities taken to be inherent in the artefact or system that are then subsequently appropriated. As such, 'some properties provided by the artifact do not exist for us as part of our technology-in-practice, while other properties are rich in detailed possibilities' (Orlikowski, 2000: 408). Thus, 'rather than starting with the technology and examine how actors appropriate its embodied structures'—the approach taken for example by Fountain—it may be more insightful to adopt a position that begins by examining the manner in which the actions of those engaged say in public service delivery and use (service commissioners, service deliverers, service users, etc.) 'enact emergent structures through recurrent interaction with the technology at hand' (Orlikowski, 2000: 407).

Ideas such as technology-in-practice and socio-materiality raise important questions concerning how technology and organization interact outwith and beyond the stages of design and development in everyday organizational practice. Moreover, they also draw attention to how the distinctions between the technological and organizational are an emergent and unstable product of that very same practice. This, we suggest, brings a renewed focus on the role of 'the user' as a key component of and indeed source of innovation, not just in the sense of reworking the materiality of the artefact or system, or of assimilating the material in different ways into their systems of meaning. Rather, the entangled nature of these processes can be seen as ways in which users are the means through which new forms of socio-materiality are constructed (Orlikowski, 2010). As Pinch (2010) has recently observed, analytical attention must now also shift to the way in which such shaping occurs during use. We return to the issue of design and use in the next section.

Before proceeding, we should note that critics of the idea of technology as an outcome of socio-material practice question the extent to which users are able to freely make sense of and shape technology in such a seemingly continuous and open-ended manner. For example, it has been suggested that, whilst organizational actors can choose to make sense of and use technologies in different ways, their capacity to do so rests in part at least on the structural characteristics of their organizational position and its context (Boreham *et al.*, 2008: 38–40). A similar point, albeit for rather different reasons, is made by Williams and Pollock (2008) who argue that studies which focus only on the actual implementation and use of technologies within specific adopting organizations tend to play up the 'heroic' attempts of users to make technologies work, seemingly against all odds, given the designers' intentions. The actions of users, though, are only one aspect of what can be termed the 'career' or 'biography' of a technological system or artefact. It is therefore necessary to understand the full cycle through which systems and artefacts evolve. This involves both the means of their design and procurement through to the manner in which, over the full product life cycle, they transfer across industry sectors through processes of adaptation, customization, and alignment (Williams and Pollock, 2008).

Both of these criticisms point to the importance once again of factors which shape the materiality of technology over time. That is not only during use, as the technology in-practice view suggests, but also through practice during design and development. Moreover, this cumulative experience enables and constrains subsequent cycles of development, design, and use in the artefact or system's 'career'.

One current suggestion in dealing with this issue has been to focus on what has been termed technological 'affordances' or 'possibilities for action' (Hutchby, 2001: 447). This idea, it is claimed, provides a 'third way' between the 'realist' view that seeks to retain room for technological effects and 'constructivism' which seeks to show how both technology and its effects are socially constructed (Fayard and Weeks, 2007; Hutchby, 2001; Zammuto et al., 2007). According to Hutchby, 'affordances are functional and relational aspects which frame, while not determining the possibilities for agentic action in relation to an object' (Hutchby, 2001: 444). Different technologies in this sense have different affordances in terms of the functions that they can and cannot be used to perform and the different ways in which such affordances might or might not be taken up by different actors. In important ways human users can learn about these affordances in their use whilst those who design technologies can seek to instantiate affordances within artefacts and systems that make their possible uses more evident to prospective users (Hutchby, 2001: 447).

As Hutchby (2001) notes, the idea of affordances does not imply a lapse back into determinism in the sense that humans are caused to 'react in given ways' as a result of the inherent characteristics of technology, but nor does it mean that attention should just be focused upon the different interpretative accounts that emerge to give meaning to an otherwise 'tabula rasa' 'technology', and the means by which particular accounts win out or not against others (Hutchby, 2001: 450). Rather, attention is turned to new empirical questions concerning how actors manage the range of enabling and constraining aspects of technological affordances in their everyday interactions with technology. This involves more than just socially derived interpretations of what the technology is and what it can do (Hutchby, 2001: 452–3).

Overall, such criticisms remind us that insights from both one- and two-dimensional approaches should not be discarded in seeking to escape the analytical and practical traps of technological determinism. As Badham emphasizes, a three-dimensional approach is an 'integrated multi-dimensional view' and not one that seeks to ignore either the way prior context conditions practise or the way broader contextual conditions bound such practice (Badham, 2005: 133). Put another way, a three-dimensional view accepts that there are different ways of looking at and making sense of the same phenomenon. One-, two-, and three-dimensional views can therefore be regarded as different views or *projections* of the same thing and not as mutually exclusive perspectives.

The terms 'affordances' and 'enactment' point, in our view, to the possibility of a new methodological synthesis around the term 'conversation'. In the digital government projects we shall be discussing in the following chapters, 'users' of many types and varieties are engaged in the enactment of their relationships through conversations—that is, the process by which intentions are negotiated and become shared. The idea of conversation also highlights the critical distinction between intentions and actions, what we do and what we mean to achieve by doing it. These are ideas we will return to in Chapter 8. For now we can note that when a technological means is deployed in a conversational setting, the conversationalists may accept it as the instrument of the conversations they intend. Alternatively, they may see it as an unacceptable constraint or impediment to their conversations. They may, alternatively again, invent new conversations which they then instrumentalize, with or without the technology, in new and different ways. By better understanding the relationship between intentions and actions, the resulting insights may provide a useful platform for new conversations between designers and users. Indeed such conversations might transform these roles and relationships within a more co-constructed and co-productive frame. However, this is to get ahead of ourselves. First we need to explore the designer–user relationship in a little more detail.

Designers and Users

A social informatics perspective pays particular attention to the relationship between the design of information technologies on the one hand and their use on the other. For example, according to Agre (1996) social informatics studies

> aim to ensure that technical research agendas and system designs are relevant to people's lives. The key word is relevance, ensuring that technical work is socially driven rather than technology-driven. Relevance has two dimensions: process and substance. Design and implementation processes need to be relevant to the actual social dynamics of a given site of social practice, and the substance of design and implementation (the actual designs, the actual systems) need to be relevant to the lives of the people they affect.'
> (Cited at http://rkcsi.indiana.edu/index.php/history-of-the-term)

In other words, a social informatics approach can be seen as an antidote to 'determinist' or 'techno-centric' models and approaches to technology and system development. Whilst the advantage sometimes claimed for the techno-centric approach tends to provide benefits for designers, developers, and the suppliers of technologies, the disadvantages of such an approach seem to fall on the intended users of these systems (see Table 2.1). A social informatics approach seeks amongst other things to redress this balance.

As noted above, in social informatics research, it is now widely recognized that users and the context of use represent a major factor in understanding the implications of digital and other forms of technology (see e.g. Oudshoorn and Pinch, 2003; Röhracher, 2005). However, exactly how and when users can engage in shaping technologies, and what the practical implications might be, depends on the analytical perspective adopted. From a one- and two-dimensional point of view, for example, the issue may be seen as one of how better to incorporate user inputs into the design process—perhaps by more user involvement through 'participatory design' methodologies (see e.g. Bødker *et al.*, 2004; Kensing and Blomberg, 1998). A more three-dimensional approach might place its emphasis on gaining a detailed understanding of the day-to-day interactions users have with the tools at hand, with the aim of using these insights to in some way inform innovation recognizing the enhanced possibilities for users as a source of innovation.

Indeed, one benefit of a more multi-dimensional understanding is that it may help us to avoid what has been termed the 'design fallacy' (Stewart and Williams, 2005). That is the analytical assumption that there is a rigid distinction between design—where designers' objectives and values are inscribed and embodied in a technology—and implementation—where this fixed technology is taken up and used, albeit in variable ways, by users in particular contexts (Stewart and Williams, 2005). This assumption seems less and less viable given

Table 2.1 Pros and Cons of a Techno-Centric Approach for Users

Pro techno-centric	Anti techno-centric
Simplifies goals and problem scope. Focuses on a limited set of problems, with clear responsibility lines.	Does not learn from history of failed IT-driven projects because difficult human, organizational, and work issues are excluded or minimized.
May be the only way large-scale information technology projects can be done in highly complex, and differentiated settings. In such circumstances it is difficult to get users to lead and agree a project.	Longer-term outcome is unlikely to provide optimal service delivery because a mish-mash of unplanned variations in use and practice are likely to emerge as the system evolves.
Could speed up the process initially, by getting technologies and systems live and on-line, leaving difficult decisions about service delivery to be made later.	It is not clear how the developing technological infrastructure will influence current organizational processes and practices in a planned or coordinated way. Assumed organization will bend to meet the requirements of technology.
Builds on previous experience because 'managing IT projects' is how professional project managers often perceive their job.	Users may become disillusioned and feel no sense of ownership, or little scope to shape developments and outcomes of the system as they affect them.
Can help to get developers 'off the hook' later, as users can be blamed for ineffective service delivery, with developers claiming they met their contractual obligations to supply the technologies and systems.	If not dealt with initially, organizational aspects may not get funded or managed, thereby reducing opportunities for improving the design of systems and the optimization of work, organizational and other arrangements around them.
Benefits accrue mainly to developers	*Disadvantages fall mainly on users*

Source: Adapted from Peltu *et al.* (2008: 30).

observations that information and other digital technologies rarely work 'out of the box' in complex organizational applications. Instead they require considerable local customization and configuration. This provides the opportunity for users to influence design as they attempt to figure out how to configure and appropriate systems to their purpose and practice. By the same token, attempts to 'configure or materialize' the 'prospective user within the product itself' are inevitably flawed, even where a degree of user participation is involved in the process (Webster, 2009: 67).

User appropriation requires enactments that involve both 'practical efforts to make technology work' and action that 'creates meaning' to enable a technology to become integrated into the identity of the individual user and embedded in the culture of the user community as a whole (Williams *et al.*, 2005: 55, 58). These 'practical efforts to make technology work', involve two processes: (1) 'innofusion' where local technical innovation takes place to configure available technologies to specific circumstances, and (2) 'domestication' whereby these technologies are creatively assimilated within 'local practices, purposes and culture' (Williams *et al.*, 2005: 7). As such, a rigid conceptual distinction between design and implementation makes less and less sense since much of the work required to produce a 'working technology' occurs 'post-adoption' through 'design-in-use' (Badham, 2003). By the same token, the social meanings and understandings of the context of use may themselves require considerable reinterpretation in order for users to 'make sense' of technology and value it as 'socially appropriate' (Williams *et al.*, 2005). How user communities interpret a technology in terms of who they are and what it means for them becomes, therefore, a key factor in the take-up of that technology.

All of this has some important implications for how the design–user relationship is understood. Stewart and Williams (2005) suggest, for example, that the notion of 'design' is rethought, with both designers and users seen as collaborating in an extended notion of the design phase that encompasses 'design-in-use', both during implementation and beyond (Stewart and Williams, 2005: 45). Others have suggested that the practical requirement for 'design-in-use' means that, in analytical terms, technology can be regarded as 'co-constructed' by users and designers (see e.g. Oudschoorn, 2003; Webster, 2009). We return to these ideas in Chapters 7 and 8 and explore how the idea of co-construction might further assist in understanding the designer–user relationship, and most importantly be given practical effect through a process of co-production.

Conclusion

From a social informatics perspective it is not enough to recognize technology as a new 'driver' of change and source of digital disruption in the the way public services are organized and delivered. Nor is it sufficient, as some public management scholars have started to do, to see the effects of such technology-driven change as indeterminate and open to variation depending upon how technologies are actually taken up and used. Whilst these are valid and useful insights, from a social informatics perspective they do not go anything like far enough in seeking to rethink the nature of the technology–organization relationship. In particular, they run the risk of viewing technology as a 'given' and as something acting outside of and upon public service organizations and those who seek to use their services. Challenging such a view, we suggest, is of critical importance if the possibilities for innovation in public services are to be realized through the engagement and involvement of those it is meant to serve. To do this, we need to explore far more fully than is currently the norm the manner in which digital technologies and the associated organizational arrangements or environments involved in their appropriation are co-constructed.

In proposing this conceptual and methodological shift, we also suggest that these 'arrangements' might usefully be thought of as conversations rather than simply functional reorganizations of protocols, processes, and resources. Technologies may provide appropriate and effective instruments for the conversations that are intended. However, how certain patterns of conversation become the intentions of communities of users is, though, a matter of social development and governance rather than technological design and control. However, this is again to jump ahead in our argument. We first need to turn to an exploration of the substantive nature of attempts to make digital government work.

3

Integration: Towards the Virtual Agency?

Introduction

It is assumed by public policy-makers that integrating hitherto dispa-rate, separate, and often-incompatible information systems and the data held on them will bring an end to fragmented service delivery (Glasby, 2005). However, as Ellingsen and Monteiro note, 'the notion of "inte-gration" has a deeply ambiguous meaning' (Ellingsen and Monteiro, 2006: 444). On the one hand it might refer to the integration of techni-cal systems themselves, on the other to the integration of services and service delivery, or again, to the actual integration of systems and serv-ices. Digital government occupies the space in which these and quite possible other meanings of integration have come together in attempts to transform service delivery (Wilson, 2012). In this chapter we explore the tension between such meanings and the idea of the 'virtual state'. First we examine the idea of the 'virtual agency'. We then unpack the idea of integration from an information systems and public service deliv-ery viewpoint. We highlight the enterprise-based/e-commerce model of information systems integration on the one hand, and the 'integration dilemma' for public services as they seek to move towards increased vertical (within agency) and horizontal (cross-agency) integration of service delivery, on the other. In exploring this tension we will begin to question the assumption that technical integration and the desired outcome of service integration actually result in better coordination of service delivery. One danger is what we term as 'over-integration'. Here too much 'digitization' or 'virtualization' of service delivery sys-tems and processes may actually result in outcomes that undermine the objective of increasing coordination of service delivery across time, space, and service discipline (Wilson *et al.*, 2011*b*).

The Virtual Agency?

At their core, public agencies revolve around the capture, processing, recording, and dissemination of information to inform policy-making, the commissioning of services based on these policies, the delivery of those services to citizens and other services users, and the monitoring and evaluation of the effectiveness of service delivery in meeting policy objectives (Gauld and Goldfinch, 2006; Hughes, 2008). The bureaucratic organizational form, with its associated features of top–down management and hierarchically arranged offices, paper-based record keeping, and filing, has historically been closely associated with improvements in efficiency and service effectiveness of information management and operations (Hughes, 2008: 183–4). Public agencies have also sought to refine the bureaucratic model over time by willingly embracing new generations of information technology. These have included earlier 'new technologies' such as the telegraph, telephone, and other office technologies and, since the 1960s, computers (Hughes 2008: 184).

Most recently, of course, the networking possibilities afforded by the internet and related digital technologies have also been embraced. Indeed, since the 1990s there has been, as we have seen in Chapter 1, a rapid development of the supply-side of e-enabled service delivery. Such developments provide new possibilities for the organization of services that appear to challenge the bureaucratic model (see e.g. Bellamy and Taylor, 1998; 6 *et al.*, 2002; Heeks, 2006; Harris *et al.*, 2011). According to 6 *et al.* (2002: 145–6) for example:

> there is now a core vision of where information integrated service provision should be moving. The heart of the vision is the single point of access for the consumer. Instead of having to know how to deal with many local, regional, national, state and federal agencies for each of the many aspects of their problem as they are broken down by function, the consumer will deal with a one stop shop, either by voice telephone to an integrated service call center, or on screen…on a mobile phone, on the World Wide Web through a personal computer, or on a dedicated channel through a digital television.

Such visions not only challenge the conventional notion of hierarchy within the public agency but also the boundaries of the 'organizational silo' that it inhabits.

For example, networked information systems would appear to enable such things as: more rapid and devolved decision-making to lower levels of the organization, down as far as the point of service delivery; decentralization of responsibility for processes whose performance can now be remotely monitored from the centre; the creation of electronic records which can be accessed by a range of people at different levels, in various roles, and located at different sites; the development of opportunities for mobile working by front-line practitioners, including working from home and in the field, as well as the remote delivery of services to a dispersed population aided by tele-care and remote monitoring devices; and the prospect of more 'self-service' and 'self-directed' service by citizens themselves using e-enabled channels and means. At the same time, the greater ability to remotely monitor and capture information affords a new visibility to operations and provides an overall picture, 'view', or 'window' within an agency or across a network of agencies. This generates, for example, information at the aggregate level on patterns and trends that can inform centralized service planning, resourcing, and commissioning, as well as feedback into the policy-making process.

The implication is that, as greater degrees of service integration become possible, agencies will increasingly have to find new ways of working together. This might involve, for example, joint working in new 'multi-agency' organizational forms, collaborations, or partnerships, in order to provide the more 'joined-up' services that government policies deem are required from a citizen or client perspective. Indeed, it is these organizational and social networks, 'enacted' through digital means in the form of single-agency websites, cross-agency portals, internal agency networks, and new forms of multi-agency organization, that many regard as the new 'virtual' organizational form of the state and its agencies (Fountain, 2009: 99–101). If all of this is correct, as Hughes notes, in the 21st century, 'formal structures designed for 19th century technology are unlikely to remain relevant' (Hughes, 2008: 185).

The idea that information technologies will mark the end of the bureaucratic form in public organizations is, however, not a new one (Harris *et al.*, 2011). Indeed, whilst public organizations have readily adopted previous generations of 'new' information technologies, they have done so only in so far as they can be absorbed into prevailing organizational arrangements. What has typically taken place, it has been suggested, has simply automated aspects of existing information management and processing tasks and activities. Indeed, Kraemer and King (2006: 3) argue that 'the main problem with the claim that information technology is an instrument of administrative reform is the lack of evidence to back it up'. Indeed, organizational elites—and those in public agencies are no different—have no interest in deploying computer and information technologies to transform their organizations. Rather, the overwhelming evidence seems to be that they have deployed new technologies to 'reinforce existing organizational arrangements and power distributions rather than to change them' (Kraemer and King, 2006: 3). Moreover, this pattern is now being repeated. Rather than being used by top management to achieve the transformational aims of administrative reform, the latest digital technologies are more likely to be deployed 'to enhance the information available to them; to increase their control over resources; to rationalize decisions to superiors, subordinates, and clients; to provide visible deliverables with the aid of the technology; and to symbolize professionalism and rationality in their management practices' (Kraemer and King, 2006: 4).

Fountain makes a similar point in more elaborate terms in her study of the virtual state. She notes that public agencies are 'embedded in an institutional environment that discourages cross agency initiatives', whilst at the same time encouraging 'competition amongst autonomous agencies for resources' (Fountain, 2001: 101). The result is 'strong institutional constraints on network formation', whereby successful behaviour in relation to such ends may even result in negative consequences in terms of resource flows and agency autonomy (Fountain, 2001: 101). Such disincentives to integration pose fundamental questions with regard to what happens when the 'networking' or integrating 'logic' interact with the embedded logics of behaviour in public institutions.

Integration and Information Systems

As we have noted in Chapter 1, the promise of *transformed* government and associated vision of joined-up, seamless public services is a core feature of public policy on a global scale. Digital technologies, much as they have been in the private sector, are seen as the means to improve coordination, collaboration, and networking in the delivery of public services. To this extent, system integration and service integration appear to be synonymous, resulting in better coordinated and more joined-up government, through virtual organizational forms. In this and the following section we unpack the meanings of 'integration' that are being brought together in this line of thinking. We begin with the information systems view of integration.

The use of the word 'integration' in the world of information systems has its roots in the 1960s when the concept of the relational database was developed. To function, relational databases require data from

55

different sources to be linked together. The centralizing of data from different systems aims to 'systematize and co-ordinate record keeping' and involves the 'design and implementation of structures of categorization and aggregation of transactions, ultimately allowing for the generation and manipulation of comprehensive virtual perspectives on the nature and flow of operations and resources' (Chapman and Kihn, 2009: 153). By combining data from multiple heterogeneous sources in this way, business functions are 'tightly integrated...into a single system with a shared database' (Chapman and Kihn, 2009; Lee and Lee, 2000: 153). This can lead to reductions in data inaccuracy and storage capacity requirements, plus improved data retrieval and currency of data. It is also, of course, the basis for providing much more sophisticated 'customer relationship management' (CRM) to customers.

The result is a more unified or 'enterprise-wide' view of an organization and its customers (see e.g. Goodhue *et al.*, 1992; Abiteboul *et al.*, 1995; Gulledge, 2006). Ideally, the preferred solution is to have 'one source' (Gulledge, 2006: 153) or a 'single point of truth' (SPOT) whereby all data is processed by a single software application. This concept of enterprise integration has been the basis for so-called 'Enterprise Resource Planning' (ERP) systems which have spread widely in the private sector from their origins in small to medium-sized enterprises in the engineering industry (see Williams and Pollock, 2008). Increasingly they have been taken up in public organizations (notably in universities) keen to improve not only 'back office' processes but also relations with their 'customers' (i.e. students) through developing e-enabled delivery of core services, including 'on-line' courses (see Cornford and Pollock, 2002).

However, the assumption that greater data integration into centralized enterprise-wide databases is universally desirable has been challenged. It has been noted, for example, that attempts to bring about such integration are far from unproblematic for the organizations that attempt it (Goodhue *et al.*, 1992; Cornford and Pollock, 2002; Williams and Pollock, 2008). In the specific case of public organizations such as universities, for example, it has been noted how, rather than making service delivery more 'virtual', the paradox is that 'non-virtual' organizational arrangements have to be rendered more 'concrete' if e-enabled services are to work in practice (Goddard and Cornford, 2001; Pollock and Cornford, 2005).

It has also been observed that what is meant by 'integration'—both analytically and in everyday practice—varies considerably (Gulledge, 2006: 5). In the light of this, various attempts have been made to offer more nuanced and precise analytical definitions (see e.g. Goodhue *et al.*,

1992; Gulledge, 2006; Hasselbring, 2000). For example, Goodhue *et al.* (1992) suggest that the appropriateness of particular models of integration should be seen as contingent on the *equivocality* and *uncertainty* of organizational environments. As such, integration (defined as the formalization of data items and integration of systems) is most likely to work best when it provides improvements through reducing ambiguity and improving predictability between parts of an organization. In this contingency-based view, integration works particularly well where there is an *advantage* to supporting the sharing of large volumes of information between highly interdependent subunits operating in a stable environment. The integration of information in such circumstances reduces uncertainty and provides a platform for planning and better synchronization of the operations of different subunits (Prencipe, 2003).

Alternatively, in more turbulent environments where the sharing of information is equivocal (or open to interpretation) and therefore requires 'richer' processes of exchange (e.g. face-to-face meetings), or where the benefits of tighter inter-organizational relationships are less apparent, then integrating information in this way might not be so beneficial and prove more problematic (Goodhue *et al.*, 1992).

In similar fashion, Gulledge (2006) distinguishes between what he describes as 'Big I' and 'Little i' approaches to integration. 'Big I' is a 'one system fits all' approach, implied by 'ERP' products and represented in the business models of vendors who offer themselves as 'system integrators', providing 'single turnkey' solutions to the problems of technical and service integration (Prencipe, 2003; Davies, 2003; Chapman and Kihn, 2009). 'Little i' integration, in contrast, refers to a range of intra-organizational integration tools and resources that allow organizational subunits to share information. These include point-to-point integration; database-to-database integration, data warehouse integration, enterprise application integration, application server integration, and business-to-business (also known as B2B) integration (Gulledge, 2006).

A common feature of all of these approaches is that they consider the problem of integration as bounded by the domain of the enterprise concerned—bank, retail organization, or whatever. Information within the enterprise, or a subunit of it, is deemed integrated, whilst that outside of it, marked by the boundary of the enterprise, is not. This is the basic form of what has been termed the 'enterprise model' or enterprise approach to information system architecture (see Figure 3.1) where the enterprise boundary is key. Inside the boundary is a trusted, secure, and governable domain where identities can be assured. Outside of the boundary are potential threats (cyber fraudsters, hackers, etc.) and opportunities, such as markets and customers.

Enterprise   Environment

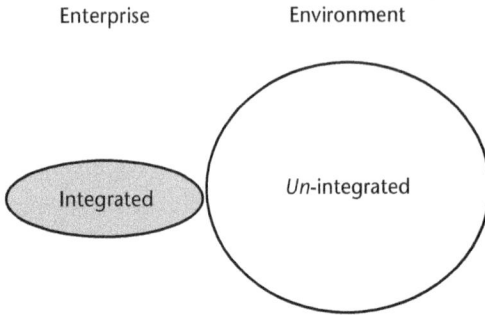

Figure 3.1 Enterprise Model of Integration
Source: Adapted from Wilson (2012).

The 'Integration Dilemma' in Public Services

The capability to create a single view of 'the customer' has proven a highly attractive model for governments seeking alternatives to existing fragmented and partial views of the citizen. Academics, keen to support the policy assumption that more cross- or multi-agency working is both useful and desirable, have explored ways in which more integrated service delivery and outcomes might be achieved. Influenced in particular by the seminal work of Leutz (1999), they have contributed to an emerging orthodoxy in countries such as the UK that has shaped the policy and professional debates in this area (see e.g. Sullivan and Skelcher, 2002; Peck and 6, 2006; Glasby and Dickinson, 2008). Beyond this 'school of thought' a wide range of other writers have also concurred with the broad assumption that integration is both useful and desirable, if somewhat challenging (see e.g. Kodner and Spreeuwenberg, 2002; Glendinning, 2003; Leutz, 2005; Hudson, 2005; Armitage *et al.*, 2009; Suter *et al.*, 2009).

The central question for many researchers has been how much integration is appropriate for agencies in a given service domain and what is the most appropriate means by which this might be established, maintained, and governed? The search for an answer to this question has been framed in terms of two dimensions (see e.g. Peck and 6, 2006; 6 *et al.*, 2006). The first concerns the number and range of agencies, organizations, and other entities involved in sharing information and partnership working—that is, the 'breadth' or the extent of 'horizontal integration' (see Figure 3.2). For example, this might be a single agency concerned with health care that is sharing information with an agency concerned with social care. Alternatively, it might be an agency (for

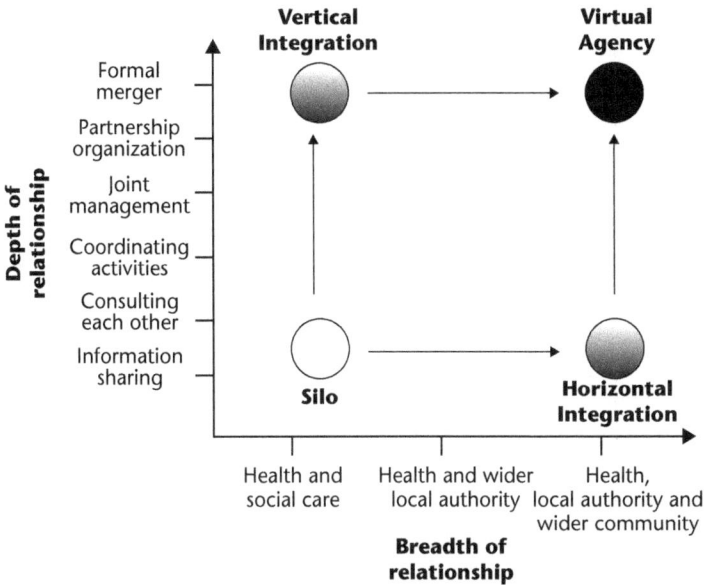

Figure 3.2 Vertical and Horizontal Integration
Source: Based on Glasby (2005).

example, a charity in the third sector) sharing information with the service commissioning body (typically central government through a local authority) where this information may, as a result of open-data policies, be made available at some point to the wider community. The second dimension concerns the nature of the arrangements underpinning partnership working, which themselves are a function of the volume and sensitivity of the information to be shared—that is, the 'depth' or the extent of 'vertical integration'. Here agencies might, for example, share low volumes of routine information of a non-sensitive nature. Alternatively, they might be engaged in much deeper organizational collaborations (either within or cross-agency) where much higher volumes of far more sensitive information are routinely exchanged.

When applied to developments in the UK public services, this framework shows that the type and extent of integration appear to vary in different service domains. For example, integration in adult social care has tended to be 'vertical' or 'deep' or the extent in character, where agencies, typically health and social care, have forged formal arrangements to work together (Glasby, 2007; Reed *et al.*, 2005). In contrast, in children's services, collaborative arrangements have tended to be of a broader and shallower nature (Glasby and Peck, 2006). In each case different challenges are involved in increasing integration towards the 'full' desired network or virtual form. In the case of services for children, for example, the task might be seen as involving the creation of deeper integration with existing partners, whereas in adult services there is a need to integrate with other agencies such as housing bodies, leisure services, and so on.

Information Systems and Care Service Integration

In the UK at least, the tendency towards thinking in terms of vertical and horizontal integration has been implicit in policies and organizational forms concerning how information systems in service domains such as health and social care should be shaped. In addressing these issues, policy-makers in both domains have seen the procurement of information systems as the means by which the integration of existing fragmented service delivery arrangements can be achieved. One factor exacerbating these issues has been the presence of legacy systems that both reflect and underpin this existing fragmentation (Sugden *et al.*, 2008).

One response was the establishment in the early 2000s of two demonstrator programmes (see Department of Health, 1998, 2001): the Electronic Record Development and Implementation Programme (ERDIP) and the Information for Social Care (IfSC) programme. The former looked at the prospects for establishing electronic health records, whilst the latter explored the deployment of electronic records in social care. One of the outcomes from the health demonstrator programme was the establishment of Connecting for Health and in turn the National Program for Information Technology (NPfIT) in the National Health Service (see Chapter 4 for further details). Arising from the social care demonstrator programme was a series of local projects that looked at the specifications of electronic or 'virtual' records in the domain of social care. We look first at one of the implications for NPfIT on local service delivery, namely in primary care.

Vertical Integration and Procurement in Primary Care

The NPfIT marked a major change in approach to how information systems were to be procured in the health service. Dubbed as the largest ever civilian IT project (Brennan, 2005) and intended as a ten-year programme with a total investment eventually estimated as in the region of £12.7 billion (House of Commons, Public Accounts Committee, 2009), it was plagued by delays, contract disputes, and increasing policy, practitioner, academic, and public criticism (discussed in Chapter 4—see e.g. Brennan, 2005, 2007; Currie and Guah, 2007; Randell, 2007; Peltu *et al.*, 2008; House of Commons, Public Accounts Committee, 2007, 2009).

The approach taken to procurement involved a move to a suite of nationally rather than locally procured solutions. In turn this effectively reconfigured the health system supplier market. The specification of system requirements was centralized, with little involvement from local and front-line levels. Similarly, the management of delivery of systems from suppliers was conducted through a rigorous set of contract-based incentives and punishments. The aim was to overcome the perceived failings of previous procurement regimes, in order to deliver a set of working information systems with the required functionality and, above all, integrated into a single overall information technology solution for the NHS in England (see Brennan, 2005).

Exactly how this was to be worked out tended to vary according to the medical specialism and area of the health care system concerned. Thus, in some cases, it was anticipated that Local Service Providers (LSPs) would provide completely new systems for areas such as mental health and community health, whilst specialist systems within hospitals would be retained but adapted to interface with the LSP-chosen core solution. In the case of primary care, it appeared that the then current broad range of choice enjoyed would become more restricted, with system options seemingly limited to a core system common to all LSPs and one alternative being made available by each individual LSP.

In primary care, the shift in procurement moved the focus of what information systems were intended to support. For example, instead of being for the individual (computers for GPs), systems were now meant to serve the needs of the collective or organizational level (systems for primary care). Similarly, rather than being there to support medical processes (prescribing of drugs), they were now to be concerned with such things as the development of single assessment processes to provide a 'one-stop' assessment of health and social needs at the start of the care pathway. In the primary care supplier market these developments caused considerable concern not least because changes swept aside existing procurement relationships and the links these provided between suppliers and GPs.

These relationships had been in place for much of the 1990s and at their core was an accreditation process (the RFA, Requirements For Accreditation, first introduced in April 1993, although revised subsequently) whose purpose was to ensure that computer systems supplied to primary care provided agreed core functionality and conformed to agreed national standards. The funding model for primary care provided reimbursement to GP practices for procurements on the basis that the systems concerned met these requirements. By the end of the 1990s the RFA had been successful in 'raising the standard of primary care systems to a baseline functionality which supported good, paper-light practice for medical records' (Sugden *et al.*, 2008: 115). At the same time the standards 'did not hinder innovation or diversity within or beyond that baseline' and 'allowed the primary care practice considerable choice of supplier' (Sugden *et al.*, 2008: 115).

Against this, however, the process of setting the standards themselves was based on seeking a balance of the interests of the various stakeholders—clinical interests, the suppliers, local health authorities responsible for commissioning services, and so on. For example, suppliers might be keen that the standards favoured their commercial interest by keeping requirements for new functionality to a minimum, thus avoiding the high costs of new system developments whilst allowing them to gain revenue from the maintenance of the existing installed base. Although checks and balances existed in the standard setting process to ensure that commercial interests did not dominate, the net effect of the process, in particular in the context of the reimbursement regime, was to constrain rather than stimulate innovation. This served to preserve an existing pattern of diverse, fragmented, and poorly connected systems, not only between practices but between the primary care and the hospital systems.

In the face of the changes arising from the NPfIT, bodies representing clinicians and doctors (the British Medical Association and Royal College of General Practitioners) sought to preserve the existing freedom of choice that existed for GPs in primary care. They issued guidelines to try and support this, whilst other professional associations with a stake in this area warned that 'previous procurement arrangements' had 'created a strong sense of "ownership" by GP practices towards their IT systems' and supported a 'close but robust relationship between practices and their IT supplier' (British Computer Society Primary Specialist Health Care Group, cited by Sugden *et al.*, 2008: 117). The fear was that the more centralized procurement approach at the core of the NPfIT, rather than bring about greater integration, would result in a reduction in 'ownership' by GPs and reduce the supplier incentive to develop solutions that met the needs of staff on the front line.

For the existing suppliers of the primary care system, the NPfIT had a varied set of implications. For example, for the supplier who at the time had the largest installed base of electronic record systems

Table 3.1 Characteristics of Information System Infrastructures

Descriptor	Infrastructural Characteristic
Enabling	Support a wide range of activities and are not devoted to just one purpose or application. Infrastructural resources open up new possibilities, not just improve existing activities.
Scaleable	Have no predefined limits to their size and are *shareable* by a large community of users and user groups who can *repurpose* them according to their needs and requirements.
Heterogeneous	They comprise networks of unlimited numbers of elements such as users, developers, and other stakeholders, along with technical elements and contexts of use.
Socio-technical	Do not have to be 'reinvented' or 'assembled' each time they are used by user communities, who learn to take their infrastructural resources for granted, where such learning is part of becoming a member of such communities.
Drift	Constitute *emergent* and *sustainable ecologies* that grow and evolve through emergent incremental adaptation rather than a planned and controlled process of top–down design and implementation.

Sources: Based on Star and Ruhdler (1996), Hanseth *et al.* (1996), Ciborra (2001).

within primary care, on the back of a highly 'user-centred' approach, was surprisingly not selected by any LSP to provide its primary care system. In contrast, other suppliers—often new market entrants—took the chance to reposition their business and technology solutions to meet the new opportunities offered by NPfIT. Ironically, in the event, the new entrants struggled to meet the challenges involved, and some ran into serious financial and business-threatening problems in meeting the rigorous terms of the NPfIT contracting regime. At the same time, mounting opposition from GPs resulted in some mitigation of the 'top–down' approach, with agreement that they could continue to use the existing systems in their practices, provided that these were compliant with the NPfIT systems.

The issues highlighted by this case of attempted 'vertical integration' are significant. It has been argued that information systems are, no matter what is intended by their designers, best regarded as infrastructure that inevitably evolve over time (see e.g. Hanseth *et al.*, 1996; Ellingsen and Monteiro, 2006; Monteiro *et al.*, 2012). New developments in information systems are in reality extensions and improvements to existing infrastructure and not constructed *de novo* (see Table 3.1). One consequence of this is that any new elements have to align with the existing installed base and that this exerts a strong influence on the specification and design of extensions or improvements.

The RFA approach, for instance, can be regarded as 'a good example of a self-reinforcing process of increasing returns and positive feedback', enabling the 'installed base infrastructure' to evolve 'to meet additional needs' (Sugden *et al.*, 2008: 122).

Of course, as in the NPfIT case, attempts can be made to seek a radical break with existing information systems configurations and their legacies. However, to do so flies in the face of the dynamics of the evolution of infrastructures and, for some commentators at least, is always doomed to fail (Ciborra, 2001). In the case of the NPfIT, the 'top–down' approach and centralized 'one size fits all' solution, as it interacted with the existing complex of technological, organizational, and other arrangements that shaped front-line practice, inevitably started to show the signs of feedback-informed adjustment that such an infrastructural view would anticipate. Ultimately, the attempt at 'top–down' change, that appeared in intention at least to hand control and choice previously exercised by users (doctors) and their suppliers to the management consultants, was after ten years to be abandoned (see Chapter 4 for further discussion).

Horizontal integration and Electronic Social Care Records

Electronic Social Care Records have been a key part of the modernization of social care in England. In the early 2000s the Department of Health sponsored a number of demonstrator projects to explore how such systems might be developed to support more joined-up working in the delivery of social care to children and adults. The broad aims of the initiative were to provide an electronic record to encourage improvements in social care practice and sustainable electronic records management. The intention was to take account of the distinctive approach taken by social workers to record keeping, with the emphasis on various forms of documents (such as structured forms, reports, letters, and photographs) rather than the shorthand coded approaches often used by medical practitioners (particularly GP records in health care). Such systems, it was assumed by policy-makers, would then enable forms of 'horizontal integration' with other service domains—for example, in the case of services for children, those of education and health, to provide better coordinated care.

One of the demonstrator projects involved the authors as university researchers working in collaboration with a Social Services Department of a City Council and a technology provider responsible for software development (see Wilson *et al.*, 2007*b*). The project had emerged out of the AMASE Children's Services Pilot (see Chapter 4 and Appendix).

As part of the research we conducted an ethnographic study of the proposed users of the system, the social care professionals and their corporate managers from the various front-line agencies who were seeking to collaborate with each other. The aim was to understand their knowledge about and expectations of the proposed e-record system and the implications they saw of such a system for their work. The study, which involved a number of facilitated workshops to discuss the design of the proposed system, revealed that there were differing views amongst participants and other stakeholders in the overall project. These reflected varying ways of making sense of what an 'electronic record system' might look like and do, which in turn derived from differing expectations, as well as motivations for engaging in the project. There were also divergent views about the other stakeholders' motivations for getting involved in the project.

One finding, for example, was that users were frustrated with aspects of their current IT system, as they felt it did not fit their working practices and instead their work had to fit into the system. The corporate representatives were also frustrated with aspects of the present system and accepted that some front-line users did not use them. They therefore wanted to explore barriers to the use of IT systems by front-line staff as well design new software tools for an electronic record. The technology providers had a pre-existing set of tools and felt that developing the electronic record could be achieved by reconfiguring these. They welcomed the chance to have user input to this process. Gaining a better understanding of the different backgrounds, expectations, assumptions, and concerns of the user group was seen by the technology provider as essential in developing a usable system.

The benefits of this kind of user-centred approach began to be revealed as the project progressed. For example, after being shown a final prototype, members of the family services team and the Social Services directorate—one of the key user groups—identified potential new ways of working that might be enabled by the development, including mobile use, different applications of the system (such as for Social Services inspectors), and 24/7 electronic access for Social Services emergency duty teams and GP 'out of hours' services. It also became clear that, for the potential of the electronic record to be fully exploited across the wider community of social services, there was a further requirement to develop a supporting set of infrastructural resources such as information policies, including authenticated access control, information-sharing protocols, and service user consent. These would therefore enable and support the horizontal integration of children's services beyond the immediate locality at a regional level.

On the face of it the project appeared to have made some significant progress in working out, albeit in demonstrator format, how an electronic record specifically developed to support social care practice might be the basis for more horizontal integration in service delivery. Indeed, some of the development work subsequently informed the national standard developed to guide the design and development of electronic records in social care. However, despite its relative maturity, the system did not subsequently get taken up and diffuse as hoped. There were ongoing issues that served to constrain the pathway to greater integration. For example, the software suppliers were unwilling for commercial reasons to adapt their systems to the extent required beyond what was involved in producing a demonstrator, whilst corporate managers were unable to provide the necessary support in the face of the demands of what they saw as competing objectives and projects. This meant, for instance, that they were unwilling to provide the level of investment needed to support the demonstrator being taken up more broadly. All these factors highlight the tensions between the competing logics of supplier business models, local service management objectives, and practitioner needs on the front line. The study, therefore, laid bare the challenges of seeking to achieve horizontal integration, even in the relatively modest and circumscribed context of a social services team specializing in supporting families.

Over-Integration and Under-Federalization

According to Bowker and Star (2002: 308), 'the toughest problems in information systems design are increasingly those concerned with modeling co-operation across heterogeneous worlds' (see also Friedman and Cornford, 1987). As we have seen, the general response in public policy has been to assume that information systems integration enables in a 'seamless' way the organizational integration necessary to bring about more coordinated or joined-up service delivery. A more nuanced form of this argument points to the 'dilemma' posed by the type of integration involved (i.e. 'vertical' or 'horizontal'), which in turn requires an understanding of the starting point for change in particular cases and an appreciation of and ability to navigate the perilous nature of the ensuing journey (q.v. Figure 3.2).

However, all of this makes two critical and rarely questioned assumptions. First, that enterprise-based e-commerce solutions developed in the private sector are, with some necessary adaptation, appropriate to the needs of service coordination in public services. Second, that the way to achieve the desired coordination is through increased integration brought about by techno-centric or technology-driven design and project implementations. In this section we begin to set out a counter view that will be developed and demonstrated in subsequent chapters. Essentially, our argument is that the assumption that integration is always appropriate can result in what we term 'over-integration'. This is particularly likely when integration is looked at from an enterprise point of view (integrated/unintegrated) and where the infrastructural nature of the evolution of information systems around an installed base is not taken into account. If we are to take the architectural properties of information systems into account this means designing systems to meet changing and unknown future needs and not just user requirements as envisaged by system designers (Monteiro *et al.*, 2012). In this light, we suggest it makes more sense to think of information systems in terms of the idea of federation, and as being federat*able* as well as integrat*able*.

The evidence we will review in the following chapters suggests that information systems need to be far more agile and configurable in multi-agency settings. Here, networks of public agencies and other organizations involving health, social care, and a range of other from different disciplines practitioners will typically be working with clients with complex needs that cannot readily be reduced to transactional principles. As we will see, the challenge in such circumstances is to create an information environment that supports particular and timely joining up by those concerned at the critical points where that 'view' of the client or customer is required. To achieve this, information systems need to be thought of in infrastructural terms and not as particular applications to meet a specific known requirement. The organizational corollary of this is that cross-agency environments need to be seen as 'federations' rather than entities bounded 'as if' within a single enterprise (virtual or otherwise).

In federated architectures, the interoperability of systems to enable information sharing between multiple agencies, rather than the centralization of standards or data to allow integration, is the key issue (see e.g. Chen *et al.*, 2008; Gottschalk, 2009). In such environments, 'hubs' of local agencies and their independent systems are federated together to form domains of local trust and syndication. In such circumstances it becomes far more difficult to specify and capture requirements for the design of information system resources on the basis of designer assumptions about existing working practices, work flows, business processes, or other organizational arrangements. Indeed, what is required in such circumstances are resources which are not defined by

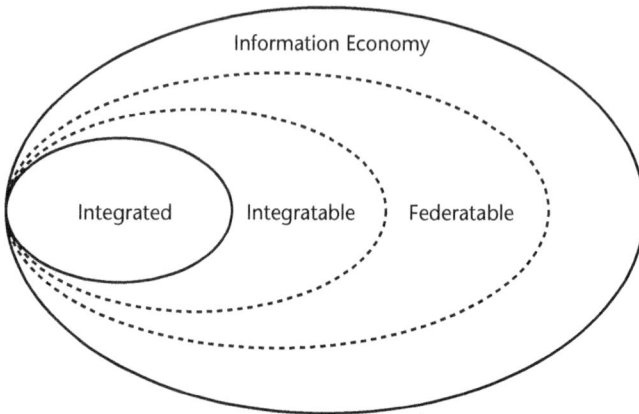

Figure 3.3 Integration and Federation
Source: adapted from Wilson (2012).

an intended application and context of use, but which are open to as yet unforeseen requirements and circumstances. Moreover, in a federated architecture the problem of integration is recast as one of *understanding the nature of individual and collective identities and relationships, so that appropriate information is shared at the point of practice.* All this serves to suggest that the idea of integration—in terms of the seamless sharing of information between multiple agencies—is misconceived. Indeed, if the primary aim is to leverage the affordances of digital technologies to increase service coordination, then the federated model may be more appropriate. Figure 3.3 depicts the federation alternative to integration for environments where high volumes of sensitive information are being shared across multiple organizational and other boundaries.

In the following chapters we will explore in more detail the consequences of the normally unquestioned assumption that greater coordination of service delivery is best brought about by increased integration as implied in concepts of the virtual agency. This, as we shall suggest, can result in 'over-integration'. This arises when inappropriate assumptions are made by designers about the everyday practices and routines of service providers and users in relation to information sharing and governance. These assumptions are then 'built into' virtual systems, resulting in unintended organizational outcomes and consequences that are sub-optimum, if not completely dysfunctional, for the everyday practice of users on the front line. Whilst the objective of integration is laudable, the reality is that its tendency to tighten the couplings between different parts of health and care networks reduces capacity and ability to respond effectively (Granovetter, 1973) and therefore points towards reduced inter-professional flexibility and inter-organizational autonomy. As we will show, the outcomes may be the unwitting sharing of sensitive information (Chapter 4); a failure to understand the nature of identity and the need for appropriate and adequate governance (Chapter 5); a new constraint on the discretion of front-line public sector workers in interpreting policy and individualizing service delivery to service users (Chapter 6); or the pursuit of 'techno-centric' visions of 'virtual care' which fail to understand the logics and context of practice in areas of complex need, such as health and social care for the ageing (Chapter 7).

Conclusion

In this chapter we have seen that what is meant in organizational or service delivery terms, by the adoption of digital technology to integrate organizational processes within and relationships between public agencies, is far from straightforward. Public agencies face an 'integration dilemma' in terms of the pathway to integration they should follow, the appropriateness of the pathway, the means of establishing the necessary relationships within and between agencies to permit information sharing under such arrangements, and, perhaps most of all, the arduous and risky nature of attempting to align both internal and external stakeholder interests to permit such a journey to be attempted, if not completed.

However, this said, there is a more fundamental question of whether better service coordination, or joined-up service delivery, is actually achieved by increased integration. Indeed, there is a danger that this objective is actually undermined by what we have termed 'over-integration'. Accordingly we have indicated that alternative models of organizational and information architectures based on more infrastructural principles may be needed. The pathway to more coordinated service delivery through information sharing may be better understood in terms of ideas such as 'federation' and 'syndication'. All of this implies that many of the integration solutions currently deployed in attempts at joining up public services, in particular in areas such as health and social care where 'wicked' problems prevail, are inadequate for the task. Moreover, even more integration of this type is not the answer to these complex multi-faceted problems. Taking this complexity seriously, we will suggest, demands a more elaborate response to the problem.

4

Joining up Children's Services and Health

Introduction

Policies aimed at joining up services to make the citizen experience more seamless have, in the UK and beyond, been a core feature of attempts at public service redesign and reform. Information sharing and multi-agency working have more often than not been at the heart of these attempts. In this chapter we consider these issues with reference to the social and health care sectors in particular. These, arguably, provide the most challenging domains for any attempt to bring about more joined-up services. They are typically highly fragmented and complex, and in principle stand to gain significantly from the greater integration offered by digital technology. Moreover, it is within these domains that vulnerable groups have suffered most from repeatedly 'having to tell their story' to multiple service providers. Unfortunately, in a small number of high-profile cases, it has turned out that the providers responsible for delivering care were simply 'not listening' and did not share information at vital times, with sometimes tragic consequences. In this chapter we examine one of the most 'highly stressed' (Dunleavy, 2010) areas of service delivery in the UK, those concerned with providing services for children. We then consider the related area of the joining up of health care or 'e-health' and in particular the seemingly intractable problems involved in the development of shareable electronic health records (SEHR). Overall, the key objective of this and the following two chapters is to continue to question the assumption that 'more integration', at least in the sense of data integration through pooling and 'warehousing', is the key to better multi-agency working and the delivery of more joined-up services. First, however, we need to explore in more detail what might be meant by 'joined-up government'.

What is Joined-up Government?

The term 'joined-up government' (JUG) now enjoys a wide currency, although it is not given the same emphasis in different national jurisdictions (6, 2006). For some at least, it represents the antithesis to the much debated and discussed phenomenon of 'new public management' (NPM). According to Dunleavy *et al.* (2006), NPM has its origins in the UK and Australia in the early 1980s before diffusing more broadly in Australasia and Europe. For the last twenty or so years NPM has 'dominated the agenda for changing or reforming public sector organizations' and created a 'substantial branch industry' in academia devoted to its analysis and development (Dunleavy *et al.*, 2006: 96). Initially at least, part of the NPM agenda was to use new technology, 'to displace previously paper-based operations' (Dunleavy *et al.*, 2006: 96). However, NPM, it seems, became submerged in a more substantial focus on promoting organizational changes, more or less influenced by perceived best private sector business practice and driven by the principles of 'disaggregation', 'competition', and 'incentivization' (Dunleavy *et al.*, 2006: 96–101). Significantly, it is claimed by some at least, this has worked to the detriment of deploying new digital technologies effectively (Dunleavy *et al.*, 2006: 96).

For the UK, it has been argued that, JUG represents 'a central element of reintegration' to counter the fragmentation that resulted from NPM and to exploit the new possibilities for integration offered by digital technology (Dunleavy *et al.*, 2006: 229). From the late 1990s onwards, 'joining up' and related phrases such as 'seamlessness' came to denote the ways in which, until its fall in 2010, the New Labour government responded to the perception that existing fragmented arrangements for the delivery of public services were no longer adequate (Ling, 2002). Policy statements and political speeches frequently urgently demanded the dismantling of bureaucratic structures and associated 'barriers', 'silos', and 'walls' (see e.g. Lewis, 2006; A. Johnson, 2007). However, despite the prevalent use of the term JUG, there seemed to be considerable ambiguity and a lack of a clear definition of what was actually meant (Pollitt, 2003; 6 *et al.*, 2007; Bellamy *et al.*, 2008). Sometimes it was an idea applied to policy-making intended to ensure greater effectiveness and avoid contradictory or unintended outcomes. In other usages reference was made more specifically to the way services are delivered and experienced within a given policy framework. At times the distinction between policy—the espoused intention to join up—and implementation—delivering joined-up services as an outcome—was not a hard and fast one.

Moreover, whilst often portrayed as a new idea, 'joining up' in some sense has frequently been a feature of government concerns in the past (Pollitt, 2003: 69), although the term coordination is more often found in debates prior to the 1990s (Hood, 2005). The available evidence appears to show that JUG, whether under its previous guises or in its more recent incarnations, is not 'an easy idea to implement' and carries with it 'some substantial risks and costs' (Pollitt, 2003: 72–3; also Bogdanor, 2005). To work in countries such as the UK for instance, it has to be accompanied by significant behavioural and cultural changes by public managers, professionals, and other front-line staff (6 *et al.*, 2007; Bellamy *et al.*, 2008). This is clearly not something that can 'be achieved overnight' (Pollitt, 2003: 73). In the domain of service delivery, whilst public managers, professionals, and other workers might have a high degree of identification and commitment within a single agency, this is difficult to bring about in the context of 'more abstract cross-cutting objectives' or in a 'temporary multi-organizational team' (Pollitt, 2003: 71). By the same token, in such situations, working out who is responsible for what in terms of, say, commissioning policy, allocating resources, monitoring their effectiveness, and being accountable for the outcomes, is more difficult to define than in more conventional bureaucratic arrangements within a single agency (Pollitt, 2003: 70–1). Both these points are particularly pertinent at the local level where JUG has been seen by central government as requiring local authorities to assume a new role influencing 'other partners' rather than exercising 'authority' (Bogdanor, 2005: 15).

Having said all of this, there are strong claims that the technologies of digital government seem to offer a fresh opportunity to address such issues and enable new organizational forms, collaborations, and on-line service delivery where they simply could not have been contemplated before (6 *et al.*, 2002: 142). However, not even the simplest 'one-dimensional view' of digital government would equate greater provision on the 'supply-side' of the means of technical integration with the 'joining-up' of services in practice. Moreover, as we have already seen in the preceding chapter, previous evidence about the application of computer and information technologies suggests they will often serve to shore up and reinforce existing organizational arrangements rather than herald the arrival of new ones.

This view would seem to be borne out by contemporary studies that have looked at attempts to join up services through e-enabled means. For example, McIvor *et al.* (2004) looked at the potential of internet technologies to enable change in service delivery in six public agencies. They concluded that lack of managerial knowledge and understanding, silo cultures, and low-trust relationships with private sector suppliers all acted as 'considerable barriers to implementation' (McIvor *et al.*, 2004: 72). Other studies point to the fact that implementing information systems to support multi-agency working across services is inherently more complex than introducing digital solutions into single-agency single-service organizations (Lupton *et al.*, 2001). This involves, for example, a reconciliation of different professional worldviews in how they see service users (Banks, 2002: 9) and overcoming different approaches to the recording, storage, and distribution of information (Green *et al.*, 2001). In the face of such apparently intractable problems, as we will see below and in Chapter 6, there have been numerous calls for the e-enabling of service delivery to be accompanied by major cultural shifts in both organizational and professional practice on the front line.

Joining up Services for Children

In the UK local authorities have a statutory responsibility for the provision of social and care services. The Children Act of 1948 established these responsibilities with specific regard for children and young people. Prior to this, dating back to Victorian times, voluntary and community organizations had played the main role (e.g. Thomas Barnardo set up his first 'Ragged School' in London in 1867). In more recent times, local authorities in the UK have been at the forefront of attempts to join up services in general, and those for children in particular. In what follows we draw upon a study of changes over a number of years (2000–7) in a metropolitan local authority—*Big City*—located in a provincial region of England (see Wessels and Bagnall, 2002; Vaughan *et al.*, 2003; Wilson *et al.*, 2004, 2007b; Wessels *et al.*, 2008). We will focus here on the most recent research, led by one of the authors with colleagues (Wilson *et al.*, 2012). This concerned the creation of what are known as service directories. In the context of joining up, such directories constitute a vital means through which information about the services available locally can be shared between providers and made available to service users. In order to understand the context in children's services we now provide a brief overview of the changing policy frameworks that have led to attempts to bring about more joined-up delivery.

Many of the problems associated with providing these services have been linked to the 'fragmentation of responsibilities for children, young people and families' (Wilson *et al.*, 2004: 541). As a result, services have been subject to significant changes in both the assumptions underlying policy and the methods and modes of delivery. During the early years of the 21st century in the UK, for example, New Labour policy thinking was that, to deal with complex social problems, such as poverty amongst children, low levels of achievement in education, and rising crime rates amongst the young, a more integrated and coordinated response on the part of the various organizations, agencies, and authorities concerned with the care and welfare of children and young people was required (Wessels *et al.*, 2008).

At the same time, the consequences of the responsible agencies failing to share vital information with each other—highlighted in tragic circumstances through the death of children whose vulnerable situations were known but not acted upon—also stressed a need for improved information sharing. In particular, the public inquiry chaired by Lord Laming into the death in 2000 of Victoria Climbié at the hands of those responsible for her care reported that, in the months prior to her death, Victoria had been known to three housing authorities, four social service departments, two hospitals, the police, and a national charity (Laming, 2003). The conclusion of the inquiry was that the agencies concerned were underfunded, inadequately staffed, and badly managed. The government response to the inquiry concurred and cited the case as an extreme example of a failure to share information across agency boundaries. 'Victoria Climbié', the government observed, 'came into contact with several agencies, none of which acted on the warning signs', whilst there was 'no one' able or willing to build 'up the full picture of her interactions with different services' (Laming, 2003: 51). Regrettably such tragedies had occurred before and have taken place since.

The Children Act 2004 extended the responsibilities of local authorities by making it a statutory requirement for providers of services to children in social care, health, and education to work together to deliver and improve their services for children. Service commissioners at the local level were also required to engage with a more diverse base of providers, such as small businesses, charities, social enterprises, and community and voluntary organizations. To bring this about, new information systems would be needed (Peckover *et al.*, 2008; Pithouse, *et al.*, 2009). These technologies included a new electronic 'common assessment framework' (CAF) which was to be linked to a national database for all children and young people (*Contact Point*) intended to protect vulnerable children. This would require personal information about service users to be made available across organizations and agencies (including statutory bodies, voluntary groups, and for-profit service providers) with different priorities, management structures, and information systems (Green *et al.*, 2001; Hudson, 2005). It was recognized that these new ways of cross-agency working would also require a programme of 'culture change' on the part of local authorities, their partner agencies, and front-line practitioners (Department of Education and Skills, 2003; Department of Health, 2004).

Children's Trusts emerged as a means through which the proposed multi-agency approach to providing care and related services to children could be rendered. Trusts in this sense might be viewed as a form of virtual public agency, offering a 'one-stop shop' to children and families seeking to access and engage with social, education, and health services (Wilson *et al.*, 2004: 542). Trusts were intended to enable such things as single assessment processes between agencies, a multi-agency approach to service commissioning and planning, and information sharing to identify children at risk. Since 2010 the new Conservative-Liberal coalition government has promoted its notion of the 'Big Society'. This envisages a much greater role for the third and private sectors in public service delivery and a more 'mixed economy' for service delivery, involving both voluntary and private providers (Cabinet Office, 2010).

Service directories and children's services

Since 2005, UK local government authorities have been required to produce a directory with information on local providers and to make it accessible to professionals working with children and young people, and where possible to the public (what follows draws on Walsh *et al.*, 2012). In the past, directories have been provided locally as a simple list of available services, although the extent to which this was actually achieved has varied. Moreover, directories had typically been produced within the organizational confines of the local authority itself, rather than on a cross-agency basis to all service providers. The emphasis on joining up services for children following the Children Act gave new priority to the responsibility of local government in making information available about services within its jurisdiction. Prior to this, the process for compiling directories was normally to request information from other service providers such as voluntary sector organizations. This was accomplished via standardized and often paper-based forms. The information would then be added to or updated over time. Significantly, editorial control over the information, for instance deciding how it was to be represented in the directory within which it resided, rested with the local authority as the 'editor' and 'publisher' of the information. However, given the wider number of service providers and the increasing prevalence of data being held on computers, fulfilling the new policy requirements brought additional challenges in updating, granting access to, and integrating this information into a single directory.

Indeed, the initial findings from our research revealed confusion and variation in approach in the practices of the local authorities located in the provincial region of the UK which was the focus of our study. There was little evidence, for example, of attempts to approach the problem across local boundaries or of an attempt to coordinate these efforts at the regional level. When it came to the audience for the information contained in the directory, there was further confusion over whether it was for the sole use of practitioners 'when they had a child in front of them' or was a resource that could be accessed by the public more generally, including, of course, children themselves. The broader the audience the more viewpoints there were, on the part of both information providers and users, about what information should be made available. Other issues involved the difficulties of verifying information, in particular to avoid 'bogus provider groups'. Users were, in effect, accessing information on a 'buyer beware' basis.

Other problems included the updating of information and the burden this created for providers such as voluntary groups. This was allied with concerns that entry in a more broadly available directory would create service demands that could not be fulfilled. There was also varied 'buy-in', with regard to interest and potential use on the part of providers more generally, and problems of making the information user-friendly for the public. A further key point was the emerging relationship between local authorities and the increasing range of service providers in the increasingly 'mixed economy of care'. The former, as already noted, saw themselves as the 'editors' in charge of the directories. The latter, on the other hand, did not see themselves as mere 'agents' of the authorities and many had strong views concerning the trust placed in them by their clients. They feared a loss of professional control over the information they held and that they felt had been entrusted to them.

All of these issues can be characterized in terms of the intended conversations between the client and receivers of services, the providers of those services, and the local authorities as information brokers. The traditional conversation had been between an applicant and a service provider (i.e. Social Services department in the local authority) who held all the information and had the right and duty to qualify and, indeed, ration supply. The new, expected conversation was between a range of care service suppliers and their clients facilitated by an information service that acted fairly and appropriately in the interests of the community and society. Put in these 'conversational' terms, the enormity of the change and of the challenge it represents to participants is made clear.

Given this, a second phase of our research sought to facilitate service providers in developing the kinds of new conversational relationships necessary to share information in a more joined-up environment. This part of the study used action research workshops to further explore the issues (see the Appendix). One strong theme that emerged from the workshops was the suggestion that providers themselves—rather than local authority staff—could play a much more active role in the management and curation of their own information, the nature and format of the actual information published, and in determining what information should be shared and with whom. In so doing, providers could maintain their independent identities and trusted relationships with clients. Other possibilities identified included a greater use of the directories to inform service commissioning and future resource allocation. This might enable directories to be 'used to manage information strategically in the interests of efficient and effective local services', and to provide 'aggregate data to reveal and make judgements about regional gaps in service provision' (Walsh *et al.*, 2012: 16).

Figure 4.1 depicts an initial mapping of local authority, service provider, and user views as they emerged out of the workshops. This

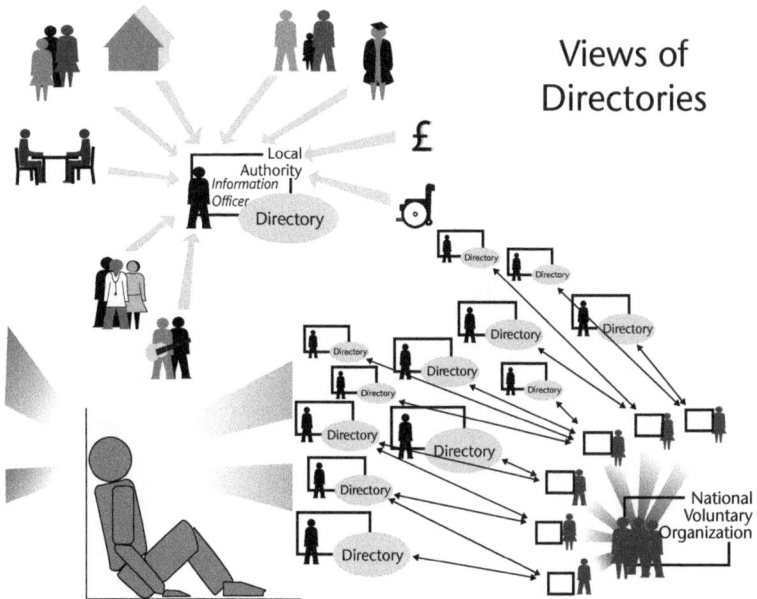

Figure 4.1 Views of Service Directories

Source: Walsh *et al.* (2012). Reprinted with permission of Taylor and Francis.

juxtaposes the local authority-centred view as editors and arbiters of the directories and their content; the view of the voluntary sector bombarded with information requests and fearful of a loss of trust with their clients; and the requirements of national policy to join up services and integrate information. Further discussion in the workshop led to better understanding of these respective positions on the part of participants. It also led to a view that the cross-cutting interests and legitimate concerns of each meant that joined-up service delivery could not be brought about simply by the integration of information into directories. Whilst this was the preference of the local authorities, combining the roles of providing, maintaining, and delivering information tended to reinforce working within organizational boundaries and 'silos'.

A further purpose of the action research phase was to provide the concepts and language in which the participants could explore different relationships and allocations of responsibility. Figure 4.2 presents an alternative approach introduced to the discussion by the action researchers. New roles, for example, of 'informant', 'editor', and 'publisher' of information are identified. Along with them come possibilities for new distributions and sharing of these roles and the 'conversational' possibilities they represent. Implementing such an approach implies

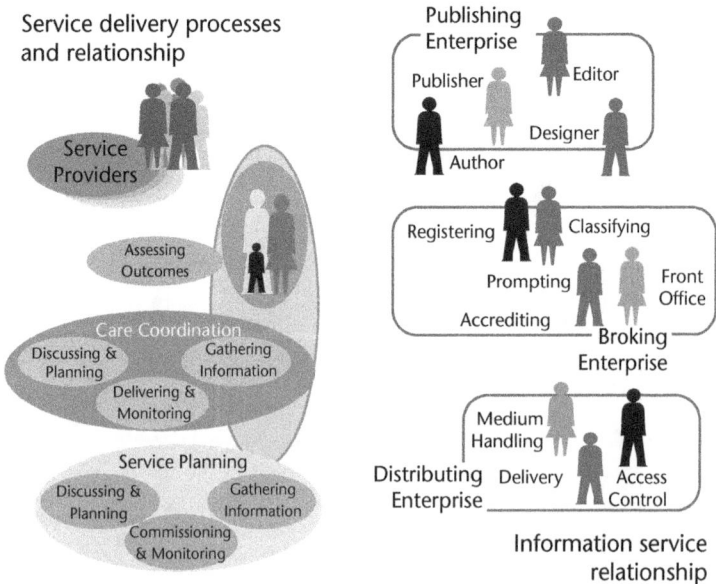

Figure 4.2 Roles and Responsibilities and Service Directories
Source: Walsh *et al*. (2012: 8). Reprinted with permission of Taylor and Francis.

the syndication of publishing across federated domains managed by a variety of organizations. Here the local authority is the 'host' rather than 'owner' of the directory, becoming an 'information broker' rather than 'the information source'. Editorial responsibility is separated from publication and from responsibility for the provenance of information. In all these aspects, service providers and users have a new voice, where in an integration model this would be circumscribed.

Joining up Health Care: e-Health

The deployment of digital technologies in the delivery of health care services—often referred to as e-health—is one of the major areas in which innovations in public service delivery have been both called for and predicted. E-health can take a number of forms. For example, much attention has been given to tele-health as a means to deliver health care services (even conducting surgical procedures) remotely. Other application areas include electronic prescribing, electronic transmission of x-rays, test results, and so forth. A key enabler of all these possibilities is the integration of information systems to enable the sharing of patient records within and between hospitals, and between primary and secondary care systems. The digitalization of the patient medical records in this way has been seen as essential to underpin many of these developments and to allow new service innovations, for example patients maintaining parts of their own record themselves, supporting public health campaigns to promote healthier lifestyles or to assist those with long-term chronic conditions to do more to monitor their own health.

Until relatively recently, all health records were kept on paper. In the UK, for example, the main system of keeping records in primary care predated the First World War in the form of brown, 5 inch × 7 inch envelopes named after their originator—Lloyd George the then Minister for Health. According to one authority, the purpose of a health record is to provide a 'contemporaneous list of the individual's physiological, psychological and social well-being' (Purves, 2002: 15). It is claimed that, in its paper form, the record deteriorated over years of practice into an 'after the fact' writing chore whose residual function was to be as an aide-memoire and provide a means of 'covering the GP's back' (Purves, 2002: 15). In the light of this, the shift to electronic records could be construed as an opportunity to restore the health record to its original purpose, whilst avoiding some of the problematic features of paper-based recording, such as the notorious illegibility of

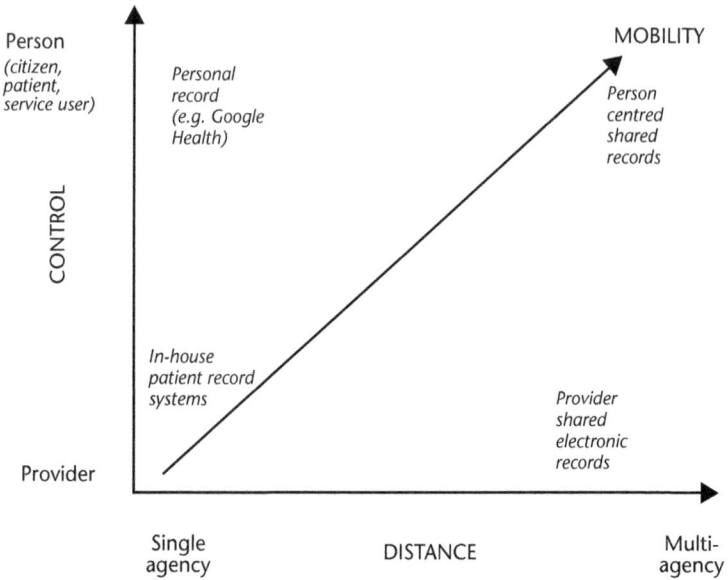

Figure 4.3 Dimensions of SEHRs

GP's handwriting and the limited availability of such records, in particular during critical medical episodes such as accidents and emergencies where access to details of a patient's medical history could be vital.

We use the term 'shareable electronic health record' (SEHR) to distinguish digital records from long-standing computer-based patient and/or medical records kept in-house, which are not specifically intended to be shared across organizational and occupational boundaries. SEHRs themselves can still take a number of forms and can in principle be differentiated in terms of the degree to which control over them is 'provider' or 'person' centred and the distance the record can travel (in temporal, spatial, and organizational terms) when shared (see Figure 4.3). As such a patient record system might be primarily provider centric (i.e. the content and access to it is determined by medical practitioners) and this content is only shared within a given boundary, whilst a patient is in hospital, and is not routinely updated once that medical episode is concluded (e.g. within a specific hospital or group of hospitals, or locally within the primary care system). An alternative, in what some regard as the most developed form, even the 'holy grail', of the digitalization of medical data, would be a situation where the content of the record and access to it is controlled by the patient. Moreover, the information on the record has complete mobility as 'an account of his/her diverse encounters with the health system as recorded in a variety of medical records maintained by various providers such as GPs, specialists, hospitals, laboratories, pharmacies etc.' (Stroetmann *et al.*, 2011: 31). It is the shareable aspect that makes the idea of electronic records particularly attractive to proponents of health service modernization and reform (see e.g. Department of Health, 2001, 2002; Wanless, 2002; EC, 2004, 2005, 2007; Deloitte, 2008; PwC, 2013).

In the UK SEHRs are seen as the 'cornerstone of a modernized health service', bringing about 'better, safer, cheaper and more integrated' health care where 'lost records, duplication of effort, mistaken identity, drug administration errors, idiosyncratic clinical decisions and inefficient billing will be a thing of the past' (Greenhalgh *et al.*, 2009: 703, citing Department of Health, 2008; Institute of Medicine, 2009). In Australia, the Labour government stated that 'electronic health records have the potential to save lives, time and money and make the health system more efficient' and would 'drag the management of health records into the 21st century' (Roxon, 2011). In the USA, in the face of the global financial crisis, a major component of President Obama's stimulus package announced in 2009 was to provide 'every American' with an 'electronic health record' by 2014 (Childs *et al.*, 2009).

These ambitious aims notwithstanding, the growing evidence is that actual attempts to deploy SEHR and related systems in many countries are proving extremely problematic, fraught with difficulty, and highly controversial (see e.g. Brooks, 2007; Deutsch *et al.*, 2010; Hackl *et al.*, 2011; Sheikh *et al.*, 2011; Garrety *et al.*, 2013). It seems that 'failed' projects are the norm and, even where success is claimed, the programmes concerned are 'typically plagued by delays, escalation of costs, scope creep, and technical glitches including catastrophic system crashes' (Greenhalgh *et al.*, 2010: 3). Even when implemented successfully, there is evidence that health care staff are 'distracted' from the 'human side of medicine and nursing' by the new tasks that are generated, such as data entry and the like. More generally, take-up and use of electronic records by patients is seemingly hampered by broader societal concerns about privacy, confidentiality, and data security (Greenhalgh *et al.*, 2010: 3), and a parallel reluctance on the part of patients to be turned into 'consumers' of health care services in the way that some would appear to wish.

Table 4.1 Transforming Information Systems in the NHS

Date	Key Events
1998	September. Government sets out long-term information strategy for the NHS, 'to ensure that information is used to help patients receive the best possible care' (Department of Health, 1998).
2000	July. New 'vision of a health service designed around the patient' published (Department of Health, 2000).
2001	July. Information and IT systems for delivering the NHS Plan set out (Department of Health, 2001).
2002	February. PM Tony Blair commits to make a 'step change' in NHS IT, setting ambitious targets to deliver substantial tangible benefits within three years.
	April. Independent Wanless (2002) review recommends doubling and protecting NHS IT spend; stringent, centrally managed national standards for data and IT; and the better management of IT implementation in the NHS, including a national programme.
	June. Department of Health's report takes first steps to establish NPfIT (Department of Health, 2002).
	October. NPfIT formally established to develop an infrastructure to support standard interoperable systems to be used by all NHS Trusts to help deliver an efficient 'patient-led' health service.
2003	December. Contracts worth £6.2 billion awarded to a small number of consortia to develop and implement standard systems, some nationally and some by local service providers, initially divided into five regions.
2007	July. NPfIT Local Ownership Programme finalizes preparations for transferring responsibility for local implementations to Strategic Health Authorities.
2008	Completion of the transfer of responsibility for local implementations to Strategic Health Authorities, with Trusts paying for implementations.
2009	Reports emerge of hospitals breaking away from the programme and procuring their own system. Key parliamentary committee voices further concerns over the programme (House of Commons, 2009 also 2007, 2011) in the wake of criticism of the programme from the National Audit Office (2008, also 2011).
2011	Conservative-Liberal coalition announces cancellation of NPfIT programme, preserving working systems only.

SEHRs in the UK and Australia

We can draw on some of our current research with colleagues to illustrate these points in the context of attempts to introduce SEHRs in the UK (England) and Australia. In the case of the former, interest in SEHRs dates from the late 1990s in the form of reviews of information system requirements for the NHS. In the case of the latter, the history of interest in electronic records goes back to the early days of the internet, over twenty years ago (Garrety *et al.*, 2013). In the NHS in England the attempt to introduce SHERS was a central element of the ill-fated NPfIT (see Table 4.1 for a chronology). In Australia, after several false starts, a controversial national scheme to introduce a 'personally controlled electronic health record' (PCEHR) went 'live' in July 2012 (see Table 4.2 for a chronology).

As we have noted, NPfIT was claimed to be the largest civilian IT programme ever conducted anywhere in the world and it took place in what is probably the world's 'largest Civilian bureaucracy' (only the Indian railways and Chinese Red Army are said to employ more people!). The aim was to provide a national system for England (Wales and Scotland developed their own arrangements) that would 'radically change the face' of the NHS's information technology. The NPfIT involved a range of systems and applications intended to provide nationally available information for patients and practitioners. This, in part, was to be through an electronic integrated care record (a key element of which was a shared summary record available nationally) and other associated digital systems, such as for electronic appointment booking and prescribing, all linked together by a high-speed broadband network. The original aim was that the systems would be implemented across the NHS by 2007 and that every patient would have an electronic care record by 2012 (House of Commons, 2011). However, by the mid-2000s it was clear that the programme was in considerable trouble, with key vendors withdrawing from the project, some facing major financial issues, and various contractual disputes. Estimates of eventual cost overruns at the time ran as high as 440–770 per cent. In one of numerous governmental and parliamentary reviews, Edward Leigh MP, the Chair of the UK House of Commons Public Accounts Committee, declared in 2007 that, not only was NPfIT the largest computer project in the world, but it was also in danger of becoming the 'biggest disaster' (Cross, 2007: 815; see also NAO 2008, 2011). On the back of such views the programme, which it was now acknowledged would never deliver the care record, was effectively cancelled by the incoming Conservative-Liberal coalition government, albeit in the midst of yet another new information strategy for the NHS (NHS, 2010).

There is a case to be made that it is too early to reach any firm and considered analytical conclusions about the NPfIT. Indeed, as some commentators have pointed out, some elements of the programme have, it appears, been successfully implemented (see e.g. Brennan, 2007). However, at this stage, at least the following observations can be made on the basis of research evidence that is currently available.

First and foremost, the project appears to have been classically framed as a 'vertical integration' with a strong 'techno-centric' orientation, which has obvious appeal in ambitious large-scale projects of this type (see Table 2.1, Chapter 2). Any benefits tended to rest with the design and development community and not with the intended users in the NHS (Peltu *et al.*, 2008). Second, and following from this, the programme took little or no account of existing and complex 'institutional logics' in the domain of these user communities (Currie and Guah, 2007). It seems to have been assumed by those sponsoring and managing the project that transferring solutions—in the form of technical deliverables—developed for and in the private sector into the health service could be accomplished in a seamless way. The project's approach to change management made little or no provision for the need to 'win the hearts and minds' of the health practitioners, especially those on the front line of care delivery, who were expected to use the various NPfIT applications (Currie and Guah, 2007: 244; House of Commons, 2007).

Third, despite the 'techno-centric focus', there is evidence of considerable *ad hoc* innovation at local level to get the new systems to work in an acceptable way and/or find alternative solutions where they could not be rendered serviceable. However, this had the potential, if left to take place in an unsupported way, to be 'dysfunctional' for the overall care system (see e.g. Harris, 2011; Eason, 2007). What may have emerged is what has been termed 'distributed change agency' (Buchanan *et al.*, 2007). The scale and complexity of the NPfIT project was such that there was in effect 'no one in charge' (Greenhalgh *et al.*, 2011), in the sense of having a grasp of the project or 'meta-project' as a whole (Alderman *et al.*, 2013). In the absence of this, what innovation there was seems to have been primarily 'user-driven' and most evident at local level. What seems to be evident is the inevitability of the infrastructural evolution of information systems outlined in the previous chapter. Indeed, the health service innovations that seem to have had most impact on the front line are precisely those incremental adaptations and 'innovations in use' which make most sense in the local context of health practice.

In Australia the aim has been to give more control to the patient over the information held electronically about them, by putting them 'in control' of their own personal electronic records. However, the PCEHR (at the time of writing the 'personal' dimension is being de-emphasized) has attracted much opposition. For example, it has not been well received by the medical profession and seems to be of little interest to the target end-user, citizens themselves. Significant concerns over privacy and data security have been raised by consumer advocates and others (Garrety *et al.*, 2013). The President of the Australian

Table 4.2 National Electronic Health Records in Australia

Date	Key Events
1991–2	Australian Health Ministers propose a 'Health Communication Network' which would be a 'public utility...the electronic equivalent of the Australian Post Office'. Public concerns over centralized databases mean concept never pursued.
1997	House of Representatives establish inquiry into 'the potential of developments in information management and information technology in the health sector to improve healthcare delivery'.
1999	National Health Information Management Advisory Council, arising from above, recommends establishment of a task force to develop 'a coordinated approach to electronic health records in Australia' and recommends establishment of a 'national electronic health records task-force' (NHIMAC, 1999).
2000	Task force report recognizes privacy concerns and recommends consumer led focus (NEHRT, 2000).
2001–5	HealthConnect, attempts to establish a 'national health information network' through a series of pilot trials and development of 'business architectures'.
2005	HealthConnect reconfigured and new National e-Health Transition Authority (NeHTA) established by Commonwealth Government to, 'identify and develop the necessary foundations for e-health'.
2007	NeHTA begins referring to 'personal' and 'individual' electronic health records, with greater emphasis placed on consumer benefits, as well as convenience for providers.
2008	NeHTA presents business case for an electronic health record to Council of Australian Governments (COAG).
2009	National Hospital and Health Reform Commission recommends a 'personally controlled' EHR (PCEHR).
2010	Federal Labour Government commits $467 million to implementation of PCEHR by July 2012; Health Identifiers Act passed which paves way for PCEHR.
2011	September. Federal Minister for Health and Ageing, Nicola Roxon, releases draft legislation for a Personally Controlled Electronic Health Records (PCEHR) Bill. November. Senate inquiry announced into a full range of issues, including long-standing concerns over data privacy and security.
2012	1st July. PCEHR goes 'live' and citizens able to register on-line amidst press reports of little interest on the part of Australian citizens in registering.

Medical Association (AMA) went as far as to refer to the consequence of giving control to patients as effectively 'de-medicalizing' the health record, and to say that the system as a whole was 'reckless and dangerous' (Hambleton, 2011). Whilst doctors will not control what is in the PCEHR, they will be required, if asked by the patient, to provide and maintain a clinical 'shared health summary' within the record. This has raised a further issue in relation to payment for the extra work perceived to be involved in this. This generated such complaint amongst clinicians that some informed commentators believe the system may not be viable (More, 2011).

With the PCEHR due to 'go live' on 1 July 2012, an Australian Senate inquiry was called towards the end of 2011 and reported in March 2012. It concluded that 'it must be a matter of great concern' that 'so many fundamental issues are yet to be resolved a little over three months from launch after six years of development and the expenditure of between $467 and $750 million' (Australian Senate, 2012: 44). Opposition senators recommended that enabling legislation be delayed for a year whilst these issues were sorted out but the incumbent Labour government elected to push on. Whatever the rights and wrongs of this decision, after a little over one month of being 'live', it was apparently the case that only just over 5,000 Australians had registered (Barlass, 2012). Indeed, despite the much-vaunted functionality of the record, that is all that visitors to the PCEHR website could do.

A comparison of the PCEHR with NPfIT is instructive. Both projects have been plagued with issues such as technical delays, scepticism on the part of health practitioners and patient groups, and concerns over privacy and confidentiality. There are, though, important differences. The most obvious of these is that PCEHR is an opt-in system. Put simply, until an entitled citizen elects to register on-line for an electronic record, they do not have one. In contrast, the NPfIT system was designed as an opt-out system and, whilst this has been moderated to some degree, the essential position is that all of the eligible UK population has, or rather would as a default have had, an electronic record. Opt-out systems are, it is argued, simpler and citizens with concerns over privacy or their medical information being shared can elect not to participate. By the same token, those in most need and likely to benefit (e.g. older people or those with chronic conditions) are automatically in the system and do not have to go through a registration process. Opt-in systems such as the PCEHR put the citizen more directly in control of whether they participate or not. However, it is argued that there may be higher costs of educating the populace about the benefits and that, if a critical mass of participation is not reached, the full benefits may never be realized (Jolly, 2012).

National Databases or Local Publication Spaces?

The above examples provide a first illustration of the ideas discussed in Chapter 3 concerning the difference between joining up services

through increased integration coordination in and a more federated information environment. Whereas the former approach might
assume that the need to publish service directories can effectively be
accomplished by developing an e-enabled application or 'integrated
solution'—perhaps a sort of electronic 'yellow pages'—the limits to this
are quickly encountered in terms of conflicting of stakeholder interests
and concerns. By the same token, the idea that medical information
previously stored locally by 'analogue' means can be digitized and put
into an electronic record, which can then be accessed and shared over
time and space, makes key assumptions about the mobility of such
information. This is not to say that database and related technologies
do not have crucial roles to play in the implementation of systems
and infrastructure to support care services. However, where the idea of
'building a database' comes to dominate the way problems are defined,
this can result in complex social conditions being ignored or downplayed for the purpose of creating an electronic catalogue or record.

For example, let us imagine the information to be recorded is to do
with bruising to a child observed on admission to hospital. From a
clinical perspective the event would be documented in a health record
noting the physical and other aspects of the injury, any tests conducted, treatments applied, and so on. However, a social worker might
record the event quite differently in terms of concerns over the parents'
behaviour towards that same child. Putting these two pieces of 'data'
into a shareable electronic record or making them shareable through
information-sharing protocols and the like is far from straightforward.
When is the parent a 'danger' and to whom, when and in what context, or with what provocation? The same 'facts' on the record might
support quite different conclusions. An assessment by a social services department, based on the parents' circumstances, need, and the
veracity of their account of an accident that they claimed led to taking
the child to hospital might result in a quite different conclusion. This
might be that the parents need a small grant to install a 'child gate' on
the stairs to prevent a similar fall happening again. By the same token,
if the same 'data' were shared to a police record, it would not have the
same status in terms of provenance as when viewed as part of a social
work assessment or the information recorded on a health record. The
point is that meaning can only be given to data when it is 'interpreted
in context' and 'framed' (Greenhalgh *et al.*, 2008: 20).

The problem here is a view of information that treats it as 'stuff'
that can be 'captured', 'recorded', 'stored', and 'shared' unproblemat-
ically, as if the record was a 'data container'. However, if information
is to be shared then this same 'stuff' carries with it a complexity of

context-derived meaning, a meaning that remains attached to the conversational settings—roles, responsibilities, and purposes—in which it was generated and in which it is or will be interpreted. It is not surprising, given such complexities, that attempts in countries like the UK to construct large centralized databases and top–down specification of systems and networks in which to put and move around this kind of 'stuff'—be it to do with health records (NPfIT) or social care (*Contact Point* cited above)—have been abandoned. Ironically, this has been because vertical integration has been attempted, in order to govern the sharing of information through a central monopoly. However, to do this in a multi-agency context is both inappropriate and, as indicated in the case of children's services, damaging in terms of its implications for front-line practitioners, with potentially dangerous consequences for those who are meant to be the subject of care. The ERDIP programme was subsequently absorbed into the NPfIT.

An interesting upshot of this in the health record domain is that there is an argument that local systems seem to 'be more efficient and effective than larger ones' (Greenhalgh *et al.*, 2008: 23). One reason may well be that the proximity and mutual understanding of context of those sharing information provides a frame through which to manage the multiple meanings and interpretations of such information. This insight is borne out to some extent by our own retrospective studies of a local electronic health record demonstrator project. This was one of several pilots conducted as part of the national Electronic Record Development and Implementation Program (ERDIP), as noted above, a precursor to the NPfIT and claimed, in the midst of what we assume to be stiff competition, to be 'one of the strangest and least understood initiatives carried out by the NHS' (Brennan, 2005: 71).

The pilot in question was conducted in a provincial region of the UK, under the technical direction of one of the authors (Martin) and took place between 1999 and 2002. The aim was to explore the concept of digitizing and sharing patient information. As part of the pilot a study of health records was conducted. This comprised technical development work informed by ethnographic study of information use in a number of health care settings (see Jenkings and Wilson, 2007).

One of the aims was to develop a design for a 'health record' that could be shared across professional, organizational, and disciplinary boundaries. The main vehicle for this was the development of a rapid prototype 'demonstrator' health record. The demonstrator used the example of a clinical scenario in coronary care, the core of which was a sequence of clinical messages (e.g. in relation to drugs prescribed, appointments, referrals, lab tests, and results, etc.) relating to the care

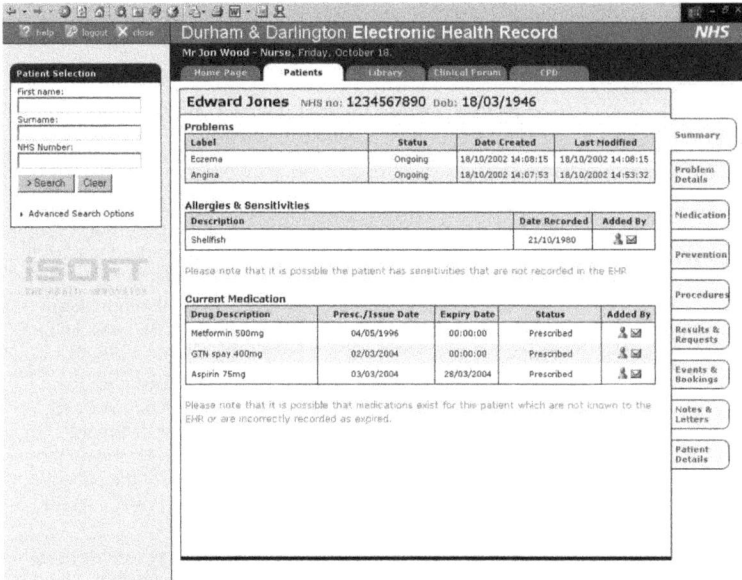

Figure 4.4 SEHR Animator and Sample Screen Shot
Source: Jenkings and Wilson (2007).

pathway of a particular patient that included an emergency admission to a hospital during a suspected heart attack. The demonstrator took the form of a mock-up animated browser window on a computer screen (see Figure 4.4). The animator tells in audiovisual form the story of Mr Jones through four linked scenarios (see Table 4.3). Each scenario is presented using a mixture of scripted dialogue between the 'actors', a representation of the activity of the various agents and health services, and a technical animation of the messaging architecture showing the processing/exchange of information between the organizations involved.

The 'animator' and the medical scenarios it depicted were constructed in consultation with clinical expertise. The animator was then used to evaluate prospective user responses. This was accomplished through ten focus groups convened with a range of health care practitioners from different areas of health practice. The groups were conducted in such a way as to provide a base line of views before and after participants had been exposed to the animation. In the main this was both supportive and positive of the potential benefits of an SEHR, although there were concerns over such things as additional data entry tasks which might arise, confidentiality of patient information, and (with

Table 4.3 SEHR Animator Scenarios

Scenario Number	Care Pathway Events
1	Mr Jones phones NHS Direct from home complaining of chest pains. He tells how he undergoes triage by NHS Direct, and how this is facilitated by Mr Jones having an SEHR that can be accessed by the health call centre nurse. The animator illustrates the type of information that would be potentially available through these records and how it is used, not only for triage, but also to transfer patient details to the ambulance crew that the triage nurse has sent to the patient's home.
2	The ambulance crew access Mr Jones's patient information that has been tailored to the requirements of the ambulance crew.
3	The ambulance crew notify the hospital accident and emergency (A&E) department of their intended arrival and through the SEHR transfer patient and current treatment details (see screen shot). This has also allowed for the printing of A&E documentation necessary for the care of the patient. The ambulance is then shown arriving at the hospital where the patient is signed over to A&E care.
4	Back in time six months to a GP consultation where Mr Jones is diagnosed with heart disease and asked if he would like to have his details on an SEHR. This, it is explained to him, would allow his medical details to be available to various healthcare professionals should they require them.

Source: Jenkings and Wilson (2007); Martin (2010).

remarkable foresight born perhaps of previous experience) 'scepticism regarding the NHS's ability to implement' such a system (Jenkings and Wilson, 2007: 98).

The clinical experts in the research team initially thought they were involved in work to construct a database. However, through their involvement in developing the prototype, they started to understand that the problem was more to do with messaging (i.e. what was shared with who, when, and for what reasons) and transaction management (i.e. how this process was regulated and governed). Again we see the situation described in terms of conversational processes and interactions. The research team and prospective users also realized that, in effect, what was being produced by the demonstrator was a 'live, evolving record', as the patient moved through the care pathway and different specialists added to the record as a side effect and consequence of their acts of care. Moreover, a high degree of reliance could be put on the quality of the information so recorded because it had come from real transactions between the specialists, rather than having been collected and input as data for the purposes of a recording system.

In fact, the pilot took a similar line to our intervention in the service directories case discussed above. In this sense, 'the record' was viewed as something that responded to the need to inform and support the intentions, processes, and relationships of those engaged in the delivery of care. Rather than being construed as a resource or application to store and share patient information, the demonstrator viewed 'the record as publication space' and as an infrastructural service. The key point here was that this allowed the participants in such arrangements to choose what, when, and where to publish in the space. The record in this sense was the 'instrument' that enabled 'conversations' among practitioners and carers and between them and their client/patients. Whilst of course it was only a demonstrator and not a live system, the reaction of prospective users to the prototype were very positive. This in part reflected the way in which the initial ethnography that had informed the prototype's development enabled the resulting system to better reflect the needs and requirements of those it was intended to assist (Jenkings and Wilson, 2007).

Conclusion

In this chapter we have seen the limitations of but have also illustrated alternatives 'integration' as the sole means of achieving more joined-up delivery of services. In both the case of service directories and SEHRs, we identified possibilities for thinking differently about the way information is shared. In particular we have drawn attention to the idea that information sharing might be better construed in terms of a metaphor of localized 'joint acts of communication and publication', where the context and meaning of information is preserved. To persist with the idea that information is best shared by treating it as a commodity to be placed in a database and then accessed as required is, we believe, a potentially dangerous and threatening trend. This is particularly so when applied to the challenging contexts of medical and social care. This is because the various and varying user needs and requirements and concerns over data security, privacy, and protection which are characteristic of these settings can be overlooked, if not completely ignored, by such an approach. We explore this issue further in the following chapters.

5

Identity, Governance, and the Citizen as 'Customer'

Putting services on line not people in line
(Bill Clinton, former President of the United States of America)

Introduction

In this chapter we explore the issues for identity management and governance raised by the sharing of digitalized information, in particular as it relates to the identity of service users, in multi-agency environments. In what follows we examine the much-vaunted role of 'smart cards' as a means of authenticating citizen identity and as a platform for providing access to cross-agency services, and the issues of information governance that this raises. We then explore the vexed question of the extent to which the complex identities and relationships we have (e.g. as citizens, patients, or clients) with public service providers can be reduced to that of a 'customer' and administered through 'customer relationship management' (CRM) systems. We begin, however, by examining debates over identity and governance as they apply to information systems and their management.

Identity Management, Governance, and Information

The increased need to share information highlights the requirement for service providers to be sure that they are talking about the same individual and that the individual is who they say they are and therefore entitled to the services they claim. It is in this context that e-commerce solutions procured from the private sector are increasingly being used to replace paper-based and/or face-to-face identification of citizens by public officials to effect transactional and relational interactions between the state and the individual (Lips *et al.*, 2009*a*). Establishing that someone is who he or she says they are—in information system parlance 'authentication'—is normally an essential first step in the provision of a service to an individual. The handling of information about that individual, including their identity, has of course traditionally been accomplished by paper-based means or through face-to-face interaction, albeit with increasing recording and storage by digital means. Identity, in this sense, is generally understood to be an outcome of the association of a collection of attributes and performative characteristics that individuals exhibit to the world and which can be recorded (e.g. date and place of birth, gender, ethnicity, parentage, signature, and so on) associated with a particular human. We can therefore understand identity as the means through which individuals are recognized or made distinct from other individuals for transactional or relational purposes.

The passport used for international travel is of course a classic means by which key identifiers are brought together in an authenticated and verifiable way to allow individuals to be identified by public agencies at border controls and allow passage from one government jurisdiction to another. Such essentially paper-based systems are fallible and open to fraud and abuse since the identity 'token'—the passport itself—is open to forgery and so on. Governments concerned about both internal and border security, and more broadly international terrorism, have therefore become particularly interested in the use of digitized biometric data i.e. physical attributes such as photographs, thumb prints, retinal scans, and genetic maps. This information is increasingly being used to identify citizens rather than the purely socio-graphic data traditionally contained in passports and the like and could also clearly be used to authenticate access to other public services. It is the apparently immutable nature of physical characteristics and the seemingly 'foolproof' capacity of digital technologies to securely and safely store and recognize them, that make such systems so attractive to politicians and policy-makers (see Box 5.1).

In general, the systems and resources that permit the capture and sharing of digitized identity data can take a number of forms, many of which are already commonplace in e-commerce in the private sector. For example, the aforementioned smart card technology is now commonly the basis for customer interactions with banks and retailing, effectively replacing cash and paper cheques, whilst CRM systems provide the interface between front and back office in many businesses and allow the tracking and guidance of customer interactions with the

---

Box 5.1 BIOMETRIC DATA AND THE UK NATIONAL IDENTITY SMART CARD

'The system works perfectly well—unless a person is disabled, has dark skin, has brown eyes, is bald, or is wrinkled. If someone makes the mistake of being bald and wrinkled, the system tells them that their head is upside down. If a person is a labourer, typist, or pianist, the system does not work. The system does not work if a person undertakes a voluntary change of appearance, which rules out every teenager in the country. If people make the mistake of ageing, identity card technology is not for them. In fact, it has been revealed that one in 1,000 cases result in a misidentification. As 13.5 million people a month go through British airports, there will be 13,500 misidentifications every month, which will do wonders for the queues at security checks.'

Mr David Heath, UK Member of Parliament for Somerton and Frome commenting on test results of the Labour Government's proposed National Identity Card System in a House of Commons debate on the National Identity Card proposals.

Source: Hansard, 8 October 2005.

---

enterprise (Taylor *et al.*, 2007). However, the spread of such systems to the public realm has raised considerable concern and debate about issues of confidentiality and citizen privacy.

For example, in relation to the impact of digital identity systems, two lines of argument have been advanced in the academic and policy debates (Lips *et al.*, 2009*a*). The first is consistent in many respects with the policy rhetorics reviewed in Chapter 1. These typically take the view that the use of digital identity management and the e-commerce solutions it supports are a key enabling component of the sharing of information between agencies, and thereby increase the scope for 'coordinating and integrating front-line service delivery to citizens and reducing the duplication of business processes in government' (Lips *et al.*, 2009*a*, 2009*b*). In this view, digital identity management systems provide the basis through which information can be safely and securely shared within and between agencies to improve service and delivery. Moreover, they also enable a more 'personalized approach' to service provision where citizen-choice, rather than bureaucratic convenience, becomes the driver allowing 'information asymmetries' between service users and providers to be corrected (Lips *et al.*, 2009*a*; Taylor *et al.*, 2007). In short, 'digitized personal identification and authentication systems' are 'the sine qua non of successful e-government' (Lips *et al.*, 2009*b*: 716) and provide the cornerstone for putting both services and people on-line.

A second, alternative view argues that 'substantial information imbalances in citizen–government relationships' are emerging whereby the state is now able, in an unprecedented way, to hold and use identity information in order to monitor, capture, and analyse the behaviour of individuals for its own purposes (Lips *et al.*, 2009*a*: 834). Digital identity management technologies offer functionality and opportunity to 'mine' different databases and to 'pool' and 'match' data between them. This information might then be used to identify behaviour that could, for instance, be fraudulent, or a threat to vulnerable sections of the population (such as children at risk), or even a threat to the security of the state itself. In this way, personal identity data can be used to segment and sort the populace into 'who should be targeted for special treatment, suspicion, eligibility, inclusion or access' (Lips *et al.*, 2009*a*: 839). In this view, such information asymmetries and functionality, rather than offering benefits to citizens, pose a fundamental threat to civil liberties, democratic rights, and freedoms. Moreover, it is claimed that the new public management paradigm is particularly disposed towards the use of such digital means as mobile devices, CCTV cameras, satellites, RFID (radio frequency identification), electronic tags, internet cookies, email records, and the like, to pay 'purposeful, routine, systematic and focused' attention to the identity and other personal information about citizens, 'for the sake of control, entitlement, management, influence or protection' (Murakami-Wood *et al.*, 2006, cited by Lips *et al.*, 2009*a*: 839).

The difference between these two views can be further illustrated in the way they tend to view data security incidents or privacy breaches (see e.g. Box 5.2). In reacting to such instances the first view typically points the finger at human and organizational failings or 'rogue' behaviours and often suggests that advances in technology and systems can assist in limiting such problems in the future. The second view points instead to the assumptions and interests built into the design of the technical systems themselves. These are often 'antiquated' and 'inflexible' and these flaws inevitably mean front-line staff having to find work-arounds to accomplish tasks in under-resourced environments. The difficulty here is with the whole concept of technology-driven 'transformational government'. This is founded on the creation of increasingly large, centralized databases to which ever increasing numbers of people, at all levels, and across a wide range of functions and activities, require access in order to do their jobs. It is impossible, argue proponents of the second view, to devise governance frameworks and protocols that can ensure that such complex information flows cannot be subject to security breach or other compromise. The issue is not, as the first view would have it, with the users, but primarily with the design of the architecture of the technological systems themselves.

Box 5.2 'DISCGATE'

On 20 November 2007 Alistair Darling the British Government's Chancellor of the Exchequer stood up in a crowded House of Commons (the lower Chamber of the British Parliament). He reported that, as a result of a 'substantial operational failure', two data discs had been 'lost' at Her Majesty's Revenue and Customs (HMRC) offices in the North-East of England. It was claimed that a junior civil servant had sent the data to the London offices of the UK National Audit Office (NAO) via the 'internal post'. The discs never arrived and subsequent searches by the police failed to locate them. The discs contained the government's complete database of 25 million child benefit claimants, including names and addresses of both adult claimants and every eligible child. In 7.25 million cases the lost data also included bank account details. Should the information fall into 'the wrong hands', Darling admitted, all those on the database—roughly half of the UK population—could be at risk of fraud and identity theft. More evidence emerged suggesting that the sending of information in this way—on unencrypted discs—was not an isolated practice but had been the norm in the agency during the preceding months. The political fallout was immediate. Instances of data loss by other agencies, some by overseas third parties to whom data services had been outsourced, also began to emerge. At the same time, severe reservations were expressed by politicians, the press, and other commentators over new national policy initiatives that were dependent on the creation of large centralized data-bases. The episode was quickly dubbed 'Discgate' by the media. Subsequent enquiries partly blamed 'rogue behaviour' by a front-line worker but also called for a radical tightening of data handling procedures and protocols.

Sources: Anderson (2007); Collins (2007); *Guardian* (2007); B. Johnson (2007); Wintour (2007); Poynter (2008).

Behind this are the policies and practices that have produced them and the 'database state' and 'surveillance society' that they seem to be bringing about (see e.g. Murakami-Wood *et al.*, 2006; Anderson *et al.*, 2009). In short, in this second view, using digital government to manage identity is about putting people in line, not on-line.

These concerns serve to highlight the key issue of information governance, which sits more broadly within the wider concerns over other dimensions of governance in public services (see e.g. Gray, 2004; Frederickson, 2005). When considering the governance of digital information it is useful to distinguish between the *use* made by government and its institutions and agencies of information technologies, including how they are procured; the management *processes* and *activities* involved in the deployment, implementation, and operation of such systems, including the management of projects; and the *frameworks* and *standards* through which it is ensured that the information so produced is shared in a manner consistent with the objectives, consents, and obligations which were the basis of its reporting and recording. It is the latter which concerns us most here but it also needs to be recognized that the other two dimensions can have a significant bearing on this third area, and indeed should themselves each consider the other dimensions of information governance.

However, in countries such as the UK, the requirement for effective data governance in the context of the digitalization required to enable greater information sharing has seemingly been interpreted with great variance. This reflects an ongoing struggle for public agencies as they seek to strike a practical 'balance' between the competing demands of transparency and sharing data, on the one hand, and data privacy and civil liberties, on the other (Bellamy et al., 2005; 6 et al., 2005). In attempting to bring some statutory framework to this struggle, the UK Government has sought to legislate around what have been seen as critical issues of transparency (freedom of information) and privacy (data protection). Concerns over these issues in the NHS, for example, were heightened by a number of high-profile health service scandals (most notably the undetected murders by GP Harold Shipman of some 250 of his patients over a number of years, which came to light in 1998, and the unauthorized retention of human organs, including those of children at the Alder Hey hospital in Liverpool first revealed in 1999). At the heart of both cases were significant issues of information visibility and transparency that pointed to the need for more appropriate governance processes.

A contributory factor in the lack of oversight was perceived to be a 'confetti' of legislation, records management guidance and certification, research ethics procedures, security, and confidentiality policies which applied to the health service at that time (see Richter and Wilson, 2013). The idea of information governance (IG) was proposed as an overarching conceptual framework aimed at solving the problem and producing an accountability system for NHS organizations. This was defined as: 'a framework which aims to support organizations and individuals in the NHS to ensure that personal information is dealt with legally, securely, efficiently and effectively, in order to deliver the best possible care' (Walker, 2001). The apparent success of the approach in the NHS soon led to the development of an IG framework and associated toolkit for local government, whilst similar approaches were also developed in social care (Hill, 2009; Richter and Wilson, 2013).

In a study of English local authorities led by one of the authors, conducted a few years after the implementation of the IG approach, we sought to establish how far this had evolved and to what extent this might alleviate at least some of the concerns over asymmetries of power and control highlighted above (see Richter and Wilson, 2013). The overall finding was that the understanding of the requirements of information governance by local officials was often a rather narrow one. More often than not, responses were driven by legislative requirements in areas of information transparency and data protection, and were normally only prompted by compliance requirements or public pressure under freedom of information legislation (Wilson *et al.*, 2011*b*; Richter and Wilson, 2013). In some instances, the changes that had taken place occurred only in the wake of the rising tide of 'data governance disasters' that seemingly plague public agencies in the UK. The struggle to strike a balance it seems has still to be resolved. We now explore some of these issues further by turning to the example of the smart card.

Smart Cards

Smart card technologies have been the focus of much interest by governments and public agencies. They provide a means of digital identity management that enables a more customer service orientated, customer focused, and customer satisfaction driven public service (Richter and Cornford, 2007: 35). The technology is not in itself new. It was invented well over thirty years ago and applications have been in evidence in the private sector for two decades or more, although many of these implementations have been characterized by 'spectacular and costly failures' (Blythe *et al.*, 2005: 47). Having said this, the technology is now regarded as 'mature' and the value to consumers in relation to private services is well established.

In contrast, for the purpose of public service delivery, smart cards represent a novel and attractive technology, albeit with distinctive challenges (Davies, 2004). For example, in Australia, transport smart card projects in the nation's two major cities, Melbourne and Sydney, have suffered from delays, cost overruns, and contract disputes. In Melbourne the city's 'Myki' card has been plagued by technical problems in getting the system to operate on Melbourne's iconic trams, and at one point it was dubbed 'the costliest and possibly the most delayed, smart card system in the world' (*The Age*, 2008, 2010). In Sydney, a smart card system—the 'Tcard'—was intended to link the city's ferry, bus, and train networks but was never implemented. In what was probably of some consolation for Melburnians, the project foundered amidst rising costs, contract wrangles, and legal disputes between the New South Wales State Government and the contractors (Clennel, 2007).

Despite such problems, the attraction for public agencies—initially at least—is that a citizen issued with just one card might be able to access a range of different service offerings—e.g. transport, education, and library services. At the same time the card might be used by public agencies and others to check entitlement to and/or collect payment for the services provided. In principle at least, the data held on, or associated with, the card by the service provider is protected from unauthorized access and use and the cards provide a means of establishing trusted channels of service delivery. As such, they have the potential 'to become *the* interface between the public' and the services local government and related providers 'put on-line' (Leibert, 2004; original emphasis). Indeed, more recent research by Lips and her colleagues suggests that smart cards and other identity management systems are having a 'substantial impact on informational relationships between the individual and the State' (Lips *et al.*, 2009*a*: 850). Moreover, they are becoming more important in their own right and not just as a supplement to more conventional 'paper-based or face-to-face' means (Lips *et al.*, 2009*a*: 837). In addition, the information generated is increasingly being used, either for later analysis or to influence behaviour, e.g. loyalty points schemes to reward healthy eating amongst the populace or for attending class on the part of school students; or by the police to track the travel patterns of individuals who are of interest to them (Cook, 2012; Dunn, 2012).

However, in illustration of our earlier discussion, the deployment and implementation of smart cards in public services raises significant identity management and information governance issues. For example, typically, the information is held on 'databases' that, although trusted, are likely to be hosted by third-party providers. This is often part of an arrangement where the 'production and issuing of smart cards, as well as the management and maintenance of identity information collected through citizens using the smart card', is undertaken by private operators (Lips *et al.*, 2009*a*: 851). The upshot is that public agencies are no longer the 'sole responsible party for managing citizen identity information', and for the citizen their relationship is now managed by a 'third party' (Lips *et al.*, 2009*a*: 851). The danger here, as Fountain has observed, is that along with such outsourcing of the supply of information system services can go an outsourcing of the public interest (Fountain, 2001).

The lessons from our own research suggest that in navigating such puzzles a number of interlocking factors need to be considered. We have captured these in what we term a 'generic framework' to guide multi-agency working (see Figure 5.1). The framework was originally developed

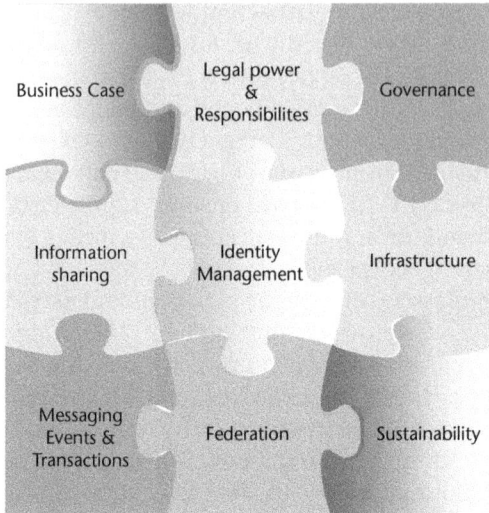

Figure 5.1 The Multi-Agency 'Joining-up' Puzzle
Source: FAME (2004).

as part of the UK Office of the Deputy Prime Minister's national programme on local e-government (see Chapter 6 and Appendix). The
intention was to provide guidance to local authorities faced with developing more joined-up service delivery through multi-agency working.
The kinds of issues this might involve include legislation and guidance
underpinning cross-agency service delivery; legal powers and duties
concerning information governance; and confidentiality and consent
for the management of identity. In addition, the framework addressed
the general questions of establishing and maintaining multi-agency
partnerships over time.

The framework identifies nine areas that public managers and others
embarking upon a multi-agency project should seek to address. These
include such things as the basic business case for the project; the legal
and ethical issues involved; the formal and informal rules by which
action can be pursued by multiple stakeholders in a multi-agency setting; information sharing within such partnerships; the design of technical systems to support this in relation to key areas such as identity
management; and a considering of how different multi-agency environments can themselves be joined together through federation and
the project 'mainstreamed' in everyday practice beyond its lifespan.
One feature of the tool was that it could be interrogated in different
ways by different stakeholders, starting from their point of initial

interest (e.g. technical matters for technology vendors or council IT departments) but then leading through the broader range of issues as perceived and understood by other stakeholders (e.g. in this instance, matters of information sharing and governance, legal concerns, and so forth).

In the case of a smart card project, a first requirement might be for public managers to develop a business case, a core feature of which would have to be the likely 'added value' that would be seen by citizens through the possession of a smart card to access a particular service (see Davies, 2004). In this simple form the business case for such a smart card is relatively easy to construct as it is an application developed for only one service which is most likely provided by a single agency. However, such a narrow focus runs the risk that any new systems developed will have purpose only within existing 'silos', resulting in a proliferation of integrated but not connected systems as each agency 'does its own thing'. An alternative approach would be to see the smart card based services of different agencies as using a common infrastructure, e.g. to manage identity and transactions. However, the business case for such infrastructural investments is much harder to establish. This is in part because the future uses to which this infrastructure might be put cannot by definition be predicted. That is, they are dependent upon innovation by future users such as public professionals and others as they devise new services or service combinations (much the same difficulty would have faced anyone seeking to make a business case for the deployment of the first telephone!). However, whether a single application for a given service or an attempt to develop an infrastructure to provide shared services to support a range of applications, most of which are not known at the outset, the perceived value in both cases also needs to be set against potential fears over such things as privacy of information and civil liberties.

The issues here crystallize around governance concerning the procurement, operation, and use of information. For example, by bringing multiple stakeholders (including service users) from within and beyond the public sector together there is a need to ensure common purpose and vision, whilst also acknowledging and respecting the integrity of individual agencies and interests. In this context information sharing needs to be thought of as a means by which members of a partnership or community can publish, with the consent of their customers, in appropriate publication spaces. One benefit is that the resulting system is likely to be more 'future proof' than a stand-alone application. It is thereby likely to assist public managers and elected officials in avoiding, *inter alia*, potential downstream political embarrassment as a result of the adoption of quickly outmoded technology or applications which are not sufficiently flexible to cope with changing citizen needs and requirements. It also recognizes that the investment in infrastructure is not about the creation of monuments to current policy which will inevitably change and require the replacement of the systems. The following provides an example from our own research of an attempt to apply some of these ideas in practice.

Building a regional multi-use smart card community

During the first decade of the 21st century the UK Government sought to promote the take-up of smart card applications by local government through the 'National Smart Card Project'. This was part of the National Programme for Local e-Government (see Chapter 6 for more details). The case study we outline here predates the start of the national programme but was to be part of a national network of projects focused upon developing smart card applications at a local and regional level. The case study itself arises from one of the AMASE project pilots (see the Appendix). The study involved a distinctive methodology where we sought to intervene as action researchers in the process of technology procurement in order, *inter alia*, to highlight issues of identity management and information governance that might otherwise have been neglected. The project involved the use of smart cards in transport. In this context smart cards provide a 'contactless' means of a user loading value onto the card and then using this to embark on multiple journeys, recharging the card as required, with debits for each journey being made automatically.

Travel transactions for public transport typically involve the collection of a high volume of low-value fares using a variety of paper-based (ticket) or semi-automated methods (travel pass) for providing proof that the holder has paid and is entitled to travel (AGIMO, 2008). Behind this typically lies a complex predominantly manual and labour-intensive 'back office' requirement to manage and process transactions and deal with refunds and other matters of recourse. From the service user point of view, such systems involve confusing fare structures and practices, long queues at peak periods to buy tickets and have them checked prior to boarding, and the need to carry other proof of entitlements whilst travelling on concessionary fares. Smart card systems promise numerous improvements, including more reliable and integrated ticketing across different transport offerings, reductions in fraud and fare evasion, automated back office processing, and an improved service user experience, with the potential for add-on services and products. In the search for such improvements, smart card technology has been deployed in many major cities and city regions over the past decade or so, most notably and successfully in London, Hong Kong, Singapore, San Francisco, and the German Rhineland (see AGIMO, 2008).

In 2000, *Big City Council* (a metropolitan local government agency in England) was designated the lead authority in the procurement of a smart card system by partner councils in the region who would be the scheme owners, governors, and card issuers—eventually all twenty-six local authorities in the region joined. A *Regional Smart Card Consortium (RSCC)* was formed, with the involvement of local transport operators (who were the transport service providers and would operate the card readers, etc.). Other stakeholders included would-be system suppliers and the varied sections of the population in the region from which the cardholders would come. The scheme would serve a region covering 8,600 square kilometres (sq km) and 2.6 million citizens, mainly living in two large conurbations—although two-thirds of the region concerned was rural. It was intended that the card would initially cover bus, rail, and light rail services in the region and subsequently would also be extended to cover other transport and also non-transport-related services.

The *RSCC* project therefore involved a wide range of agencies and service applications. As such it was, arguably, far more challenging in technological and organizational terms than contemporaneous developments in the UK such as the London 'Oyster Card'. The Oyster Card is now used by citizens to prepay for access to public transport in the UK's capital city. However, much of its success rests on the 'captive demand' provided by London commuters (meaning sufficient volumes to support citizen value and a viable business case) and the fact that the system itself has proven sufficiently scalable to cope with increases in demand above the levels initially predicted. The system has also been shown to be sufficiently infrastructural in concept to allow new applications, unforeseen prior to implementation, such as web-based ordering of cards and on-line top-ups, to add value for the citizen (Dunleavy *et al.*, 2005: 21).

However, unlike the *RSCC* smart card, the Oyster Card was conceived as a single-application deployment that involved only one local government authority ('Transport for London'), in partnership with the various transport operators. In contrast the *RSCC* project was neither solely concerned with transport services nor exclusively the province of a single local authority. In fact it aimed to integrate transport, education, and eventually other services (subsequent applications covering health and social care, general concessionary travel, and culture and tourism were also developed) across an entire provincial region, embracing all local jurisdictions. In addition, transport operators, the regional passenger transport executive, and the regional economic development agency were also involved. The overall objective at the time was to have nearly all eligible citizens as users by 2010.

At the start of the project a *Large Consultancy* firm was engaged to explore technical issues and assess the commercial viability of the proposed multi-application smart card. In May 2002, a major *Smart Card Supplier* made a proposal to deliver a complete 'integrated solution' for the region. This was met with reservations from public sector representatives in the consortium. The action researchers' diagnosis of the underlying cause of this rejection was that the proposed approach did not embody a concept of public sector governance and the responsibilities associated with the public sector brand. The researchers were then invited to work with the consortium with the aim of assisting them in developing a framework appropriate to a situation where citizen identity and other information would be collected and available for sharing across a wide range of public agencies and private suppliers.

Initially, discussions amongst the consortium members had been dominated by the technicalities of co-hosting different applications on to a single card. Discussion was focused upon the specification of service applications that would link transport and education—e.g. concessionary bus journeys to school. Moreover, there was also political pressure to move quickly to demonstrate some 'live' implementations of smart cards within the region. For example, it was claimed that some local politicians became excited by the prospect that cards could be configured to prevent young people travelling after a certain hour—a sort of 'curfew card' as they saw it! Gradually, however, the consortium started to realize that trying to identify which combination of applications and associated business cases would provide the best value on which to base a procurement decision was not the most appropriate approach.

As a result, attention shifted towards a consideration of the issues of identity management and governance. Facilitated by the action research team, a different language began to emerge which sought to specify the architecture for delivering 'shared' and 'trusted' services—in other words a 'build once and use many times infrastructure'. At one important stage in this process, the action researchers coloured in an emerging technical architecture diagram and an interesting terminology of the 'pink stuff' and the 'blue stuff' was spontaneously adopted by consortium members. This signified the distinction between functionality that was to be shared in use and in governance—the federation services—and those functions that were to be provided in cooperation

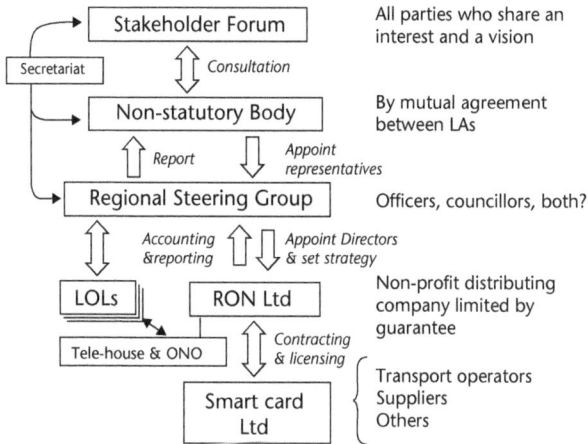

Figure 5.2 Governance Structure for a Regional Smart Card

or in competition through an emerging market. The envisaged infrastructure which emerged from this was seen as the platform for the creation of a range of offerings through the regional smart card that would be able to support 'multiple brands and multiple applications'. Accordingly, in order to inform its procurement decision, the consortium developed region-wide objectives, provided regional-level coordination across organizational boundaries, and outlined a model of 'federated services' to manage identity, recourse, and settlement, and the publication of information.

For example, in relation to governance frameworks, Figure 5.2 provides an example of proposed relationships between a stakeholder forum, a public sector 'Steering Group', a legal vehicle for commissioning and contracting which is non-profit-distributing and limited by guarantee, and a set of daughter joint-venture vehicles to deliver services. An important principle embodied in this approach was that the public sector interests had the means and mechanisms to sort out their collective priorities and policies among themselves. This in turn would enable them to present a coherent view to private commercial entities that were partnering with them in the provision, operation, and use of a common smart card infrastructure. Under the auspices of the Regional Development Agency and a Regional Strategy Board a number of these entities were established.

However, the local authorities were unable to reach an agreement on how to work together in this framework (they had never managed to do so on any other issue in the region and, indeed, two of the major councils located on opposite banks of a river were, for a limited period at the time, barely on speaking terms following disputes over previous projects). In the event, therefore, no procurement ever took place, although smaller scale projects in the region emerged out of the work. Moreover, whilst the project itself did not come to fruition in terms of either the agreement of a governance framework or a successful implementation, at least on anything like the scale originally envisaged, the activities involved in building the consortium assisted in avoiding the kind of mistakes which might have led to citizens in the region holding multiple smart cards from a variety of separate local schemes and initiatives. We now turn to the question of whether the intended users of smart cards and other such systems are more appropriately regarded as 'customers' rather than citizens.

From Citizens to 'Consumers': CRM

E-commerce enterprises, such as Amazon, and social media sites, such as Facebook, are often cited as exemplars that provide 'personalized' and 'customized' service delivery by virtual means that stand in stark contrast to the 'mass-produced' public services typically provided by public bureaucracies (Taylor *et al.*, 2007). More generally, in the private sector, e-commerce solutions have emerged as a powerful commercial tool (Taylor *et al.*, 2007). They allow the capture and analysis of information that reveals the tastes and preferences of consumers and allows the construction of personal 'profiles' of their customer-base is clearly a significant benefit to the sellers of products and services. The investment in the supply-side of digital government is to a great extent predicated on an assumption that such capabilities would also be beneficial if deployed in the delivery of public services.

The appeal of such systems is central to the modernization project of many governments. For example, the UK Cabinet Office has stated that:

> Achieving widespread citizen acceptance and take-up of services via new channels presents an urgent and important challenge if we are to realize the benefits from these new and innovative ways of working. In order to do this, we need to improve our understanding of customer preferences, as well as their needs. (Cabinet Office, 2006: 52)

Customer Relationship Management (CRM) systems are one of the principal means through which this objective has been pursued. CRM 'refers to a collection of techniques and technologies that help organizations manage their interaction with their customers by providing the

Channels	White Mail	Fax	Telephone	SMS	In person	Email	Web	Other Future Channels

Consistent Service

Front Office	Contact Centre CRM	One-Stop Shop CRM	Self Help: Online

Integration

Back Office			Laptops
	Office Based	Field Based	PDAs

Third Parties (examples)	Contractors	Government Agencies	Policies	Consultees/ Experts	External Agencies

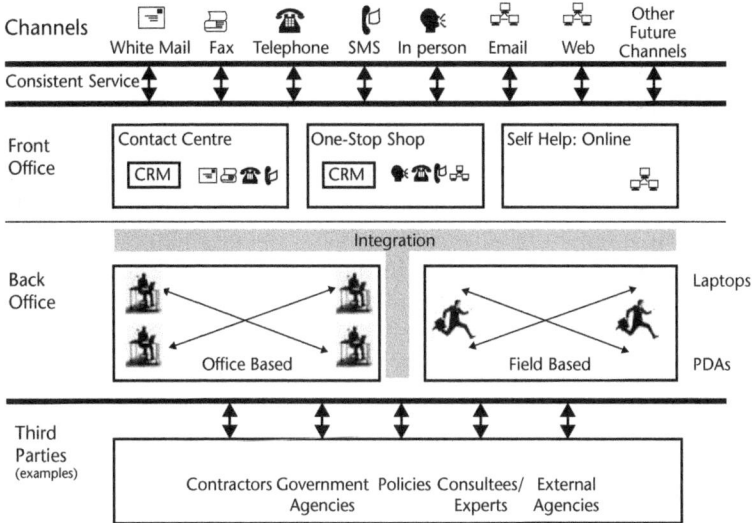

Figure 5.3 Component Elements of a CRM System

Source: Cornford and Richter (2008). Reprinted with permission of Cambridge University Press..

organization with a better knowledge and understanding of customer "needs" and by providing the customer with a consistent interface to the organization' (Richter and Cornford, 2008: 212). The information gathered by such systems can be used to support 'front office' interactions with customers, to analyse and model aggregate trends concerning customer behaviour, and to enable 'self-service' by customers and disintermediate relationships with them (Richter and Cornford, 2008: 212).

A government depiction of how such systems might operate in public services at the local level is provided in Figure 5.3. This illustrates the multiple channels available to 'consumers' to interact with a local council 'front office', either 'walk-in' through 'one-stop shops' or 'virtually' through contact centres. The 'front office' operation provides a consistent set of service standards and a 'seamless' customer experience, whilst 'joining up' the various 'back office' service-providing areas. Above all, CRM provides the basis for gathering information about 'customers' and for 'tailoring' and 'personalizing' services according to their specific needs and requirements (Richter and Cornford, 2008). How effective is this model of the relationship between citizens and public agencies? As we have already noted, notwithstanding the substantial investment made by many governments in the supply-side of e-enabling services, the target end-user or 'customer' does not seem to have responded by taking up these opportunities as enthusiastically as might have been expected. As our colleagues Paul Richter and James Cornford have put it, how are we to explain 'e-government without e-citizens' (Richter and Cornford, 2007: 35)? Digital government seems to be creating a world where, if citizens and business users of public services are not being put 'in line', as Bill Clinton suggested, they seem to be showing a significant reluctance to go 'on-line'! In order to explore these issues we return to *Big City Council* and research on its own attempts to develop CRM.

CRM at Big City Council

This study again arose as an extension of our initial research into the procurement of CRM software at the Council as part of the AMASE project (see the Appendix). Accounts of the initial study can be found in Pollock (2004) and Williams and Pollock (2008). The extension study, conducted between 2003 and 2005, is reported in Richter *et al.* (2004) and Richter and Cornford (2007, 2008), on which the following draws. The procurement of the software was part of a broader CRM strategy being developed by the Council. This strategy established a 'customer service division' which was populated by both council workers and a large number of new managerial and other recruits from the private sector, with experience in customer call and contact centres. A central customer service centre to handle face-to-face, telephone, email, and web enquiries was set up, followed quickly by a number of satellite operations. This new 'front office' was eventually to handle 90 per cent of interactions with council service users. As in private sector applications, interactions with customers by front-line staff in the service centre were structured according to 'scripts' embedded in the system software. Whilst observation of the work of the front-line staff suggested that these scripts were only 'quite loosely' followed, managers reported a concerted attempt over time to move the interactions with customers from a 'mainly reactive' mode to become more proactive. For example, there was an attempt to seek to anticipate future needs of 'customers' on the basis of forthcoming 'life events' (e.g. house move, birth or death in the family, or child starting school), to which specific services could be targeted.

One interesting feature of this approach was the implicit notion of 'the customer' that lay behind the council's strategy. This was very consistent with, and no doubt had its origins in, national government thinking at the time. First, there was an assumption that the 'customer' wants to be 'satisfied' and that the objective of the CRM strategy, and the means by which its performance was evaluated, was delivering this 'satisfaction':

> Customer Services is part of [Big City Service] and is a customer focused organisation aiming to deliver high quality and easy to use services in a place and time to suit you. We want to provide you with modern services that meet your needs and give you a choice about how, when and where you want to get in touch with us. This is achieved through our network of local Customer Service Centres and the launch of the councils first Contact Centre. (Big City website; cited by Richter and Cornford, 2008: 217)

Second, this view was evidently internalized by service centre staff who viewed their 'customers' as demanding, in terms of their expectations, and keen to drive down the cost of services and to get value for money. In other words, as far as the council and its service centre staff were concerned, the citizens it served were 'assumed to be no different than the customer of any commercial service—both demand excellence in customer service in their pursuit of self-interest' (Richter and Cornford, 2008: 218). Third, the view of 'customer-focus' involved adhered to the notion that public service was now about satisfying personalized and individualized needs. There was no recognition of a more general notion of a 'wider public good' that public agencies were obligated to serve. Indeed, the 'citizen' and the 'customer' seemed to have been merged together in the council's thinking.

Social citizens or rational consumers?

A number of explanations have been offered for the apparent reluctance of the end-users to embrace e-enabled service delivery. For example, the assumption of policy-makers appears to be that this is the result of a failure to communicate clearly and fully enough the availability of new e-enabled channels to their target audiences, a task hampered by a need also to change the culture of front-line bureaucrats. However, once addressed through 'cultural change' programmes and the like—something achieved with apparent aplomb by Big City—the full impact of the new systems will be delivered. On the other hand, others have suggested that the problem may lie in the design of the systems themselves and the 'design-mismatch' that is resulting from systems developed in the private sector for e-commerce when adopted in the rather different setting of public services. Problems identified here range from the poor usability of service user interfaces, the ability of public agencies to manage the implementation of complex projects intended to provide such interfaces, and a tendency for private sector suppliers to 'over-sell' the capabilities of their products to 'naïve public sector adopters'. Again, *Big City* appears to have managed the procurement and deployment of CRM in a manner that avoided these potential difficulties (see Pollock, 1984).

Finally, a third set of explanations focuses on the dynamics of customer satisfaction itself, and in particular the extent to which this is a function of expectations. Simply put, the problem is not that public agencies are failing to adopt a customer focus and to communicate this to their customers, or that the e-enabled systems and channels for doing this are not 'fit for purpose'. Rather, the real problem is that customers' expectations are being set by more rapid advances and developments in the private sector, and it is these that act as the benchmark in their assessment of improvements in public services (see Richter and Cornford, 2007: 38–9). As the study of CRM in *Big City Council* did not involve 'customers' directly, it is difficult to evaluate this, although such a view certainly seems consistent with the perceptions of 'what customers wanted' articulated by front-line workers in the service centre.

A further explanation, advanced by Richter and Cornford, is that the problem lies in the representation of 'the customer' developed by service providers such as *Big City*, in the context of broader government policies. It is these representations, gleaned and selected from data derived from a variety of means and sources that, it is claimed, are deployed to confirm an organizational view of who 'the customer' is. As they put it:

> while the concept of customer focus is intended to orient the organization externally, to do this it must first orient the organization internally, towards its own processes and techniques and the categories and narratives which underlie them. Before the organization can turn outwards, it must turn inwards. Strictly speaking, then, public services thus cannot be built 'around the customer'—they must be built around a *representation of the customer*. (Richter and Cornford, 2007: 40)

Moreover, whilst public agencies have always had to engage in the construction of such representations, the effect of digital government has been to impose 'a new requirement for a much more explicit and shared representation of the customer' as assumptions about 'the customer' have to be embodied in and represented by system software (Richter and Cornford, 2007: 40). If this argument is accepted, then the key issues become the ones of who is responsible for the construction of these representations, what tools and resources they use and how these constrain the activity, and what are the implications of the 'consumer identities' they create as a result? Richter and Cornford are clear that, as things currently stand, 'the public service user is envisaged as an individual, characterized by means–ends rationality, coherence, self-knowledge and self-interest' and, to boot, 'time pressured, demanding and constantly susceptible to rising expectations' (Richter and Cornford, 2007: 42). However, it can be questioned whether the identity of service users themselves is readily embraced in these terms. Typically, citizens live their lives, it has been suggested, in broader terms and the notion of 'consumer' does not embrace all aspects of the connections they feel they have with public services (Clarke and Newman, 2005, cited by Richter and Cornford, 2007: 38).

One way to address such issues might be to seek to increase the involvement of citizens in the governance and management of public agencies, to ensure that their 'voice' is heard more clearly. However, this assumes citizens want this level of active engagement as the price of being listened to. It also assumes that the views they might wish to convey would readily result in alternative modes of operation and technological configuration at the level of service design and delivery. For Richter and Cornford (2007) the question is one of how to change the representational models of the customer that obviously do not resonate with the identities that citizens hold of themselves. The way to address this, they suggest, is not to find better ways of getting the 'customer's voice heard' but rather for public agencies to learn how to listen better to citizens who may well wish to say things outwith the representation of them as a customer by the agency (Richter and Cornford, 2007: 43). This line of reasoning opens up some interesting questions about how to better engage 'users' in the design of services and the information systems that support their delivery: an issue we focus on in Chapter 7.

Conclusion

It is clear that information governance and identity management are now a fundamental part of the business requirements of all public service providing organizations. The academic and policy debate on these matters, however, has polarized into an argument between what is required to deliver the 'service state' and what is tolerable to avoid the emergence of a 'surveillance state'. We suggest that such 'one-dimensional' arguments only highlight aspects of the dilemmas and issues involved. What is at issue in the debate between the 'service' and 'surveillance' views is whether the 'truth' assumed to be embedded in centralized databases and the like is being deployed for positive or negative purposes. However, as we have sought to show, such 'truths' are relative and are associated with the relational contexts in which such associations are made. This takes us to the heart of the problems of identity management and information governance. When delivering public services it is necessary to know what the specific relationship is between the service provider and the client who is the subject of the information to be shared, and the contexts of the service providers' activities within that relationship. In other words, we need to understand the nature of the conversation that is taking place, who the conversationalists are, and what their role in the relationship is. In short, if digital identity management is the 'sine qua non' of digital government, we need to be extremely careful about the concepts and practices of 'identity' and 'governance' associated with it. We will have more to say on this issue when we revisit Mrs Cannybody's dilemma in Chapter 8.

6

On-Line on the Front Line: FAME

Introduction

Earlier, in Chapter 2, we reviewed claims that the effects of techno-logical change on public organizations were best understood as a process of technology enactment. Here choices over the deployment, implementation, and use of new technologies may reinforce existing 'organizational, political and institutional logics', whilst other more entrepreneurial behaviours may—although it seems seldom do—lead to fundamental organizational change and institutional transformation (Fountain, 2001). The idea of enactment places those on the front line in public organizations—be they public managers, professionals, work-ers (in some cases working for external providers in the not-for-profit or private sectors)—at the centre of putting services on-line. In this chapter we explore the role of local service providers on the front line and the implications of the e-enabling of services for their work. We consider this issue through the largest of the projects within the UK Government National Programme for Local e-Government—FAME. In particular we consider the question of whether there are immutable institutional bar-riers to innovation in public agencies, or whether it is possible for actors to overcome these—and, if so, in what circumstances? Before consider-ing all of this, we explore the debate over the effects of digital govern-ment on those on the front line of service delivery.

Street-Level Bureaucrats and Digital Government

Government policies are implemented by managers, professionals, and employees who interact directly with citizens in the delivery of public services. They are the groups first designated by Lipsky (1980, 2010) as the 'street-level bureaucrats' through whom most citizens encounter government and whose actions constitute the services delivered by government. Street-level bureaucrats, according to Lipsky, struggle with heavy workloads and competing demands from policy-makers and from their clients, patients, and citizens more generally. Their characteristic dilemma across public services is to 'find a way to resolve the incompatible orientation towards client-centered practice on the one hand and expedient and efficient practice on the other' (Lipsky, 1980: 45). The decisions they make, the routines they establish, and the devices they invent to cope with daily work can mean that official priorities may not be followed in practice. In an updated version of his book published thirty years later, despite the substantive changes to the context, process, and content of public service delivery, Lipsky still claims that such discretion is the enduring and defining feature of front-line work (Lipsky, 2010).

The notion of street-level bureaucracy therefore strongly suggests that many workers in front-line public services have discretion to create their own versions of their jobs in ways that contrast, say, with services in the private sector (Kerfoot and Korczynski, 2005). Indeed, it has been claimed that it is in the discretionary practices of 'street level bureaucracies' that 'policy comes alive' and 'reality is shown to be far more complex and varied than legislators had ever dreamed' (Bovens and Zouridis, 2002: 175). This seems to have been borne out in many studies of front-line work. For instance, Maynard-Moody and Musheno's (2003) classic ethnography of working on the front line in US public services, found that the stories told by the police, teachers, and counsellors conveyed 'a strong orientation toward faces, or who people are, and towards the worker's own beliefs, their value systems, in explaining their decision making', whilst at the same time seeking to balance their 'beliefs about people' with the requirements of prevailing policies, rules, and procedures (Maynard-Moody and Musheno, 2003: 4).

However, it has been argued that such discretion on the part of street-level bureaucrats is increasingly curtailed by the introduction of digital technologies. One influential thesis, for instance, is that the onset of digital government will transform the front-line worker from a 'street-level', to 'screen-level', and ultimately a 'system-level' bureaucrat:

Window clerks are being replace by web sites and advanced information and expert systems are taking over the role of case managers and adjudicating officers. Instead of noisy, disorganized decision-making factories populated by fickle officials, many of these executive agencies are fast becoming quiet information refineries, in which nearly all decisions are pre-programmed algorithms and digital decision trees. Today, a more true-to-life vision of the term 'bureaucracy' would be a room filled with softly humming servers, dotted here and there with a system manager behind a screen. (Bovens and Zouridis, 2002: 175).

In such a scenario, relations between front-line staff and citizens become disintermediated by digital technologies. In 'screen-level' bureaucracies, 'contacts always run through or in the presence of a computer screen' and 'public servants can no longer freely take to the streets'; and, as perhaps in the case of the customer service centre outlined in the previous chapter, 'they are always connected to the organization by the computer' (Bovens and Zouridis, 2002: 177).

As a result, the task of the front-line worker is essentially that of a data entry clerk, completing on-line forms and assessments to a predetermined template. This information is then acted upon in many instances, not by the front-line worker, but through an automated process enacted through decision rules embedded in the computer system. However, even the discretion that remains under these circumstances can be further circumscribed. The further development of digital technologies involves the entire process of dealing with the client being automated, that is, executed and controlled without the involvement of front-line staff. Here interactions, at least routine ones, between the citizen and the state are entirely virtual and conducted through e-enabled means such as websites, email, etc. (Bovens and Zouridis, 2002: 177).

These arguments were developed over a decade ago and, at their authors' admission, applied mainly at that time to large centralized executive agencies (such as the student grants and loans or traffic violations agencies they studied) that typically deal with high volumes of mainly transactional interactions with citizens. However, it would be reasonable to suppose, given the pace of technological development over the past decade, that such arguments may well now apply more widely. One might expect, for example, that face-to-face relationships are increasingly being supplanted by far more impersonal virtual means of communicating and interacting beyond the mainly transactional dealings between public agencies and citizens. In areas such as health or social care where service provision is more relational than transactional, such disintermediation might bring a new—and perhaps unwelcome—character to the service provider–client/patient interaction (an example of which we provide in the following chapter).

Such developments would seem to threaten to undermine the discretionary practice of those on the front line in these kinds of service domain. In fact numerous studies have noted a growing trend of adverse consequences following the restructuring of care services. Such changes have often but not always been underpinned by technological developments. The outcomes have been reported as including: casualization, work intensification, loss of job security, and increasing monitoring and distrust by senior management (see e.g. Hebson *et al.*, 2003; Cochrane, 2004; Law and Mooney, 2007). There is also evidence that front-line employees sometimes perceive digital technologies in the workplace as undermining their autonomy and expertise (Harrison, 2002; Haynes, 2003; Henwood and Hart, 2003; Nettleton and Burrows, 2003; Stam *et al.*, 2004). However, there is other evidence to suggest that the effects of 'automating' (Zuboff, 1988) on front-line workers has been limited, that they are still able to exercise discretion, and are not simply being turned into 'screen' or 'system' bureaucrats.

This is evident, for instance, in the example of the effects on social workers of the new information systems to support the joining up of services for children in the UK (see Chapter 4). A two-year research programme using ethnographic methods to explore the implications of electronic CAF in England and Wales found that, despite the intentions of system designers and policy sponsors, there was nonetheless in practice a 'continuing relevance of professional discretion' (Pithouse *et al.*, 2009: 604; see also e.g. White *et al.*, 2010). One reason for this appeared to be the poor design of the system itself, which was found to be technologically 'over-determined' (a phenomenon analogous to what we have termed 'over-integration'). Thus the 'explicit assumptions of some standardizing' and a 'shared sense-making template' that were designed into the system could not be brought about in practice. This seemed to ignore the different perspectives, viewpoints, and ways of making sense of the multiple service users who could write to the CAF (Pithouse *et al.*, 2009: 604).

In fact, rather than provide a 'straightforward assessment architecture of the common assessment framework' that would support a common language of assessment across different service specialisms, the CAF record resembled more a 'reflection in a maze of fun fair mirrors' that distorted as much as revealed these multiple viewpoints. As a result:

> Far from compressing writer knowledge into bites of uniform information, the CAF of practice as a hybridized and mediated local system, allows a multitude of responses (including avoidance and non-compliance) that for some may amount to a referral, for others an internal memorandum to progress some planning, for most a means to register less the explicit needs of some child but more the particular concerns of the writer constructed in light of their own professional standpoint. The CAF as a classification system has to some extent been designed without much anticipation of

its situated use. It inevitably fails to grasp how its ambition of a shared language cannot realistically corral and make common the variable orientations that stem from occupational groups differently trained, tasked and conceptually located. (Pithouse *et al.*, 2009: 609)

Murphy *et al.* (2009) provide a somewhat more positive slant on the way in which front-line practitioners can use their discretionary power to shape the outcomes of e-enabling services. In a comprehensive literature review and large-scale tightly controlled study of client responses to 'cyber-counselling' (i.e. on-line as opposed to face-to-face consultations), it was found that, with certain caveats, on-line counselling improved the home and work lives of clients and that this could be achieved in much the same way as through face-to-face interaction (Murphy *et al.*, 2009).

One view that has significant popular and public support is that, amidst such complex dynamics, the front-line worker appears as a barrier to change and technological progress. For example, if the benefits of 'cyber-counselling' can be clearly demonstrated, why do social workers seemingly resist its widespread adoption? Similarly, if social workers, as Pithouse *et al.* (2009) claim, purposefully engage in 'subversion as a tactical device' when they perceive digital technology is 'fit for their purpose' (Pithouse *et al.*, 2009: 604), is this not a further indication of occupational and other barriers to e-enabled service improvements? Indeed, the autonomy exercised, especially by those in the ranks of professional and semi-professional occupations, may act as barriers to 'culture change that transforms the way in which individuals and organizational units perceive the role and purpose of information' (McIvor *et al.*, 2004: 66). For some commentators, and many policy designers, such factors appear to lie at the core of the public sector's apparent failure to embrace digital technologies in the same way as (it is believed they have been) in the private sector (see e.g. *The Economist*, 2008).

However, others, in seeking to explain the apparent 'resistance' to change of front-line workers and professionals, put much more emphasis on the pressures of everyday workloads, under-resourcing, and the constraints that keeping existing operations on the road in such circumstances places on the easy acceptance and engagement with innovation and change. For example, in the context of multi-agency working, it has been observed that services tend to be overburdened with their own schedules and deadlines (Wigfall and Moss, 2001). Similarly, factors inhibiting rapport, trust, and willingness to share information and knowledge are rarely purely cultural, according to Easen *et al.* (2000), but include different conditions of work, resources, and status, as well as cutbacks, reorganizations, and short-term funding initiatives. Others have pointed to the pace of reform and change itself, which is often rapid and leaves little time for adjustment or consolidation (Robinson and Cottrell, 2005).

In Chapter 2 we discussed the idea of 'technology enactment' and the question of the scope that this suggests front-line practitioners actually have or do not have to shape technological and organizational change around their practice. It will be recalled that those with a leaning towards institutional theory suggest that such agency is ultimately constrained by conservative and stability-oriented sets of institutionalized structures, norms, and practices which can also become inscribed in enacted technology (Fountain, 2001: 88). In other words, factors that are typically identified as 'barriers to change' in public services, such as professional and workforce norms and values, lack of training and skills reflect broader, more institutionally embedded characteristics. On the other hand, there are some more agency-orientated perspectives, such as those which emphasize the constitutive role of practice, which would seem to give far more scope for such local action and influence. Here, everyday interactions with the 'technology at hand' are stressed rather than the constraining (or for that matter enabling) characteristics of technologies assumed to be embodied with 'structures, norms and practices'. Moreover, these ongoing interactions between the material and the social in everyday practice can become a significant source of innovation in themselves (e.g. Orlikowski, 2000; Boudreau and Robey, 2005). We will now explore these issues in the context of the major programme of reform in the UK (as applied to England) to transform local government by digital means and join up the delivery of local services.

Digital Local Government in England

As we suggested in Chapter 1, the mid-1990s was a period during which many Western governments began to promote the benefits of the 'digital revolution'. Accordingly, many adopted policies which embraced 'the idea that new technology might be exploited to "re-invent" their own activities' (Bellamy and Taylor, 1998: 4). In many national contexts, it is the local level of government that has been the locus of many of the subsequent attempts to bring about such transformation, in particular where this has involved the aim of improving services through increased information sharing and the development of more joined-up delivery. In order to explore the nature of the technological and organizational changes involved in such developments, therefore, we now focus on the experience of local authorities in England over the past ten or so years, and of course the vital role played by front-line workers within them.

Examining the British Government's response during the 1990s to the promise of digital technology to transform government and service delivery, Bellamy and Taylor, in their review of prospects at the time, described the response to these issues as 'patchy and cautious' (1998: 7). However, by the end of the decade, this had changed. The British Prime Minister Tony Blair (whose first New Labour government had been elected in May 1997) pledged in 2000 that 100 per cent of public services would, where possible, be made available electronically by 2005. Digital government rapidly became a central plank of the government agenda to modernize public services (Bloomfield and Hayes, 2009). This pledge applied to all public services. However, estimates at the time suggested that in Britain some 80 per cent of interaction between public service providers and the public were managed at the local or regional, rather than the national level (Cornford *et al.*, 2003). The then 388 local authorities in England (and their Welsh, Scottish, and Northern Irish counterparts) were the central players in coordinating and delivering this local and regional provision—sometimes as a consequence of statutory obligations, as in the case of the provision of services for children (see Chapter 4). As a result, they were inevitably cast as the lead actors in the new strategy to deliver public services by digital means.

This role was emphasized by the *National Strategy for Local e-Government* published early in the new century. This declared:

> Local e-Government offers a chance to breathe new life into local democracy
> and to transform local services. E-Government is central to our ambitions
> to reform and modernize all our public services and local e-Government is
> an integral part of the overall UK Online programme to realize the benefits
> of the Internet for all our citizens. (ODPM, 2002: 3)

The strategy also identified clear and broad objectives which extended the purpose of e-government beyond the mere e-enabling of services to: (1) service transformation by making them more accessible, more convenient, more responsive, and more cost-effective; (2) the renewal of local democracy by making councils more open, more accountable, more inclusive, and better able to lead their communities; and (3) the generation of economic vitality by promoting a modern communications infrastructure, relevant skills, and support for new e-businesses.

These objectives were ambitious and it was clear that to achieve the range and scale of outcomes identified would take a number of years.

This was borne out by initial assessments of progress that suggested that the most significant early outcomes and effects tended to be focused on the provision of e-enabled information (the first 'cataloguing' or 'bulletinboard' stage of digital government—see Chapter 1) rather than more complex e-enabled services involving supporting transactional relationships with citizens (see Cornford *et al.*, 2003, for a summary of early research on progress towards government targets). The more complex organizational changes required to 'e-enable' services were still in their infancy. By the same token, early studies of progress also highlighted that local authorities were more likely to have increased the provision and take-up of their own information and service provision than to have sought to e-enable services that were jointly provided with other agencies and bodies. This may have reflected the problems encountered in devising and implementing joint solutions and the difficulties around information sharing across existing agency and professional boundaries. It also points to the danger of new digital technologies being deployed by local authorities to do the same things differently, rather than to do new things that would result, for example, in multi-agency working to deliver more 'joined-up' services (Cornford *et al.*, 2003; McLoughlin and Cornford, 2006).

It was against this backcloth that the then Office of the Deputy Prime Minister (ODPM), at the time responsible for local government in England, launched the National Programme for Local e-Government. Twenty-three national projects were created with funding of £80 million. These covered what were then seen as the key priority services provided by local authorities. The aim of the projects was to ensure that all local authorities had access to digital government services and associated 'building blocks', without having to 'build them from scratch'. The programme involved local councils, central government, the private sector, and others to define and deliver projects that offered national solutions. On conclusion of the programme in December 2005, products from the national projects were then 'migrated to safe homes', mainly within local authorities.

The National Programme and FAME

The FrAmework for Multi-agency Environments (*FAME*) was by far the largest and most ambitious of the twenty-three national projects (Baines *et al.*, 2010). The ODPM provided £6 million in funding for *FAME* Phase One. The project was led by the London Borough of Lewisham, in partnership with several other local authorities, technology vendors, and

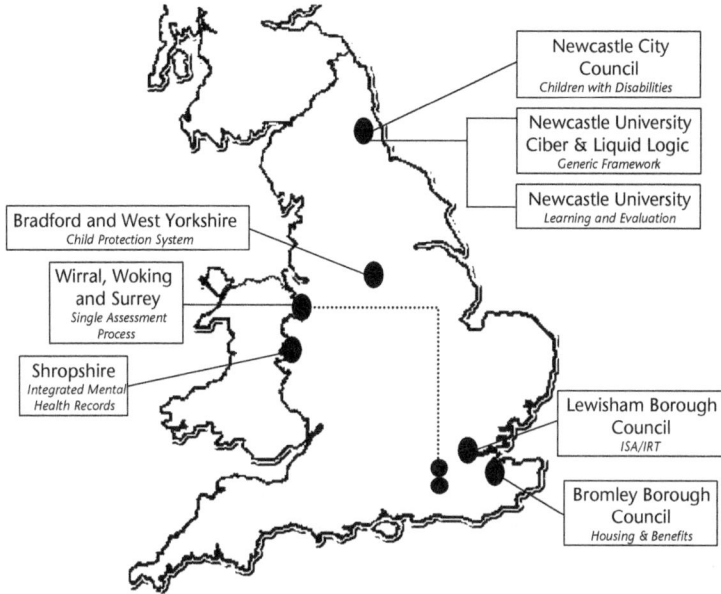

Figure 6.1 FAME Strands and Lead Local Authorities

the authors with colleagues as university research partners. A second phase of *FAME* consisted of dissemination activities, and a third phase was concerned with demonstrating a transition to a multi-agency, multi-service shared infrastructure in a regional context. In this chapter we are concerned primarily with the experience of *FAME* Phase One (the following draws extensively on Baines *et al.*, 2010, see also Baines *et al.*, 2005; McLoughlin and Cornford, 2006; Gannon-Leary *et al.*, 2006).

The aim of this phase was to implement information systems at a local level in six pilot sites, in order to support information sharing in specific services (see Figure 6.1). The overall objective was to establish a multi-agency approach to meeting the challenge of transformation in the delivery of local public services. The lessons from the *FAME* project, as with the other national projects, would then provide a basis for more general adoption of multi-agency working at the local level. The first phase of *FAME* ran from April 2003 to October 2004, with six discrete projects (known as strands) led by local authorities throughout England. Each local strand worked with a technology vendor (referred to as a technology partner) to produce a technical system for the exchange and management of client/patient information across agency and professional boundaries in the service domain concerned.

All the strands involved at their core some combination of social services, health, education, and the police, plus one or other of the supplier partners. In addition, voluntary sector agencies also participated as partners in some but not all strands. Some strands had more than one local authority partner. The university research team, along with other partners in the project, worked to link participating agencies and their systems, with secure and timely exchange of information according to locally agreed protocols.

The timescale for FAME Phase One, given the scope and complexity of the work being undertaken, turned out to be over-optimistic. Only two of the six projects—one concerned with promoting the independence of vulnerable older people and the other of integrating mental health services—achieved the promised implementation of live systems on schedule by May 2004. Two projects, one concerning information sharing and the assessment of children at risk, and the other joining up services for children with disabilities, went live later in 2004. In the case of a project concerned with interworking to deliver housing benefit payments to citizens, the lead authority decided not to proceed with the building of the required IT system. Finally, a project concerned with developing an information system to assist in child protection services had a live system working within the lead authority by the end of 2004 but faced a series of setbacks, as a result of which there had been little progress with the objective of sharing information as intended across neighbouring local authorities.

On the front line in FAME

It is against this background that we consider the experiences of front-line workers in the FAME project. Was their experience of the attempted disintermediation of service delivery one that curtailed or in some way enhanced their discretionary practice on the front line? Did they react to such a prospect in a way that was a significant barrier to change, or did their role in using of the systems to provide new services allow them to be important source of innovation in service delivery?

To explore these questions, we now focus upon two of the four FAME strands which did eventually result in live system implementations: (1) *Promoting Independence of Vulnerable Older People* and (2) *Services for Children with Disabilities*. We draw on the evaluation research that was one of our responsibilities as the university partner (the other responsibility concerned the capture of general lessons from the project—see Chapter 5). It is important to note that our engagement with the FAME project enabled us to do this from a slightly different vantage point than that of the effects of digital technologies on front-line workers in public services. That is, we were seeking to evaluate front-line practitioner buy-in to 'joining-up' projects as they progressed over the project life cycle, rather than assessing their reactions entirely retrospectively. In addition, our status as project partners enabled us to interact with this issue from 'inside' the project and not purely as 'external' academic observers. Whilst such a stance, if engaged in without due reflection, has its dangers and biases, a key element of our methodological approach was precisely the additional insights that could come from the ability to bring data to bear on issues from working simultaneously 'for', 'inside', and 'outside' of live projects (see the Appendix).

The aim of the *Promoting the Independence of Vulnerable Older People Strand* was to facilitate improvement to services for older people across health, social care, and the wider range of council services. The strand produced an electronic version of a *Single Assessment Tool*—typical of the trend towards 'screen-level' disintermediation of relationships between the front line and citizens—in order to improve the way older people are jointly assessed for their health, social care, and housing needs. The electronic tool allowed front-line practitioners across all participating agencies to assess the needs of older people. Assessments were accessed as web pages via an internet browser. The information collated as a result of these assessments was then fed into an overview 'assessment summary' to give a full picture of that older person's needs and involvement with other agencies. The strand included two separate (but cooperating) sites, one in the north of England and one in the south. It was the first of the FAME strands to go live (in May 2004) and involved 80 practitioners in the southern site and 130 in the northern one.

The *Children with Disabilities Strand* was based in a City Council that had a long history of trying to join up services in this service domain. In 2003 the council received funding as a partner in FAME, which gave it the opportunity to develop an 'electronic multi-agency assessment tool' to allow agencies working with disabled children and their carers and families to share information and to support the coordination of service delivery processes. Traditionally, practitioners from different specialisms only deal with certain aspects of a disabled child's needs and, as a consequence, only have partial information about them. This results in fragmented delivery of care and the experience for parents and carers is typically that they have to repeat information over and over again to different specialists and professionals. The aim of this strand was to bring practitioners together as if they were a 'virtual team', with access to all the necessary information they required in order to better coordinate the care they could provide. Parents, carers, and children were involved in the project and 'reference groups' for practitioners and parents were used to reflect on and discuss numerous issues such as information sharing, confidentiality, and the assessment tool that would form the basis of the IT system. The resultant system went live in October 2004 with thirty to forty practitioners trained to use it.

Enacting FAME

As already indicated our evaluation research and overall high level of engagement with the FAME project allowed us to follow the process of change as it unfolded in both of these strands in considerable detail. Here we review key issues that emerged in terms of practitioner 'buy-in' to the projects, the interplay between the projects and front-line practitioners, and the take-up on the front line of the new systems produced by the strands.

Practitioner buy-in

In the view of all the local project managers of each strand, 'buy-in' from practitioners was both essential and fraught with difficulty. At the onset of the projects, they typically expressed the concern that hard-pressed health care/social workers would simply 'see it as more work'. Practitioners on the front line, the researchers were told, get blasé and weary and often suffer from 'project fatigue'. In some instances practitioners were struggling with the implementation of other new processes and systems in parallel with the FAME project. One project manager explained that she was 'dealing with reluctance and resistance'. The term 'culture' was repeatedly invoked by project teams to denote obstacles in the way of the project. Another project manager, for example, explained that, although there was 'some level of consciousness' among front-line practitioners, the 'cultural issues' would be difficult. When asked to expand on what he understood by culture in this context he responded that culture for front-line staff means: 'I am up to my backside in agitators already and you are asking me to do something else—how does it help me?'

Such was project managers' concern about 'buy-in' that they formally logged this as a serious risk factor in their official reports to the National Project. Interestingly, their 'theories of change' were underpinned by the perception that there was a range of possible practitioner responses, from 'resistance' to 'buy-in'. They were convinced that the latter must be secured in order to ensure that the potential benefits of the projects would be realized.

In response to these concerns we developed a questionnaire to ascertain practitioner attitudes and expectations. The results from this suggested that practitioners who had been introduced to the FAME project understood and supported its aim; the vast majority shared the view that lack of coordination and exchanging information across agencies leads to less-than-optimal services to clients/patients; there was similarly very high agreement that users would benefit from closer working between agencies; and a majority of respondents also agreed or strongly agreed that they relied on service users for information about other agencies (Baines *et al.*, 2010). In short, the results were indicative of widespread positive attitudes in principle to closer work with other agencies and sharing information with them. On the face of this evidence the project managers' concerns did not seem to be well founded.

The interplay between practitioners and projects

Once the FAME projects got under way we were able to gather more observational data on how practitioners were engaging with the projects that they were associated with. In each pilot, technology partners and project teams arranged workshops with practitioners in order to start to develop the technical solution and ensure that its functionality and the 'look and feel' met their needs (researchers attended fifteen such workshops as observers). In general our observations revealed that the practitioners who attended were invariably interested and enthusiastic about the promise of an electronic system to improve the quality and timeliness of information. Some of them, however, expressed anxiety that the new ICT system would reduce personal contact and trust.

For example, one of the workshops for the *Promoting Independence of Vulnerable Older People Strand (South of England Site)* brought health and social care practitioners together for the first time, previous workshops having been conducted by specialism. Some attendees seemed surprised at what they heard from practitioners in the other specialisms. A district nurse explained that she always left her records with patients in their homes. A social worker responded that he would never leave any record with a client and asked her why she did so. One reason, she said, was security—it is not safe to keep confidential records in a car between visits. Another reason was to 'empower' patients—'it is the patient's record'—it was claimed. This dialogue continued for some time.

Another workshop, conducted for the *Children with Disabilities Strand*, brought together project staff from the city council, a representative of the technology partner, and practitioners in pediatric therapy, speech and language therapy, educational psychology, social work, psychiatry, community nursing, and the equipment service. The project staff asked participants to comment on the multi-agency joint assessment form that would be the basis of the electronic tool designed to allow agencies to share information. The form consisted of sets of headings that would ultimately be produced via the FAME information system. Information under a heading may be filtered into another document such as a Core Assessment. These headings, however, caused difficulties for some participants and provoked a lively debate. One particularly awkward issue that emerged in discussion was that speech and language therapists have continual assessment processes, whereas social services have set time frames imposed on them. The speech and language therapist spoke up to say that there were too many crossover areas that did not fit under one heading, so it would be better to change these headings. The council IT manager said it would be difficult for Social Services to use the system if the standardized forms were changed. Other professionals took exception to this, making the point that there are more services than just Social Services. The IT manager also felt that changing headings would be problematic for other initiatives being introduced to align with government policy and that the problem perceived by the speech and language therapist could be 'got around' by training. The latter insisted that training was not going to help: 'Is the aim to look at the needs of the child or to fit into the system?'

The two workshops emphasized how the professional values and ways of working differed across specialism and agency boundaries. In the first workshop, for instance, there was a reciprocal exchange of ideas about practice across agencies and this seemed to confirm that practitioners, in principle, valued increased knowledge of the work of other agencies. The second workshop revealed more difficult consequences arising from the participants' different perspectives on service users' information. This event surfaced the different perceptions of assessments by service practitioners and suggested that some at least saw the proposed technological solution as lacking the flexibility to accommodate their various and distinctive contributions to the care of the child.

Take-up and use of new systems

We now turn to the experience of the two strands after their FAME IT systems went live. Observations here are based on practitioner participation in project events and a range of interview and documentary sources. In the case of the single assessment system for vulnerable older people, the district nurse team were the first users. They were very positive about the system from the outset. Their experience was showcased in public at a 'Demonstration of FAME SAP Electronic Solution'. One nurse, for example, explained how she welcomed the fact that she could now 'see the story progressing'. Another said she found the build-up of assessments and their visibility fascinating. In trying to convey her experience of being able to see better, more complete information about patients, she likened the process of accessing it electronically to 'putting flesh gradually onto the skeleton...I can see this old lady.'

The northern SAP site (which had trained the largest number of practitioners in any part of FAME) also went live in May 2004. Implementation there had faced more troubles than in the south. The most dramatic setback occurred when the system went live and GPs discovered that they could see names of each other's patients. This was a direct outcome of 'over-integration' (see Chapter 3) where system designers, seeking to provide an assessment tool that provided the 'full picture' of the client, had failed to understand the practitioner context or the nature of their practice. Indeed, over-integration had in effect created a 'view from nowhere' unrelated to, and in this instance in direct conflict with, norms of medical professional practice. In this case the GPs demanded angrily to be disconnected from the system at once and the project team immediately complied.

Such errors notwithstanding, at the northern site, three months after initial roll-out, just under a third of the practitioners were found to be using the system in some way. However, most of those who had accessed it had done so fewer than three times, although there was a very small number of heavy users. This was in stark contrast to the far better take-up figures in the southern site. In order to understand and address the low usage, the FAME strand team invited practitioners to a 'review day' in a local hotel. About forty practitioners attended. The project team asked practitioners to articulate their concerns and barriers to using the SAP electronic solution. Practitioners were extremely forthright:

This is just another project—it will not last.

Uncertainty over the IT strategy of the National Health Service discourages buy-in from health workers.

It takes time to use the system, and taking that time means giving a worse service and imposing burdens on colleagues.

I worry that we will have a fantastic electronic system and no service to give people!

A new 'user perspective' is needed...we must see the big picture—we are all one team.

These comments notwithstanding, recommendations from the day sought to develop positive ideas about how such concerns might be addressed. In the event, they were not taken forward as the agencies concerned were unwilling to spare the time or staff resources to put the recommendations of the front-line staff into practice. In the case of the *Children with Disabilities Strand,* a year and a half after implementation, the story was largely one of dashed hopes and frustration with a technology that was perceived as a poor fit with every day working practice. Perhaps surprisingly, there was still persistent enthusiasm for the project in principle. Practitioners continued to say that they agreed with the logic of the project as an aid to multi-agency working and 'joined-up' referral and information sharing. However, levels of usage of the system remained low and a cause for concern. A variety of attempts to improve take-up took place, including an incentivized distance learning training programme for users. According to one service manager, whilst there had been success in promoting multi-agency working from these efforts, the use of the IT system was still low because staff perceived it to be 'not as user-friendly as it needs to be'. Practitioners who were expected to use the system reiterated this point, citing such things as complex log-in procedures, delays in fixing technical problems, and the inability of practitioners to make changes to material entered onto the system without asking for technical support.

Beyond Institutional and Agency Views

To what extent does the FAME experience we have outlined fit with the view that digital technologies are progressively eroding the traditional discretion exercised by front-line practitioners in the execution of their roles? Alternatively, to what extent are the findings better understood as indicative of an unresolved tension between the policy-driven requirements of a national e-government project and the day-to-day pressures upon individual agencies and workers on the front line? An institutional reading of technology enactment might interpret these findings as evidence of the strong influence of deep-seated and institutionalized barriers to change. It was certainly the case, on the part of project managers for instance, that professional 'cultures' were invoked rhetorically as being 'barriers to change'. Likewise the delays and low take-up, and abandonment in one of the strands of the attempt to implement a system altogether, would all seem to support a view that the 'culture' on the front line was obstructive to the kind of innovation and change required.

However, a closer reading of the experience of the FAME strands suggests that the conditions that lay behind low levels of system usage accord with an interpretation of harried 'street-level bureaucrats' whose coping mechanisms included avoiding or deferring difficult tasks in order to make their workloads manageable. In one site the main barrier was the perception of the new system demanding more work with no direct benefit. In the other the technical characteristics and capabilities of the system itself were emphasized as a major barrier to take-up by front-line staff. In both instances, the system was seen as a workload burden despite the initial promise of high-quality, timely information that should help them improve services by seeing the 'full picture' of the patient/client. Arguably these observations are indicative of ongoing interactions with the technologies and other material circumstances at hand, rather than an enacted and embedded set of constraints destined to shore up the status quo in a 'virtual iron cage'.

In general, front-line workers across the FAME pilot sites listened enthusiastically to promises about the capacity for more joined-up working enabled by new digital systems. The promise of a technical solution that would make information available across professional boundaries was appealing. Indeed, it seemed to offer an answer to the street-level bureaucrats' classic struggle to reconcile the competing demands from clients for services and from the state for efficiency. Practitioners were positive about opportunities afforded by the project to learn how other professionals worked with client/patient information. We would therefore argue that none of this suggests that implementation was stalled by institutionalized resistance to digital technologies and new forms of multi-agency working that they enabled. In general, within the various agencies in the FAME pilot sites there was widespread agreement that service silos must be demolished through more cooperative working and joint access to information. Moreover, there was continued expectation that digital solutions could and would deliver better and more holistic 'pictures' of service users, even in the face of some disappointing experiences.

The FAME experience, then, supports a more nuanced reading than the technology enactment view—at least in its more institutionalist manifestations—would suggest. Multiple agencies of the state interact with service users in different ways; that is to say, they engage in different conversations. Each has an implicit model of the user that works in a context, for example, medicine, education, and social care. Movements towards joined-up service delivery centred on the citizen can throw these into sharp relief for practitioners. It can emphasize for agencies how different these models or 'pictures' of the patient/client are from those of other agencies. It can also surface different assumptions about what information practitioners need to have about patients/clients and how this should and should not be used. The FAME projects revealed considerable willingness on the part of practitioners to engage with their counterparts in other agencies in understanding and working through these differences and which, if harnessed effectively, might have been expected to result in due course in some innovative ideas about how to address these issues. In other words, they seemed willing to engage in conversations with each other about the conversations they have with their shared clients.

On the basis of this in-depth, although admittedly limited evidence, our inference would be that the assertion that there is deep-seated 'cultural' resistance to closer interworking with other agencies and sharing information should be treated cautiously. The main instances of resistance from practitioners, in this example at least, were in relation to specific attempts to embed information sharing into a new system in a manner consistent with the notion of 'over-integration' (e.g. the negative reaction of GPs to the visibility of other GPs' patient records in the SAP electronic solution but also the response from practitioners to standardized assessment headings in the system for Children with Disabilities).

This significantly, in our view, reflected a failure of system designers to adequately understand the practice of the practitioner and the context of the service domain. This failure was not due to any wilful misunderstanding or shortfalls in capability or capacity on the part of the designers and the technology suppliers they worked for. Rather it was due to the expressive inadequacy of the available technical methods and language that were at their disposal in seeking such an understanding. That is, the language of rational system development methods and practice only admits concepts such as function, technical capability, and capacity. In this discourse, conversations on the exercise of roles and responsibilities of client relationships (such as the professional requirement for doctors to keep patient information confidential) are necessarily relegated to the category of 'non-functional requirements'. In other words, they become secondary and ultimately can disappear from the designer's view, with, as we saw above, disastrous results. Yet, as we have also seen, these are precisely the issues that are at the heart of user concerns and interests.

Conclusion

The experience from the FAME project would suggest a more complex picture than implied by the thesis that putting services on-line will inevitably erode the discretion of the street-level bureaucrat. Similarly, neither did the image of front-line service providers as a barrier to innovation seem an adequate representation. Indeed, their resistance, where it occurred, seemed to arise for reasons other than antipathy to change and a desire to defend institutionalized bureaucratic working arrangements and work practices. In fact, in general, the possibilities of service improvement through the use of digital technologies were welcomed rather than shunned. However, there were significant objections to technological solutions that were badly designed and thereby did not meet the perceived needs of practitioners or reflect the requirements and context of the services they provided. Front-line staff did seem to be aware that digital technologies, to use Zuboff's (1988) terms, had 'informating' as well as 'automating' effects, and as such could create new tasks, skill requirements, and work roles that might transform rather then reduce the discretion of those in front-line roles. The question we are left with, though, is how, in the context of digital government projects, the space for such enactments might be nurtured and facilitated? An answer to this might provide opportunities for the kind of entrepreneurial and innovative actions that Fountain saw as the only means by which institutionalized barriers might be transformatively overcome. We begin to explore such possibilities in the following chapter.

7

Co-Production and Tele-Care for Older People

Introduction

In this chapter we explore the designer–user problem through the example of tele-health and social care services for older people. Our main aim is to explore the idea of the co-construction of technology through practice (see Chapter 2) in combination with the currently in vogue idea of the co-production of public services. If the idea of co-production can be extended to the co-construction of socio-technical systems, does this have potential for improving the outcomes of digital government projects in term of their utility and value to those they are intended to assist—the users? We begin by looking in more detail at the idea of co-production. We then explore the policy and other contextual factors that have stimulated the vision of virtual tele-care for vulnerable segments of the population, such as the growing ranks of the elderly. Finally we consider how social informatics interventions in digital government projects might enable technology suppliers, service commissioners, service deliverers, and service users to co-produce more valued outcomes.

Co-Production and Public Service Innovation

Co-production has been defined as the 'joint production of public services between citizen and state, with any one of the elements of the production process being shared' (Mitlin, 2008: 339). Whitaker (1980) suggests three ways in which citizens can participate in sharing the production process in this way: first, by requesting assistance from practitioners, second, by providing assistance to practitioners, and third, by 'interacting to adjust each other's service expectations and actions' (Whitaker, 1980: 242). Pestoff and Brandsen (2007) also identify three dimensions or levels of co-production—co-production with service users, co-management with user groups, and, finally, co-governance. Policy-makers and academics in the UK (e.g. Bovaird, 2007; Boyle and Harris, 2009) and Australia (e.g. Alford, 2002, 2007) have identified co-production as a potential approach to bridging some of the gaps between the needs of individuals and communities and state provision. Also in the UK, the government-established independent 'think-tank' NESTA has published several reports with case study examples of co-produced local service design, delivery, and funding innovations which it sees as the most appropriate way to address the 'crisis' in many areas of public service delivery (see e.g. Needham and Carr, 2009; Slay, 2011; also Parker and Parker, 2007).

Significantly, the literature on co-production has focused upon the role of citizens as users in the redesign of services and/or their involvement in the delivery of services. The involvement of citizens in the design and development of the information and other technological systems that might underpin this has not been extensively discussed or researched. This is slightly surprising, given the large and long-standing literature on the involvement of users in design, although the 'users' in question in much of this are 'employees' rather than 'citizens' or service users *per se*. However, although the engagement of users is widely regarded as a prerequisite to creating more user-friendly and usable artefacts and devices, the variant of a co-production approach we wish to advocate suggests that this is not sufficient in and of itself. That is, whilst much attention has been given to finding ways of better engaging 'users' with the process of designing and developing new systems, for example, through the many variants of 'participative design' methods, this only considers that part of the innovation process that occurs before a product or service is taken up in-use. An insight offered by the idea that technology is co-constructed (see Chapter 2) is that opportunities also exist for user participation in the visioning and rethinking of the context into which such systems and devices are to be specified, procured, and deployed. Co-production in our terms shifts the focus of seeking user participation from the 'prior stage of design' to the arena of user appropriation in the domain of use (Williams *et al.*, 2005).

Co-production, in the sense of its application in service design, is not without its problems. As with any participatory endeavour, there can be issues surrounding the legitimacy of participants representing the community or service users. What is taken to be representative or what constitutes representation can also be problematic. Further to this, Needham (2008) questions whether it is possible that a proportionally small number of representatives can ever fully represent the views of the broader community in any given context. Furthermore, as citizens (service users) become increasingly part of the service delivery process, it has been suggested that some dilution of public accountability may occur. Similarly, Ostrom (1996) and Needham (2008) also point to the challenges that may be associated with the distortion of boundaries between public and private interest.

In addition, with reference to the communities, groups, and individuals who take part in a co-productive process, there are issues of how it can be assured that their participation is not clouded by a desire to promote an action purely to benefit their personal interest. Whilst it is expected and desired in a co-production approach that individuals will bring personal experiences and perspectives to the process, such private interests must also be identified and managed. Another challenge to co-production can be the unclear division of roles. As a co-productive approach will be long-term, it is understood that, after preliminary activity—likely to have focused on defining objectives—there is the possibility of confusion between the public agents and individuals as to their subsequent roles in the process. Bovaird (2007) and Needham (2008) also discuss the challenges that a co-productive process might have for front-line public agents with regard to their work roles and identity. We will return to some of these issues below.

Tele-Care for Older People: Social and Policy Context

It has been observed that the ageing of the global population is 'one of humanity's greatest triumphs' (WHO, 2002: 6). By 2020 it is anticipated that older people will outnumber younger people for the first time in human history (Kinsella and Wan He, 2009: p. iv). In the European Union, 23 per cent of the population will be aged 65 or over by 2020, and 31 per cent by 2050. It has been recognized that this ageing demographic has major implications for 'the labour market and the health and long-term care sector' (EC, 2005: 19). Similar trends are evident in most other advanced countries (see e.g. APC, 2011).

However, this undoubted 'triumph' brings with it new problems, issues, and challenges. For example, in order to deal with the onset of medical and other conditions that arise from the ageing process, older people frequently require access to public and other services to support them in their daily lives. Many of these conditions (e.g. dementia, which is manifested in both a decline in the ability to remember and to think) are, or could be, treated or supported in the home (Powell, 2009). Moreover, many aspects of the ageing process can progressively reduce the degree of personal autonomy of older people and therefore their ability to care for themselves or each other in such circumstances.

At the same time the ageing of the population is inevitably accompanied by a growing number of older people living alone and who desire to continue to do so, as 'care homes' are increasingly seen as an option of 'last resort' (Milligan *et al.*, 2011). These changes place new pressures on both formal health care and social service resources, and the extensive networks of informal and voluntary care that frequently underpin or compensate for these arrangements. It has also been noted that, as demographic change increases the proportion of the population who are older, the same processes will reduce the proportions of those in younger generations who are currently engaged in informal care (Powell, 2009: 86).

These demographic and social changes emphasize the need in many policy-makers' eyes, as in the case of other areas of service delivery (see Chapters 4, 5, and 6), for a more joined-up approach to the delivery of care for older people. For example, this might occur in the way that information about services is made available to older people and others by providing a web-based portal or 'gateway' to available services. This might extend to the way the needs of the elderly are assessed by service providers, through for instance single assessment processes, which obviate the need for older people to 'tell their story' over and over to different service professionals (Wilson and Baines, 2009). Further, an integrated approach might also include how and where care services are delivered to older people—such as virtually in their homes in place of attendant care, or instead of face-to-face after travelling to attend a GP's practice, clinic, or hospital. Finally, the approach might also go as far as to increase individual choice through the allocation of personal budgets which the elderly can spend on services as they choose, whilst at the same time giving more responsibility to older people in monitoring their own health and well-being (see e.g. Foresight, 2000). For many the affordances of digital technology, by providing care services in a virtual or remote way, or by supporting service providers in joining up service provision, provide the essential means through which such integration might take place.

In the specific case of the virtual delivery of services to older people at home, it has been suggested in trials that tele-care applications can result in benefits such as reducing hospital admissions, unblocking beds, and better management of chronic diseases (Kings College and

University of Reading, 2004; Inglis *et al.*, 2010). When digital technologies are deployed in the home-based health care of the elderly, such studies also point to reduced health care costs, improved quality of life, reduced prescribing costs, and the likely reduced burden on pension financing as the elderly are able to remain in the workforce longer (Colmer, 2007; Inglis *et al.*, 2010). In addition, it is claimed that the care systems of the future will also contribute to the individual empowerment of older people, stimulate their learning, and increase the possibility of independent living at home (Hardey *et al.*, 2008). At the same time, resources released by the provision of virtual services may also improve opportunities for meeting the general care needs of the population by reducing the pressures on existing public, private, and voluntary providers. However, whilst some benefits have been identified, there does not seem to be a 'hard evidence base' to suggest, in terms of either cost or care outcomes, that tele-care and the like offer advantages or even equivalence compared to existing more face-to-face approaches. One problem, as Blaschke *et al.* point out, is that, 'by the time adequate research evidence documents the impact of a given tool, the technologies themselves' have inevitably changed and developed, such that it 'may never be possible to establish a solid evidence base' (Blaschke *et al.*, 2009: 651–2).

What is clear is that, despite many years of trials, pilots, and the like, tele-care systems—in particular where health care is involved—have not become established in mainstream practice and are rarely scaleable beyond small highly localized settings (May *et al.*, 2001; Halford *et al.*, 2008; Mort *et al.*, 2009). A variety of problems have been identified which seem to contribute to this. For example, a lack of understanding can exist between the various stakeholders typically involved in such projects—such as system developer and suppliers, service commissioners, professional practitioners engaged in service delivery, and service users (Blythe *et al.*, 2005). It has also been reported that the needs of the potential users tend to be neglected by designers in preference to meeting other criteria such as ease of design and operation for service providers (Dewsbury *et al.*, 2002; Oudshoorn, 2008). In addition, little research has been done on the actual experience of users or view of potential users in relation to tele-care (Percival *et al.*, 2009), although there is some suggestion that users are not enthusiastic about managing their own health conditions (Novak *et al.*, 2008).

By the same token, whilst a variety of virtual applications of relevance to the well-being, mobility, and engagement with the community of older people already exist, they have not always been designed explicitly with the needs of older people in mind, or have been driven by clinical interests rather then the needs of older people themselves. As a result, their functionality and user interfaces are rarely as yet appropriate to the requirements of older people (Blythe *et al.*, 2005; Whitney and Keith, 2006; Colmer, 2007). Finally, whilst tele-care is often presented as eliminating the requirement for face-to-face interaction, prolonged hospital admissions, and travel to see medical specialists, there are suggestions that in reality new requirements for human action are introduced. In particular, these are a result of the delegation of responsibilities to cope with the now remote clinicians, not just to other medical professionals, but also to patients themselves (Oudshoorn, 2008).

Such issues notwithstanding, bodies such as the European Commission have not held back in viewing e-health in general and tele-care in particular as a key part of their vision of the 'Information Society' (see EC, 2004, 2005, 2006, 2007). Similarly many individual countries see virtual services as the key to dealing with the challenge of an ageing population by improving the quality and effectiveness of services, whilst lowering cost and increasing efficiency. For example, in the UK it has been suggested that:

> It is safe to imagine that the pace of technological change that we have seen over the last 20 years will continue, and that by 2030 the kinds of technology that will be available to us will be far beyond anything we know at the moment. Those using the care and support system will increasingly expect technology to play a part in helping them decide what care to choose and helping to improve their quality of life, and the care and support sector will need to be positioned to take advantage of these innovations. (HM Government, 2010: 50)

Extensions of such a view can readily be found in the popular and grey literature. There is much evident excitement about the world of super-fast broadband and smart ambient 'media-info-com' devices, where e-health is frequently identified as the 'killer app' (see e.g. Howarth and Ledwidge, 2011). Here coffee tables 'dispense medicine' and robotic pets take the role normally assigned to cats and dogs in providing companionship to the elderly. The respected Joseph Rowntree Foundation Centre for Usable Home Technology, for example, recently gave credence to such views by highlighting the potential of assistive devices, such as talking walking frames that remind people where they are going, set-top boxes so people can consult nurses, doctors, and social workers, or contact friends and relatives, using 3-D video technology, and special exo-skeleton suits to help infirm people climb stairs (Publicnet Briefing, 2009).

An Over-Integrated Model of Tele-Care for Older People?

The idea that digital and related assistive technologies can support independent living for the elderly in fact predates electronic computers themselves. For example, an electro-mechanical community alarm bell system terminating in a warden's quarters was first incorporated into the design of sheltered accommodation built in the South-West of England in the late 1940s (Hardey *et al.*, 2008: 7, citing Parry and Thomson, 1993). Of course solutions of this type have increasingly been surpassed by successive generations of more 'intelligent' electronic and digital systems. As these have become more sophisticated, they have moved beyond being emergency and alarm-raising devices to support new functionality that allows so-called 'lifestyle monitoring' (Hardey *et al.*, 2008). We now appear though to be on the verge of developments that might go well beyond current possibilities. What, then, might a virtualized care system of the future look like?

In Figure 7.1 we depict a 'mock-up' of a hypothetical virtual health and social service (it was produced as a 'provocation' as part of the OLDES project reported below). The idea is that a new tele-care system would be able to automate and extend existing telephone-based care services into the homes of a much larger number of older people, especially those living alone. The technical means to accomplish this are provided, for example, by a variety of remote monitoring and electronic assistive technologies that can be installed into the homes of the elderly. Sensors and other devices are used to capture and transmit information about the medical condition (e.g. vital signs and other indicators such as sleep patterns and so forth) and well-being (e.g. providing for remote visits to check on the individual's status, automatic reminders to do things such as take medication, alarm systems to detect movement and falls or other mishap, etc.). Health care and other professionals monitor the status of these systems remotely, whilst older people themselves are educated to use the information to take more responsibility for their own health and well-being. Table 7.1 depicts a 'story board' of how the system might operate in a typical day for an older person living at home.

However, from a social informatics perspective, there are broader issues which such a scenario does not appear to address. These concern the service environment and context within which such a virtual care system might exist and, of course, the role of users (both service providers and service end-users) in the development of this. Indeed, in the context of some of our discussion in the previous chapter, some might see this scenario, if taken at face value, as confirming visions of

(A)   TV screen display in Apartment

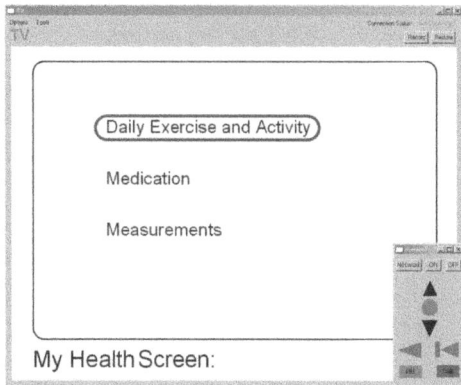

(B)   Information Channels and Apartment layout

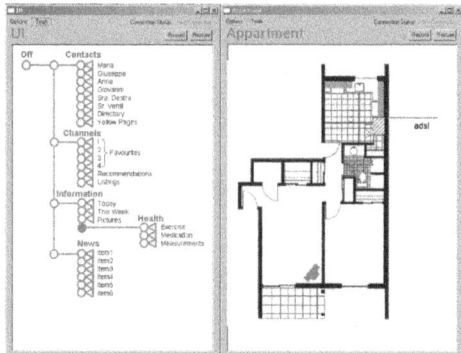

(C)   Operators Screen in Tele-care Centre

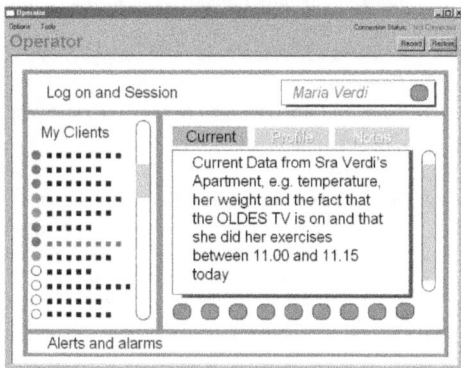

Figure 7.1 Mock-up of Tele-Care for Older People at Home

Table 7.1 Story Board—A Day in the Life of an Older Person in Virtual Care?

Time	Event/Activity *(Tele-care function)*
06.00	Room temperature and activity is being monitored in 2 rooms. *(Data transfer every 15 minutes which also serves as an 'idle channel, equipment functioning' signal). Signora Verdi (SV) wakes up.*
08.30	SV gets up (activity sensor records), steps on scales (data transfer).
09.00	SV goes to kitchen *(Monitor movement between rooms).*
09.15	SV turns on TV with remote control *(Switch on a channel).* *(Switch on. Home page with the top-level options displayed.)* SV uses remote control to select radio channel from favourites. SV listens to radio.
09.30	**'Reminder: do your exercises'** *(on-screen message displayed)* SV sees on-screen message screen/sound but does not respond.
09.35	**'Reminder: do your exercises'** *(on-screen message displayed)* SV accepts by pushing 'OK' on remote control. *(Apply pedometer dumb-bell with accelerometer and Bluetooth)*
10.05	SV performs light exercise routine. **'Well Done'** *(on-screen message displayed)* *Time passes*
11.00	VOIP call from Tele-care operator. *Ringing* SV speaks with Tele-care operator.
11.15	**'Look at Diary'** *(on-screen message displayed)*
11.20	SV uses remote control to grant Tele-care operator permission to view diary.
Noon	*(remote clinical data collection schedule)* *(Measurement sequence)* Tele-care operator reminds SV of school concert this afternoon and sets system reminder.
12.15	SV closes connection with Tele-care operator. *Time passes*
15.00	**'Concert Reminder'** *(on-screen message displayed.)*
15.30	Children singing.
18.00	*Switch off* **'Medication Reminder'** *(on-screen message displayed on close)* Room temperature and activity continues to be monitored in 2 rooms. *(Data transfer every 15 minutes which also serves as an 'idle channel, equipment functioning' signal.)*

Source: OLDES Project Deliverable.

the 'database society' and 'surveillance state'. Here private information—not just about an individual's health but about their 'lifestyle' in
general—is being 'lifted out of the body' and digitized for the purpose
of the 'clinical gaze' (Webster, 2009). This might justifiably be seen as
posing threats to citizen privacy and civil liberties and as involving
fundamental ethical questions about the deployment and use of such
technologies (see Mort *et al.*, 2003; Anderson *et al.*, 2009; Hardey *et al.*,
2008; Hanson *et al.*, 2009; Percival *et al.*, 2009). In turn, issues over the
governance of such care systems and the identity management relationships within them are highlighted. For example, how will consent
be given by service users or those authorized to act for them to capture,
store, process, share, and act on such information? What protections
would be given in relation to the privacy and confidentiality of service
users and how might adequate security be provided against 'data loss'
or misuse of entrusted information?

Broader organizational issues of how the agencies working to deliver
services in such a scenario are to be 'joined up' are also involved. For
example, what are the roles, rights, and responsibilities of the service providers who use and share the information captured in the system, and how (and by whom) are these relationships to be defined in
the first place, and regulated and maintained over time? Would the
greater service integration implied by the availability of such information and the sharing of it between care professionals really result in
more cost-effective and yet citizen-focused services when delivered by
virtual means? There is growing evidence, for example, that in virtual
health care environments, the importance of contextual understanding and face-to-face contact remain critical in providing a 'dialogue of
care' (Mort *et al.*, 2009; Powell, 2009; Hanson *et al.*, 2009), whilst at
the same time challenging the spatial assumptions of Western medical
practice (Nicolini, 2007).

Of course, without a full consideration of such issues and an attempt
to address them in an appropriate way, this mock-up has many of the
hallmarks of the 'one-dimensional', 'techno-centric', 'over-integrated'
approach to the development of digital government that we discussed
in Chapters 2 and 3. The technological capabilities and capacities of
assistive and other technologies are taken as given and as the principal
enabler of change; the understanding and influence of the culture and
practice of users is weak. In particular, it is unclear what changes to
organizational arrangements in the delivery of care—in particular in
relation to identity management and information governance—would
be required to translate these technological affordances into a safe and
appropriate practice. Indeed the mock-up privileges the judgement of

the expert designer, and work that service providers and users might have to do remains 'invisible' (Oudshoorn, 2008). How, then, might the issues in designing and developing virtual services for older people be better understood and by what means might pitfalls be more effectively avoided? The remainder of this chapter considers these issues through the lens of a European project—OLDES (**OLD**er Peoples **E-S**ervices @ Home)—intended to develop a co-production approach to developing tele-care systems and services for the elderly.

The OLDES 'Digital Experiment'

In Europe e-government strategies at the national and pan-European levels have brought private sector suppliers together with a wide variety of public sector agencies to develop and implement specific projects and applications in so-called 'digital experiments' (Williams *et al.*, 2005). Here the objective is not so much concerned with the 'creation of new artefacts' but the 'effective configuration' of existing technologies and their 'integration with work practices' (Hartswood *et al.*, 2002: 12). The OLDES project involved a collaboration of local government, public health and social care providers, system suppliers, and intermediary research organizations and the authors as part of a team of university researchers (see the Appendix). A key project objective was to take full account of 'users' (defined as both those who provide services as well as service end-users) in the process of system development.

Consistent with the idea of a digital experiment, the aim was not to design and develop new technology *per se*, but rather to configure a platform from existing and available 'off the shelf' technologies. From a social informatics perspective, the project could, in theory, achieve an acceleration of the appropriation of the system by users. That is, by involving groups of intended users in the configuration process, they would be able to engage in 'design-in-use' and assist in the local customization of the platform to produce a 'working system' which could then be more broadly appropriated. Obviously, the platform itself would take the limited form of a pilot system, with a view to it being implemented in two European municipalities. However, by this means some of the issues and pitfalls involved in the design–use relationship, noted in our discussion of the social informatics approach in Chapter 2, might be overcome. The lessons learnt might then be applied as the system was rolled out beyond the pilot stage. The 'experiment' also provided the opportunity to foster a model of 'co-production' that went beyond the confines of conventional participatory design (see e.g. Bødker *et al.*, 2004). That is, it offered the prospect of developing a 'shared situated practice involving users and IT professionals' that was 'grounded in the lived experience of users as they grapple with the problems of applying IT' (Hartswood *et al.*, 2002: 13).

Objectives and context

The formal objective of the OLDES project was to offer new technological solutions based on 'ambient media-info-com devices, channels and capacity' to improve the quality of life of older people:

> OLDES aims at developing a *very low cost and easy to use entertainment and health care platform* designed to ease the life of older people in their homes. In order to achieve this, new concepts developed in Information Technologies will be integrated and adapted. The platform will be based on a PC corresponding to *Negroponte's paradigm* of a € 100 device, giving the guarantee of an affordable system. (OLDES project proposal to European Commission, original emphasis)

As well as applications in the home, the platform was also intended to enable enhanced communication and information sharing between health and social care agencies. Alongside these objectives was a commitment, stated in the project objectives, to 'user-centred' development, that 'puts older people at the centre and makes their needs the main priority in all developments'. The primary focus for the project was the municipality of Bologna in Italy. A second pilot site was located in Prague in the Czech Republic (further details can be found in Busuoli *et al.*, 2007; Ponsard *et al.*, 2008; Mráz *et al.*, 2008; Novak *et al.*, 2008; McLoughlin *et al.*, 2009, 2013; Rinaldi *et al.*, 2011).

The established practice in Bologna was that social care for older people was provided by the municipality in the home, through day centres, and in sheltered residences. One relevant service innovation that had taken place was a call centre-based 'contact centre' (the *Tele-accompany Service*). This served 500 isolated and vulnerable older individuals who were contacted by telephone every week by one of four dedicated operators in order to check on their health status and to maintain personal contact and companionship. The municipality was keen to support the OLDES project. It felt such a system could radically increase the numbers of older people who could be accommodated, enhance the range of health and care services offered, and extend this support not just to vulnerable older people, but the older population in general (e.g. by providing entertainment and social networking

143

services alongside health and social care). From the point of view of the municipality, therefore, the OLDES system would provide the basis for an affordable and more efficient means of meeting the needs of an ageing populace, whilst providing better quality and more targeted and customized services.

Developing a user-centred approach

Our intervention in the OLDES project was based on a view of 'digital experiments' as a potential 'space' or 'occasion' where the denizens of an actual or prospective community of practice could be brought together to engage with the design and development process in novel ways. As we pointed out earlier, what is intended here is the creation of a 'design space' to support co-production and user appropriation. In this metaphorical space, the 'architectural discourse' is not just 'technological' but also involves the design of the ethical, organizational, professional, social, and cultural aspects of a technological artefact or system as well (our thinking here is very much influenced by Lefevre's ideas about how users might appropriate the built environment—see e.g. Lefevre, 1991 and Chapter 8). This space is a facilitated environment where users can articulate their needs and requirements in naturalistic language. In turn these views can then be expressed alongside the formalized language of 'requirements capture' and 'use cases' that system development methodologies involve, and that typically constitute the worldview of system designers and developers. However, in order for this to happen, it has to be accepted by those involved that, whilst designers and developers are present in the space, they *do not* have a privileged position as 'experts' and 'solution providers'. Such an acceptance is of course not pre-given and is a major challenge confronting those seeking to facilitate the space.

An initial task in the OLDES project was to map the service environment and interests of the stakeholders involved. Investigation of the viewpoints of the various stakeholders revealed the following. First, a strong *technical development perspective*; this was held by the technology providers of course and was the driving feature of the project proposal. This view was focused on getting the new platform to work. It involved a concept of the system framed exclusively in technical terms, with little or no notion of the service environment in which such a system might be deployed. The user need and requirement (and support) for such a system was largely assumed. Second, a strong *clinical perspective*; this was held by medical professionals and to a lesser extent other professional groups in the care community. This, whilst declaring a formal commitment to the project at an organizational level, was characterized by deep suspicion and scepticism on the ground. For example, general practitioners were concerned with such things as financial incentives for using such a system and whether the elderly really wanted such virtual services—or, as the GP warned, older people were more interested in 'sex and religion' than 'social networking [websites]'!

Third, a *municipality perspective* was held by political sponsors and public managers supporting the project. This was framed by the city's role as the provisioner and manager of health and care services. In this view, the enrolment of user support through collective representatives was seen as unproblematic (Bologna had been a Communist municipality for a long time!). It also assumed that the entertainment and social media content for OLDES virtual services could be acquired or created without much difficulty.

Fourth, a *system-level bureaucrat* (see Chapter 6) *perspective* was held by the *Tele-accompany* operators. They felt that their relationship with their elderly clients was a familial one. As interviews with them revealed, they regarded their clients as 'aunts and uncles' and they felt the older people saw them as 'nephews and nieces'. We observed, for instance, a noticeboard next to the operators' station with a 'thank you' note from one of the older people who came to visit them because she wanted to see them and where they work; there was also a photograph of a cat sent by another client. In addition, as the following quotes from operators illustrate, the relationships often extended beyond that formally prescribed by the operator's roles:

> we are not the emergency service, but sometimes we do get involved in critical situations. For example, I had an appointment with an 85-year-old lady who has enormous problems. She did not respond to the phone call for a long time. Eventually she answered and said that she was on the floor unable to get up. We called her neighbour who is also an old lady who checked but could not move here. So we had to call the emergency services.

> Our discussions with the older people are not limited to the script and to protocols for monitoring their health status. We are, for example, collecting their recipes for publication and this is preserving some of their knowledge and experience.

Finally, there was of course our social informatics *intervention perspective*, a key objective of which was to shift the understanding of the OLDES system from its mainly technical starting point, albeit tempered with a stated objective to deploy a more 'human-centred' approach and if possible to do this by introducing ideas about co-production.

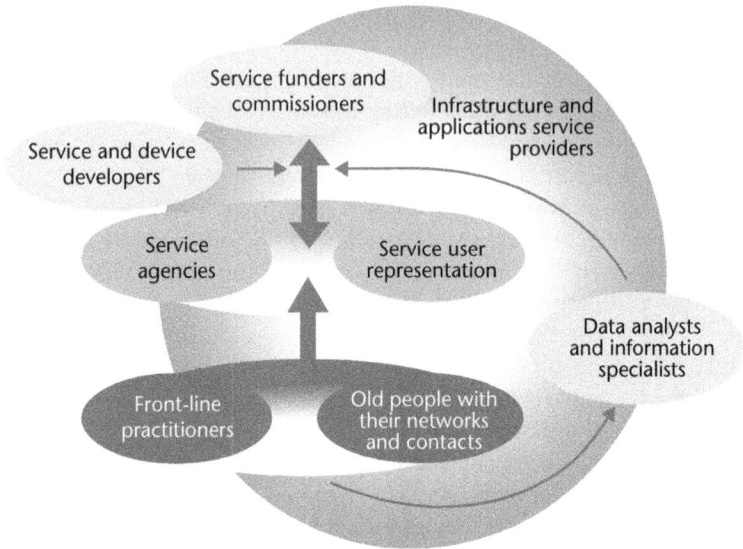

Figure 7.2 OLDES Reference Architecture

The results of this mapping provided one of the inputs into what we termed a 'reference architecture' for the OLDES system and the service environment into which it would be deployed and used. This 'architecture' comprised a series of linked socio-technical projections/diagrams representing various aspects of an envisaged system, including technical networks and inter-organizational relationships (an example is given in Figure 7.2). The aim was to inform, at the outset of the project, a strategic debate on the ways in which the OLDES partners and the local actors in the environment might coordinate their activity on the ground to make best use of the available resources.

However, having developed this reference architecture, the technical developers and other stakeholders promptly refocused their attentions on technical issues to do with the technology of the virtual platform. However, there were problems with the reliability of the core hardware technologies (in particular the low-cost INK computer) that failed to operate as specified. Ironically, the ensuing delays then provided an opportunity to spend more time developing user-generated data on needs and preferences. This in turn allowed the project to develop relations with a wider network of users (including voluntary organizations) and provided some useful insights for the priorities of the design of the system. For example, one issue was the ability of the older people to gain an understanding of and learn how to use the system. Focus groups with carers and others in day centres suggested that this issue would be better tackled if the project focused on older people in their community setting and not just as isolated individuals in the home. In other words, it needed to understand how older people learnt about other things in their lives and could be assisted in managing their fears and worries over 'change' and something that was 'new'.

As interactions with users continued to develop they took on the form of 'OLDES Lab' events. These were occasions at which OLDES users or potential users were brought together around some issue of interest or value for discussions, presentations, and exercises. These activities generated content and relationships that could be further deployed and developed through the user network. By the end of the project, the technology problems had been sufficiently resolved for a Beta Prototype to be built. This was still plagued by technical problems but judged sufficiently stable to be rolled out. At this stage the system was installed into the homes of the final users participating in the project—although around 10 per cent of the installed systems continued to experience technical difficulties.

Co-production—getting beyond techno-centric design?

Co-production has been identified as an approach to citizen participation in service redesign with a number of potential benefits. Some have gone as far as claiming it as a solution to many wicked problems and societal challenges (Bason, 2010). We have suggested that such an approach might be extended to cover the design and development of information systems and that it is important to see this as not just a process of engaging citizens in service and system design but one that applies to all stakeholders. There are, as we noted, a number of potential problems that have been associated with a co-production approach. The OLDES experience offers some insights and reflections in relation to these issues, in particular with respect to the role of legitimacy, representatives, and representation, and implications for the division of roles between public practitioners, citizens, and the impact on front-line staff.

First and foremost, the issue of legitimacy confronted by the project was one of challenging the conventional language and frameworks of systems development methods and practice. It was this expertise that was the dominant voice within the OLDES project at its inception. The architectural discourse was based around the task of developing a technological application and provided the means of articulating what the functions of the OLDES system would be and how these might be distributed over the network and platform resources that were available. Our intervention challenged this view by arguing that, if these were the only concepts to be used for explaining and discussing what the OLDES project aimed to do, then any resulting system faced the very real danger of alienating most of its stakeholders in the user domain.

Of course, this begged the question of the legitimacy of the 'user voices' themselves and a significant part of the story of the project's dynamic is about how different stakeholder interests were drawn into the development process from initially sceptical starting points. As we have seen, direct contacts with older people themselves initially took place only through their collective representatives. Ironically, delays caused by technical difficulties with key platform components opened up opportunities to build deeper and more direct relationships with the user community over the lifetime of the project. Arguably, co-production was far more 'representative' by the end of the project and the kind of activity that had developed (e.g. the OLDES Labs) a better form of 'representation'. Finally, the approach to co-production we advocated, and the tools and resources deployed to facilitate this, were intended to support a rethinking and recasting of the roles, responsibilities, and relationships in the system of care in the municipality.

We can illustrate this by examining the kinds of outputs that were possible when the discourse was opened up to all participants. Figure 7.3 provides a 'people and places' projection of the OLDES system from a 'user and service-centric' perspective. This projection was extrapolated from the initial ethnography developed by the action researchers. The contrast with the 'techno-centric' representations of the OLDES system was immediate. This 'projection' can be viewed as a co-produced animation of one of many different possible scenarios of alternative organizational and technological architectures for a federated service environment. The production of such projections involves the segregation of entities and relationships, represented in models of the service context, into separate graphical representations. At its simplest, the 'people and places' projection acts as a 'mirror' to users of their practice and provides a 'window' into the practice of other stakeholders. It is therefore the basis for a first step in a dialogue between users (as both service providers and end-users) in an attempt to build common insights and understandings in multi-agency settings.

Such projections are developed and further evolved by asking users to create scenarios through story-telling, making lists and tables, drawing diagrams and pictures, and so on. This provides a way of making

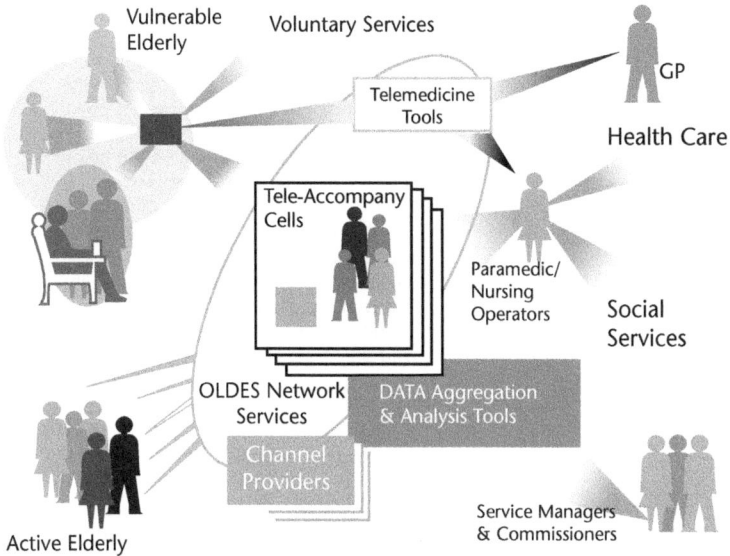

Figure 7.3 OLDES Service Environment

visible current practices and attitudes. At later stages these initial models can be further analysed with the users to identify more abstract 'functional' and 'deployment' projections. These projections present potential system 'solutions' to the 'problems' of service coordination as they emerge in the projection concerned with 'people and places'. However, these more technical projections represent a 'solution' only in the sense that they are iteratively posed as questions to the other stakeholders. They are not 'solutions' presented by 'experts' to 'users', as meeting their requirements as 'captured' by the designers. By articulating both technical and social dimensions in this way, we suggest, informational and organizational architectures can start to be defined and specified, where users are actively engaged in a process akin to 'design-in-use'.

These ideas notwithstanding, project realpolitik meant OLDES never fully escaped its technology-drive focus. However, we would suggest that, as a result of the deployment of the co-production approach, it was possible to go some way, and certainly further than might otherwise have been the case, to overcome the 'benefits the developer' bias of a 'techno-centric' focus. Some influence beyond a narrow techno-centric view in the functionalities inscribed in the OLDES technology platform prototype is indicated in Table 7.2. Arguably, the social informatics intervention succeeded in providing a basis upon which user needs

Table 7.2 Prototype Alpha Tele-care Platform Functionalities

Low-cost computer-based system	The elderly persons are provided with a low-cost computer-based system (the INK computer) that works as the access point for OLDES functionalities and services. The computer is connected as a set top box to a classic television set that displays all the information provided by the platform by a simplified graphical user interface (GUI).
Adapted graphical user interface	The graphical user interface is especially designed to meet elderly person usability requirements. An easy to use remote control is used to select options and access content.
Tele-health monitoring system	The elderly persons are provided with communicant Bluetooth medical devices. The INK set top computer installed in elderly persons' houses automatically collects the data measured by these devices and sends them to a central repository in a secured way.
Entertainment system	Through their INK computer, the elderly persons are able to access entertainment services provided by *Tele-accompany*: Audio/video content: The elderly persons are able to access audio and video content. Discussion groups: Using an adapted handset connected to the INK, the elderly persons are able to actively participate in discussion groups with an animator helping to create reactions and discussions. Voice-over-IP calls: The elderly persons can easily call their relatives (using a classic PC connected to the internet) and friends connected to OLDES system using their INK and their handset.
Automated health decision support system	The data stored in the central repository are automatically analysed by two different intelligent tools. The first one is based on fuzzy logic and the second one is based on a Support Vector Machine. These tools may generate a warning or an alarm if an abnormal situation about health or social condition of the patient is detected.
Web portal	Prototype alpha integrates a web portal which provides interfaces for: System administrators GPs and professionals Discussion groups animators *Tele-accompany* members

Source: OLDES Project Deliverable.

could be articulated and represented, and shifted the focus of attention to how to appropriate the platform in the context of use.

It can also be argued that the fact of the intervention itself nurtured an approach that sought to find ways of engaging the user as something more than a 'passive' actor and 'object' of the project. The approach in turn provided resources to assist users to start to 'acquire the skills and confidence' to become 'systems builders/intermediaries in their own right' (Williams *et al.*, 2005: 175). Second, in contrast to the normal PD approach, the intervention on this occasion was aimed primarily at the specification and design of the service environment in which the application was to be deployed, rather than at building user engagement with the technology application model. This is consistent with the point we made in Chapter 2 that, in a three-dimensional view, it makes more sense to nurture and facilitate user engagement, not in relation to the development of technological applications in-use, but in the development of use scenarios—for their deployment and appropriation in everyday practice. In the event, delays in the project prevented the extended development of these iterations in the co-production approach to a level where specifications were developed that would have fully reflected the users' own projections of a new service environment.

However, a final evaluation study to assess end-user perceptions was conducted once a critical mass of installations was achieved. This revealed some suggestions of what might evolve. The evaluation was based upon focus groups, a questionnaire survey, and a virtual study of the anonymized system interaction log files that recorded the interactions of the older people with the OLDES system. The evidence gained from the study presented a varied picture. Some users were clearly not supportive. This seemed due, in part, to their frustrations with the instability and lack of content of the barely established system and also a lack of perceived value in some if its proposed functionality—as one older man put it in an evaluation focus group, 'I don't need any new friends!' Other users, however, found the system useful and one man declared his pride at the fact he 'had found the information' by using the system rather than having, as he normally had, to ask his son. Others had appropriated the system as a means of engaging with grandchildren or children in a new way, and some had reportedly used it collectively as a group at one of the community centres, rather than as something to support them whilst 'at home'. A small group, amongst the users of the telemedicine element of the Bologna project, had begun to see themselves as 'innovation champions'. Having said that, the evidence from the log files indicated that in fact they did not use any of the Tele-accompany service or network tools!

The survey of the views of elderly users found that (notwithstanding the medical opinion relating to their preferred interests noted earlier!) the social networking and entertainment functionality of the systems were the most appreciated by users. They were valued for keeping them informed and up to date in relation to their everyday lives and general health and well-being. However, users tended to perceive the system as an additional TV channel, which also meant they tended to view the content as 'passive recipients', much as they would a conventional broadcast, rather than as an interactive system. Finally, there was a report from the medical partners on the project that one of the telemedicine users had been admitted to hospital on the basis of information generated from the telemedicine monitoring devices, suggesting that providers of services, as well as those using services, were starting to experience and in some instances see value in the system.

The ultimate implication of taking a co-production approach was that it enabled stakeholders in the OLDES project to begin to question, or at least raise the possibility of them questioning, what exactly was in 'use' (a technical platform or a socio-technical environment for delivery of care services?), what 'use' it might have (a means for providing existing Tele-accompany services 'virtually' or the basis for broader and as yet unknown emergent innovations by users in the service environment?), and 'who' were the 'users'—a stereotype of older people 'at home' or a more differentiated grouping of older people and their associated networks of care, including service providers themselves?

Conclusion

As we concluded the writing of this chapter, the headline results were published from what is claimed to be the largest ever Randomized Control Trial (RCT) of tele-care systems (involving over 6,000 patients and nearly 240 GP practices in the UK). The trial, unsurprisingly to us, concluded that the key to realizing the benefits of tele-care is 'to integrate these technologies into the care and services that are delivered' and to accomplish this by 'putting people at the centre and in control' (Department of Health, 2011: 2; see also Stevenson *et al.*, 2012). In this chapter we have examined one attempt to do just that in the form of a tele-care project intended to provide virtual services to older people living at home. We have suggested that the user–designer problem is not best addressed by increasing user participation in the design of technologies—although, where there is opportunity and it is practical and possible to do so, then this is of course desirable. Rather, we have shown that the issue requires users and designers to become engaged in the ongoing co-production of the service environments into which systems and other technological applications are to be deployed. We have also shown that this might result in more sustainable and federable service innovations. We extend this insight in the final chapter and explore its implications for the future of digital government at work.

8

Making Digital Government Work

Introduction

A recent report for the European Union has observed that, after a decade of policy development and public investment, the modest take-up of e-enabled services is 'undeniably a clear policy and supply-side failure' (Codagnone and Osimo, 2010). Whilst there has been considerable innovation in terms of 'digital products', this has not been accompanied by the refashioning of roles and responsibilities underpinning service relationships and their governance. Despite the fact that in countries such as the UK the majority of citizens are now on-line—as the UK government has recently acknowledged—they rarely use e-enabled government services (Cabinet Office, 2012: 2). For some citizens at least, for some, the meaning of digital government may well be the threat of more, not less, control by bureaucracy (see e.g. Systems Thinking for Girls, 2013). In this final chapter we develop the insights offered by the social informatics approach a little further. We outline the case for what we term a new 'architectural discourse' necessary to enable the co-production of a more *federated* and *infrastructural* information system and organizational arrangements. We go on to set out some of what we see as the broader implications of the social informatics approach for more general debates over the future of digital government and bureaucracy. Finally, we return to Mrs Cannybody and her dilemma. What have we learnt which might assist our volunteer social worker and better meet the needs of Mary in the context of digital government?

Digital Government and the Rules of Virtuality

Before coming to these issues, we first consider some of the conclusions that emerge from the previous chapters. In order to frame our

154

discussion of why bringing about of the 'virtual state' has been so problematic, we evoke what have been termed the 'five rules of virtuality' (see Woolgar, 2002). One of the key tenets underlying the rules is the key social informatics principle of 'analytical scepticism' towards the 'cyberbole' often associated with digital technologies and their effects on social relations and institutions. The 'rules' are intended as broad guidelines through which to subject 'determinative claims about the effects and impacts of any new technology' to scrutiny and questioning (Woolgar, 2002: 13–14). For our purpose they allow us to assess claims concerning the 'transformational effects' of digital government.

The first rule is: 'the uptake and use of new technologies depend crucially on local social context' and how this affects the 'reception and deployment' of new artefacts and systems by users (Woolgar, 2002: 14). The idea that non-technical circumstances are a key factor in understanding digital technologies at work is, of course, a key feature of the social informatics perspective (Introduction and Chapter 2). Moreover, this is a lesson that seemingly has had to be learnt time and time again, since the pioneering insights of socio-technical theory well over half a century ago (Trist and Barnforth, 1951). In the contemporary 21st-century example of digital government, we have observed at a number of points how the social context has played a critical role in deployment and take-up—or 'enactment' (Chapter 2)—in specific contexts and domains of use. For example in the case of electronic health records, we have seen how citizens as potential users may not always want to be in charge of their health information, and that medical practitioners have in some instances reacted in ways that illustrate their desire to closely guard what they see as their professional responsibility, if not right, to control clinical information (Chapter 4). The take-up of electronic records and related e-health technologies is, in critical ways, being shaped by such factors, albeit in varied ways, across a range of national jurisdictions.

The second rule is that 'the fears and risks associated with new technologies are unevenly socially distributed' (Woolgar, 2002: 15). In order to give meaning to new technologies, relevant social groups make sense of them in terms of prevailing expectations, perceptions of opportunities, or threats and dangers. Such sense-making varies across different groups. It is clear that politicians' and policy-makers' optimism for the transformational potential of digital government is not shared across all the various stakeholder and user groups that are implicated. For example, citizens and their representatives often seem resistant to the idea that the complex needs and identities of the 'service user' can be captured in the seemingly more transactional notion of the 'consumer' (Chapter 5).

The third rule is that 'virtual technologies supplement rather than substitute for real activities' (Woolgar, 2002: 16). In practice and contrary to what is often portrayed in the popular, if not policy, imagination, 'the virtual' has a habit of coexisting with, rather than replacing, 'the real' (Woolgar, 2002: 16–17). This can give rise to novel and unanticipated effects. For example, the unthinking assumption that key decisions concerning matters of consent and governance, which are vital to the safe and secure sharing of information, are either not relevant to the system development process or, if they are, can adequately be taken care of within its accepted boundaries, can give rise to the potentially serious phenomenon of 'over-integration'. For example, in considering digital identities, there is a strong tendency to confuse the data contained in the electronic record or database with the realities or attributes that it refers to outside of the system (Chapter 5). This gives rise to the misleading idea that what is 'in the system' is always what is 'really out there' and that the information in the system is the 'single point of truth' (Wilson *et al.*, 2011*b*: 380).

The fourth rule extends the previous rule by stating that 'the more virtual the more real' (Woolgar, 2002: 17). The claim here is that attempts to render activities virtual sometimes have the paradoxical effect of intensifying the 'reality' of what has hitherto been ignored or taken for granted—in effect making it more, not less, 'concrete'. This is clearly evident, for example, in the issues involved in making information about services available in virtual directories (Chapter 4). This is not just a question of digitalizing information about what is 'out there' and 'posting' it on-line in a sort of 'virtual yellow pages'. Rather, partners involved in the service delivery domain need to first rethink their rights, roles, and responsibilities within an information environment that involves the syndication of publishing across federated domains managed by a variety of 'real' organizations.

The fifth and final rule is: 'the more global the more local'. That is, the more digitalization supports the 'death of distance' by making information available in a more mobile or 'global' way, the more the communication enabled and the identity of those engaged in it depend on 'local ways of managing the technology' (Woolgar, 2002: 19). This aspect is clearly illustrated by the mobility associated with digitalized information—such as that pertaining to identity—and its inherent propensity to be shared across time and space. However, information derives meaning from context and treating it as a commodity (stuff) that can be put into containers (records, databases) and moved (shared) over space and time can have potentially disastrous results. To avoid this, the relational basis of identity needs to be recognized and associated governance arrangements put in place that will allow information with its context preserved to be shared (or better 'published') appropriately and safely (Chapter 5).

The Social Informatics Insight

How then might better heed be taken of these 'rules' in the future development of digital government? A major theme of this book has been to argue for a revised conceptualization of the relationship between technology and organization. We now wish to flesh out this argument a little more, albeit in a slightly speculative fashion. We do so by outlining the foundations of a new form of 'architectural discourse' through which this relationship might be recast (see Martin *et al.*, 2009; Martin, 2011). At its simplest, this idea seeks to address the absence of a common language and means of effective communication between 'technical experts' on the one hand and the 'lay members' of user communities on the other. The problem in the case of digital government is that this discourse is frequently one where what is designed often fails to meet in practice what it turned out was required by the user. As we have emphasized throughout, the particular conditions that characterize public service delivery pose specific challenges and place particular demands on the means of communication and interaction between system designers and service providers and users (including citizens themselves). This is particularly so in instances of emerging cross-agency delivery of services in general and those involving meeting complex social and care needs of citizens in particular. In such circumstances, the established means of 'capturing the user requirement' in system design and development, even the very notions of 'capture', 'user', and 'requirement' are, we suggest, insufficiently expressive to the point, sometimes at least, of being entirely inadequate.

Towards a new 'architectural discourse'

Our starting point is that the discourse between designers and users can usefully be regarded as an architectural one (in the same way as the architect/client discourse in the case of the built environment). The language associated with architecting is mostly diagrammatic, comprising such things as concept drawings and models, technical plans, inventories, and the like, and it is these that figure in conversations between the architect and client and to a lesser extent those who will eventually use the building (i.e. its 'implementers'). This architectural language has the purpose of supporting what can be termed the *instrumentalization* of these conversations (in the sense that an 'instrument' gives voice to the player's intentions). *Instrumentalization* allows the architect and client, at the very least, to elicit and express requirements (what is desirable and not desirable, or technically possible or not). That is, to express to each other what they regard as significant for the architectural process and, as these conversations develop, to establish mutual understandings and agreements which can be expressed and recalled through these *instruments*, as progressive commitments and discharges of responsibilities between the parties unfold. Ultimately, the concept drawing, model, or other form of instrument can be held up to the finished building and the client can assess whether the material artefact exceeds, meets, or fails to meet expectations. That is, whether it represents to them some kind of value.

A central characteristic of this process is its under-determination (Garud *et al.*, 2008). The client can never really know or fully articulate what they want. The architect can never fully know what is or is not possible. Whilst existing knowledge and ability to predict outcomes provides a degree of certainty of outcome, architecting is also an emergent process that recognizes the possibility of new and as yet undiscovered opportunities or needs. In short, knowledge is always incomplete and evolving, and as such the roles of architect and client are subject to a vulnerability that arises from the fact that things could go wrong or right for each of them and that their relationship has to manage both risk and ambiguity. What is important in this situation is the quality of the conversation in terms of the commitment between the parties to authentic exchange. Such commitments stand, of course, in ambivalent relationship to other more institutionalized aspects of the conversation that seek to resolve ambiguity and reduce risk through legal and contractual devices.

Architectural discourse in this sense can be seen as founded on *conversations*. The idea of *conversation* brings together the *intentional* world of meanings, values, and purposes, on the one hand, and the *extensional* world of material things and their behaviours, on the other. In this sense, *conversation* provides a formal means of linking *intentions* to *extensions* in a semiotic process that enables the creation of shared visions, purposes, and plans in the production of the socio-material world. In other words, *intentions* provide a basis for establishing, in a particular context by any given community of practice, what counts as counting in that situation. *Extensions* are the technical means by which such *significations* are given material expression. A key requirement affecting the quality of the architectural discourse is the extent to which it can deal with the relationship between the *intentional* and the *extensional*. That is, how far does it provide both an effective means through which what counts as counting (*signification*) in a given situation can be translated through a process of systematization into material outcomes, as embodied—or *instrumentalized*—in the technical characteristics and capabilities of an information system.

Given this framework with its abstracted generic roles of architect, client, etc., what does this mean for the way the architectural process could proceed in order to improve the quality of the discourse? For example, how might the architectural process be rethought and what would a different model of architecting and building based on ideas of co-production look like? In such circumstances, what alternative forms of service and information system architecture might emerge and how would these better suit the needs of users? One element of such a conversation is not only a commitment to the possibility of open discussion about the reformulation of the design itself, but also the nature of the conversation itself and the roles and responsibilities that are being exercised (e.g. how the abstract roles of 'architect', 'client', and 'implementer' might be combined, shared, and allocated in practice).

In the context of digital government, of course, we are concerned with the possibilities and conditions that might generate service innovations and the information systems required to support them. However, we can perhaps assist the reader by providing further insight into our arguments here by considering the more tangible example of co-construction and co-production of a built (rather than information) environment. Box 8.1 provides an example of exactly such a process involving a community-based project to build domestic dwellings, involving a reallocation of conventional roles and responsibilities. This, we suggest, provides some interesting indications as to the form answers to the above questions might take.

In the terms of our previous discussion, we might say, for example, that the self-build project represents an instance where a new architectural discourse developed around an alternative approach to design and build consistent with the idea of co-construction of material artefacts and systems. This allowed a redistribution of roles, the development of new conversational relationships, and the emergence of a self-build community able to co-produce their own housing needs solution. The design approach also enabled the community to build dwellings which were both scalable and could be repurposed as their needs, circumstances, and times changed both during the design process and beyond, 'in-use'. Indeed, we might say that the built environment had key infrastructural properties that enabled this. The new architectural

Box 8.1 THE HEDGEHOG CO-OP PROJECT

The Hedgehog Co-operative was a legally incorporated entity inspired by a traveller fed up with the insecurity of living on the road and the limited opportunities this offered for his growing child. Together with like-minded and motivated members drawn from the waiting list for local council housing, the co-operative invested 'sweat equity' in a project to build each other's homes. The project began in late 1997 with the aim of constructing ten houses of a common design but of varying sizes on the outskirts of Brighton on the south coast of England. The funding of the build was provided by a Housing Association (a private, not-for-profit organization whose aim is to provide low-cost housing for those in need). The plan was that, having built their homes, co-op members would then rent them from the Housing Association. As a result they would have a secure tenancy and a quality of life not achievable through the standard provision of social housing by local authorities.

The co-operative determined to build not just homes but a community 'designed with their needs in mind'. Each family was required to commit to thirty days labour on site each week. If not able to keep the hours up they ran the risk of losing their house. Nobody could move into their home until all others were complete. The co-operative consisted of ten families of seventeen adults, with no building experience. Their efforts were supported by a site manager (a veteran self-builder) for three days a week and monitored by a clerk of works on a weekly basis, both funded by the Housing Association, as was the work of a skilled carpenter. However, community members determined the overall strategy of the build and day-to-day operations democratically.

The chosen method of the self-build was based on the approach first developed by 'community' architect Walter Segal (1907–85). The Segal approach originated from his need to build a temporary home in the garden of his house in Highgate North London whilst his main home was rebuilt. The techniques he used were intended to allow self-building without the need for wet trades or significant building skills and expertise. The essential philosophy was that 'anyone could do it' and all materials were to be bought 'off the shelf' and assembled on site. A key feature of the design was that the buildings constructed with this method used the corner posts to bear loads rather than the internal walls as in more conventional construction techniques. This meant it was easy to reconfigure the detail of the design, move doors and windows, and change the layout of internal walls, and easily extend the original build, as changing needs and requirements demanded. Over the years these basic principles have been developed by other architects, in particular to develop the ecological and sustainable possibilities of the approach.

In the case of the Hedgehog project the method provided the self-builders with both skills and purpose and the simple construction techniques meant they could learn by doing on the job. The implementation of the design used sustainable materials that also lent themselves to customize the aesthetic appearance of each dwelling by the builders/occupiers. Because of the flexibility of the Segal method, community members were also able to keep changing their mind over the layout and configuration of their houses during construction. This was particularly valuable for the novice designer/builders who, unlike experts, were less able to envisage from plans and drawings what something would look like until it started to assume its materiality in practice. The end results were a safe and governable community in which all members, including the children in the families (there was an on-site crèche to assist with the demands of childcare), had been included in the construction and thereby community-building process. The end result may not have been home ownership but the members of the co-op felt that they had gained something more enduring and of value.

Sources: Grand Designs (2009); Ward (n.d.).
http://www.selfbuild-central.co.uk/first-ideas/examples/hedgehog-co-op/
http://www.segalselfbuild.co.uk/projects/hedgehog.html (both consulted July 2012).

discourse provided an effective means through which what counted for the community as relevant and appropriate to their housing needs and requirements (e.g. secure tenancy and not ownership, which was beyond their means) could be articulated and appropriated into a set of material outcomes that were of value to them in-use and in both a socially and ecologically sustainable way.

Moreover, the discourse raised questions and posed different solutions to how roles such as those of 'architect' and 'client' were to be allocated in practice and the relationships between them managed and governed. The 'client', for example, was involved in the process of design, a process which was not just limited to the pre-construction stage but one that extended into post-construction and use. This was not just a case of the earlier engagement or participation of the user in the process of design. Rather it raised the prospect of all parties being able to recast, not only their roles within and the outcomes of the development process, but also the very nature of the process itself.

In techno-centric approaches to system design, user requirements are assumed to be susceptible to capture to the extent that all the roles and responsibilities and intentions have been agreed and expressed in terms of work-flows and business processes (where appropriate, 're-engineered'). Resolving contradictions and ambiguities, should they be detected, is not deemed part of the system architect role. However, our contention is that, to improve the architectural discourse in the development of digital government, such matters must not only become the province of system architecting but must also be the basis for a reconfiguration of the process of architecting itself to reinsert the social or intentional. In other words, consistent with the idea of co-construction, the boundaries between the functions of the 'architect' and 'client' need to become more fluid and their configuration itself part of a co-produced process of socio-material architectural design.

161

The Future Evolution of Digital Government

Dunleavy *et al.* have argued, somewhat against the grain, that hitherto dominant managerial paradigms of public sector management such as NPM are 'stabilizing' and 'wearing thin' (Dunleavy *et al.*, 2005: 9). Future developments will, they suggest, usher in a 'new era of digital governance' (Dunleavy *et al.*, 2005: 12). Moreover, they have suggested that this process is gathering momentum as more recent technological developments such as Web 2.0 and social media start to have their impact (Dunleavy and Margetts, 2010). In advancing their thesis, they claim that digital technologies have the capacity to 'colour' future developments and overcome the kind of embedded institutional and other barriers that writers such as Fountain see as so constraining. In this scenario, digital technology and e-government emerge as the main source of innovation and change in public service organization and delivery. Information technology-driven changes ('digitalization') enable greater integration of previously desegregated ('reintegration') public services and government functions, support a more 'holistic' approach and structures based on citizen and other service user needs ('needs-based holism'), and e-enable the delivery of many of these services and associated administration (Dunleavy *et al.*, 2005; Margetts, 2006: Dunleavy and Margetts, 2010).

Whilst we recognize the power of such an argument, our take on its efficacy is itself 'coloured' by our three-dimensional analysis as presented in Chapter 2. First, we would not support a purely 'one-dimensional' interpretation of this thesis. That is, a view that either digital technology itself will in effect determine the path and trajectory of such changes, or that these impacts can in turn be seen as socially determined, where technological capacities and capabilities are marginalized and seen at best as mediators of socio-economic effects. To be fair, this is not the position adopted by Dunleavy and Margetts and their colleagues, who themselves clearly state that they wish to avoid crude determinism of either the technical or social variety (Dunleavy *et al.*, 2005: 248; Dunleavy and Margetts, 2010: 4). Two-dimensional interpretations of course stress the contingent and enacted nature of outcomes and the mutual shaping of the technical and the social. However, as we have seen, researchers differ on the emphasis they give in this dynamic to the power of social action versus embedded structural constraints. The likes of Fountain (2001) lean towards the constraining influence of embedded institutionalized values, norms, and behaviours. Dunleavy and Margetts and their colleagues, in contrast, prefer in our view a variant of the two-dimensional perspective in the form of what has been termed 'soft determinism' (Badham, 2005: 119). This stresses the enabling characteristics of technology in opening up the possibility of transformational change in public institutions and services, but denies any determining effect.

However, as we argued in Chapter 2, aside from the issue of 'determinism', a three-dimensional view questions any notion of 'technology' as something that at some point is 'fixed' and definitively capable of such enabling 'effects', whether deterministic or not. Thus the claim, for example, that information and communication technologies have 'centralizing network effects' and 'decentralizing data base effects', in analytical terms attributes independent technical influence to technology even if these 'impacts' are not seen as determinative in their organizational outcomes (Dunleavy and Margetts, 2010: 4). As we have discussed, in contrast, the alternative or practice-based view examines the socio-technical process through which technologies are appropriated and given meaning in particular contexts. This in turn results in a reshaping of these resources. It is not a question of 'effects', however qualified, but an issue of what sense and use is made of technological possibilities to affect their practice by the 'denizens of communities' (Lefevre, 1991) in particular circumstances. Rather than seeking to avoid 'determinism' by suggesting technical effects are subordinate to non-technical influences, such as 'organizational and budgetary factors', 'user influence', and 'societal adoption and cultural adaptation' (Dunleavy and Margetts, 2010: 4), we suggest these factors along with materiality are both sides of the same socio-material coin. In this chapter, we have sought to capture this argument more precisely by suggesting that this process—or conversation—can be understood metaphorically as an architectural one and that what is central to it is the quality of the discourse through which such architecting is conducted. If there is any 'colouring' to be done, we would suggest that it will be neither 'technology' nor the 'social' alone that will be responsible but rather the quality of the conversations through which the two are constructed.

We can further illustrate this point by returning to maturity models of the development of digital government considered in Chapter 1. It will be recalled that these have a strong tendency to make 'one-dimensional' assumptions about the technology-driven nature of such evolution. These models implicitly stress the need for public agencies and the like to adapt their organizational forms to meet technological requirements if progress is to be achieved (see Chapter 1). However, both two- and three-dimensional views suggest that any stages in the evolution of digital government should be seen not as indicative of technological impacts leading to greater integration, but as socio-material phases involving ongoing appropriation and social learning in practice by users. In turn, such learning by users inevitably reforms and reshapes technological possibilities.

In the four phases typically identified in current maturity models, many of the lessons that must be learnt in order to make initial progress are to do with understanding new responsibilities for electronic publication and information channel management as face-to-face and paper-based methods are replaced. Initially, such developments do not appear to have significantly challenged the services and the silos, or vertical organizational structures, through which they have traditionally been delivered. However, recognition does seem to have emerged that service users typically do not access a single service at a time. Rather the life events that generate a need normally require packages of several services in order to be addressed. As a result, the idea of 'joining up' services to better meet user needs has in many instances gained ground and previously distinct activities and processes within agencies have begun to interact (see Figure 8.1). In countries such as the UK, and to a lesser extent perhaps Australia and the USA, the need for interconnection and cross-cutting functionality in information systems to support such 'joining up' has arguably been firmly established. In this phase, policy-makers and public agencies have started to learn how to run digital information services and channels, the culmination of which is the citizen portal which provides the external evidence and symbol of a process of both technological but also internal organizational change. The 'front office' side embedded in the portal, for example, is comprised of multiple channels of citizen access, such as the call centre, the community outreach or drop-in centre, internet kiosks, and the web portal, while internal reorganization of service processes and data management provides a 'back office' where the individual content and transaction elements required to deliver these service and administration functions are accomplished.

It is important to note that the social learning that is taking place is essentially 'first order'. The aim is to effectively manage the risk created by new uncertainties posed by the digitalization of existing channels and means of service delivery through developing appropriate visions, plans, implementation, and evaluation bounded by existing organizational silos and working arrangements. In the light of Fountain's institutional analysis it could be suggested that this is all, in the main, that is possible. As we have seen in earlier chapters of this book, reaching even this stage of socio-technical transformation appears to be far from easy or straightforward. Moving beyond this may well require external

1st Generation e-Government

Publish services on the WEB

Make services interactive

Make services transactional

2nd Generation e-Government

Transform services

Learning to transform
the organization

3rd Generation e-Government

Learning that you don't
build a new application
for each new policy

Learning to run
information
services and
channels

CRM and
Enterprise
Solutions

Single Agency
Multi-service

Learning to work
in partnership

Multi-Agency-single
service client group

Shared
Regional &
National
Services

Multi-Authority
Multi-Agency
Multi-Service

Reusable Public Servie
Infrastructure

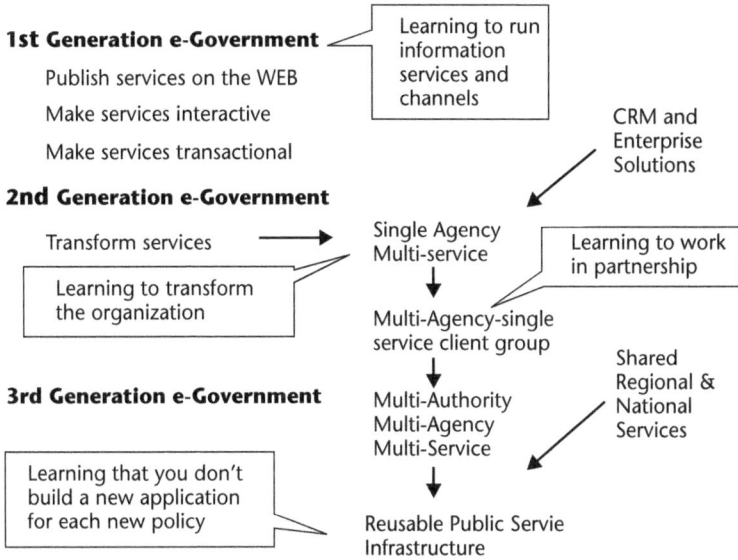

Figure 8.1 Digital Government Maturity Model
Source: Martin (2006).

shocks and crises as Fountain claims, along with strong, even perhaps heroic, acts of leadership and entrepreneurship to counter prevailing institutional and other constraints. If this is the case, the transferability and diffusion of digital government innovations is likely to be highly problematic. While it is clear that principles and approaches that are of wide application can be identified (be it health records, smart cards, CRM, etc.), their applicability and take-up is extremely sensitive to the local context, history, and practice. 'Solutions' cannot simply be 'shrink wrapped' and 'rolled out'. Moreover, if such solutions are presented to users as applications that dictate a particular business process, rather than as infrastructures to support their conversations, then the likelihood of significant innovation (e.g. through co-produced design-in-use) is even more limited. In short, policy-makers and public agencies are still struggling with framing the challenge of digital government as one of transforming the technologies through which service delivery is accomplished but also developing appropriate organizational and governance arrangements to underpin this as well.

Given this, what might we envisage as 'second generation' digital government? In this phase further emphasis is placed on the goal of coordinated service delivery in order to better meet the needs of

165

different segments of the population such as children, older people, those with disabilities, or the unemployed (perhaps as proposed more recently in the UK under the 'Big Society' rubric and more recently in Australia in relation to disability services). This may involve the growth of a 'mixed economy' of private and third sector service providers (in some circumstances, this may be coupled to the state playing a less significant role and personal budgets being allocated to individuals empowered to engage in self-directed care). In this scenario the demand from government is for service delivery to be joined up, not just within an agency but across public agency and increasingly public/private/third sector boundaries where, in the future, services will increasingly be provided from.

The challenge here is to develop information and governance systems able not just to support integration within single agencies, but rather to support partnerships in multi-agency and cross-sectoral settings. Moreover, these need to be configurable and capable of being repurposed as part of a new 'mixed information economy' supporting a personalized care marketplace (see Codagnone and Osimo, 2010). If the argument we have advanced in this book is correct, such developments will place overwhelming stress on single-enterprise integration solutions to information sharing, which will prove insufficiently flexible or agile for the task. An important change in thinking needs to take place involving a recognition that within new multi-agency and cross-sector partnerships concepts of integration (involving e.g. the aggregation and cleansing of data and the standardization of functionality) are not appropriate, desirable, or even safe.

If this challenge is accepted we would suggest that a 'third generation' stage of digital government emerges as a possibility. Here, building a new system for each new policy will be recognized as a no longer sustainable practice. Instead, a more appropriate response to policy change will be a reconfiguration of existing infrastructural capacity and publication spaces in the face of inevitably changing patterns of social need, legal context, and political priorities. A new application will not be needed for every change in policy direction. To enable such a development the nature of social learning will have to change. Indeed it is the nature of social learning, rather than the simplistic notion of improvements in technology, that we stress again is what drives progress in digital government. Here then, learning assumes a new 'second order' dimension where existing strategies and approaches to implementation are questioned, and it is ambiguity rather than uncertainty through risk that is to be managed. This requires new sense to be made of changing circumstances, new concepts, ideas, and language to be evoked and, as a result, a new set of commitments established (see e.g. Codagnone and Osimo, 2010). Finally then, even more speculatively, we can glimpse perhaps a further 'fourth generation' of maturity characterized by partnership working across a mixed economy of public, private, and third sectors, and supported by an infrastructure of federated information and identity management systems and shared service environments.

Mrs Cannybody's Dilemma Revisited

The final point we wish to make in the light of our discussion about the nature and properties of architectural discourse is that we can now identify a sixth, perhaps all embracing, rule of virtuality. We summarize this rule as: *virtualizing the instrument does not virtualize the conversation*. In order to explain this, we now turn back to Mrs Cannybody and her dilemma with which we began this book.

It will be recalled that the proposal within *The Charity* was to introduce an e-commerce solution to better enable information sharing between front-line service workers' complex needs, as well as satisfy reporting requirements to the local authority and central government. From the point of view of the IT manager's proposal for an e-commerce solution, the data warehouse and its associated 'enterprise information architecture' offer an opportunity to rationalize and clean up the data currently held across different databases and document management systems. In order to do this the *The Charity* will need to work with system suppliers to elicit use cases from Mrs Cannybody and her colleagues, map work flows and business processes, define data sets, and devise appropriate security policies. This would then permit the objectives of *integrated* delivery, *integrated* planning and processes, and *integrated* governance, embedded in national policy requirements and the strategies of service commissioners, to be realized in practice.

However, in contemplating her dilemma in relation to her concern over Mary, these proposed changes are also a source of additional concern to Mrs Cannybody. In particular, she is worried about the effects that the planned data warehouse will have on how and where the identity and relationships of her clients will be represented in the case management, recording, and reporting systems of *The Charity*. In the current system, client cases are effectively managed locally by the relevant caseworkers through customizable arrangements around record keeping that make sure details of identity and particular relationships are only shareable between the front-line workers in the local Sure

Start centre. But how will this operate if all information is pooled in a large centralized database accessible by a wide range of users, where access may be controlled by role and relationships to clients? How will identity information and information about different relationships with *The Charity* and its various services be safely governed and the interests and consents of clients be understood, managed, and respected?

The rules of virtuality outlined above and our analysis of architectural discourse clearly question whether the language of system development involved here is adequate for expressing the concerns of the likes of Mrs Cannybody, let alone the interests of clients such as Mary and Derek. For example, as we have already seen in Chapter 3, the assumption that integration has a universal, monotonic value where more is always better can be questioned. Indeed, rather than attempting to over-integrate by capturing and cleansing data for a central database, a more 'user-centred' and context-dependent set of requirements needs to be explored. One aspect of this is the way in which identity is conceived. Typically the architecture of e-commerce systems adopts a simplistic inscription of a 'dyadic logic' of identity (Wilson *et al.*, 2011*b*). Here identity is conceived as an attribute of the identified—for example, in an information system database a system identifier is linked to a demographic attribute (e.g. date of birth). In this way an individual's identity becomes a set of facts, such as given names, a date and place of birth, and so forth. However, in this dyadic approach, the identity of the identifier is implicit in the role of the owner of the information system or database as designed by system developers.

An alternative 'triadic logic' (following Pierce, 1998) views identity as the attribute of a relationship in which both the identifier and the identified and, as a consequence, their relationship, remain explicit. In other words the identity of the identifier in all instances is made clear and kept so (Wilson *et al.*, 2011*b*). As such, identity is the three-way linkage between the means (information) by which a recognizer (person, institution, agency) recognizes an individual (person). The purpose of the recognition is to maintain and make use of a shared history that is to support a relationship. Triadic logic means that the representation of identity and of relationship are not separated but always operate in conjunction. This notion provides the scope, we would suggest, for developing appropriate governance of electronic records and digitized information. That is, rather than being digitalized and disintermediated in dyadic terms, there is now a possibility to make decisions about the architecture of information systems and governance frameworks that take better account of the 'real-world' diversity of the practice of front-line practitioners.

In the case of *The Charity* this might, although of course we cannot say for sure, result in an architectural decision to separate identity management into a separate service. This would hold 'Mary's' preferences and consents in relation to what information about her and her situation were shared or not. Thereby this would ensure that the coordination of the care plans and assessments between two service or project domains would be a matter of governance (as shown in Figure 8.2) and not an unintended side effect of the existing design of the record management system (Figure 0.2) or 'over-integration' in the proposed 'data warehouse' (Figure 0.1).

Such an architectural solution would recognize that, if there is to be any resolution to wicked problems of the kind presented by Mary's situation, then that is most likely one that will be produced by the individuals involved within the context of the individual cases and relationships (conversations) in which they are engaged. It is not something that can be embodied a priori into 'integrated systems' (*instrumentalized*) and realized through electronic means of sharing information. The *virtualization* implied by the *instrumentalization* of information in databases, data warehouses, electronic records, and the like may well change the nature of conversations in such complex service relationships through their disintermediation. However, contrary to what is assumed by proponents of ideas such as digital era governance, this does not make those conversations (and the roles, responsibilities, and rights within them) virtual.

Mrs Cannybody intends to publish her concern about Mary's welfare to anyone in *The Charity* who has a relationship with the individual she knows as Mary. She wishes to do this on the understanding that Mary may have relationships which she wants to maintain quite separately from the one Mrs Cannybody has with her. What the recipients of this 'narrowcast' and specific 'publication' do about it is up to them and Mary, and Mrs Cannybody may or may not get a direct answer. Mrs Cannybody must look to her experience, recommended practice, and her relationship with Mary to formulate her next moves. To leave the governance of such complexities to the decisions of suppliers, IT personnel, and others concerned with the technicalities of database design and system architectures—whatever their merits in solving the information sharing problems of the likes of Marks & Spencer, Tesco, and Walmart—would seem to be a folly of the utmost proportions.

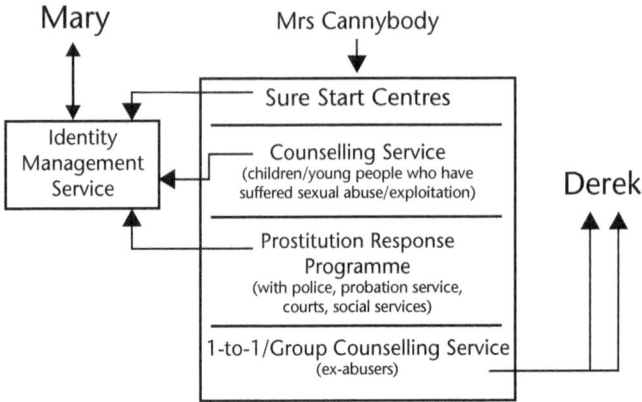

Figure 8.2 Alternative Identity Management System.
Source: Wilson *et al.* (2011). Reprinted with permission of Cambridge University Press.

Conclusion: The Puzzle with no Picture on the Box

The continued development of both the power and the pervasiveness of digital government is resulting in a situation where many aspects of our lives as citizens and consumers of public services are becoming dependent on *how* information systems and the organizational arrangements around them are constructed and operated (Martin, 2006). Gregory Bateson defined information as 'news of a difference that makes a difference' (Bateson, 1972). Increasingly, in the world of public service delivery and the functioning of the state more generally, 'it is *information in systems*, rather than *information in the real world*, that is making the key differences in peoples' lives' (Martin, 2007: 51; original emphasis). These developments cannot be halted. What does need to change, if we are to avoid repeating the many mistakes of past and present, is the way that systems are designed, deployed, and governed and who gets to participate in their co-production. Information and organizational architectures need to change from those which focus on integration through structures to ones which emphasize infrastructure and emergence, and seek alternative means of coordination such as through federation and federability. To accomplish this we need to evolve the language that is used to talk about, give meaning to, and enact the socio-material things we call artefacts and systems. The challenge for both students of and those engaged in public service delivery is to work out how to do this puzzle with no picture on the box.

Methodological Appendix

A social informatics perspective is about making the design of information systems, 'relevant to people's lives', through both affecting the process of design itself and the substantive outcomes which emerge from that process. This requires a particular mode of research that involves a commitment to

1) immersion in the design and development process in a conscious attempt to change that process in order to increase its relevance, and
2) understanding what is relevant to the above in the lived experience of the social actors information systems are supposed to benefit (Agre, 1996).

For us, one of the key practical implications of this is a need to conduct research from the inside of 'live' projects, preferably as they unfold, and to capture and reflect upon the experience of doing so from the point(s) of view of all those involved (including of course the researchers themselves). Such commitments, we suggest, cannot be delivered from within one disciplinary frame. Accordingly, our preferred research frameworks and methods are cross-disciplinary, involving methodological inputs ranging from action research, ethnography, through to information system modelling and architectures.

The Projects and Participants

The principal vehicle for the research reported in this book has been provided by three major projects.

1) *AMASE—Advanced Multi-Agency Service Environment (funded by the UK EPSRC, 1999–2003)*—examined how local public agencies were confronting the issue of integrating systems to support multi-agency working (McLoughlin *et al.*, 2004). The aim was to (*a*) understand the practice of public agencies as they worked together in emerging multi-agency environments; (*b*) assist agencies in their attempts to make sense of and act differently in their new policy and service delivery contexts; and (*c*) produce a socio-technical model of the information and organizational architectures required to support information sharing in cross- or multi-agency environments.

Three digital government projects in emerging multi-agency environments (with the same city council—*Big City*—at their core) were studied:

- *Services for Children* which involved the development of a new strategic partnership between health, social services, education, and voluntary sector agencies for the delivery of services to children (especially those with disabilities). The study was subsequently extended to cover electronic social care records and service directories (see Chapters 3 and 4).

- *Regional Smart Card* which involved working with members of a consortium of local authorities, transport providers, and technology vendors who were seeking to develop a multi-function smart card that would support a variety of transport, education, and potentially other offerings in a provincial region of the UK (see Chapter 5).

- *CRM Software Procurement* explored the roll-out of new customer contact centres and the attempt to procure software to assist in the integration of back and front office operations through the novel (for the council) device of a partnership with the private sector. The CRM study was extended, following implementation of the system, through a doctoral research project (see Chapter 5).

2) *Framework for Multi-agency Environments (FAME) (funded by the UK Office of the Deputy Prime Minister, 2003–2007).*

Our role in this major government project was twofold: (*a*) conducting a formative evaluation of the front-line experience in developing multi-agency partnerships (see Chapter 6), and (*b*) using the findings from the project evaluation, other academic studies, and grey literature to generate a 'generic framework', i.e. a multi-faceted guide, resource, and tool for subsequent adopters of multi-agency working and associated information sharing technologies (see Chapter 5). Full details are available at www.fame-uk.org.

3) *OLDES (Older People's e-Services @ Home) (funded by the European Commission 2007–11)* was part of the European Union's Information Society Technologies (IST) Framework 6 Programme (FP6) for *Ambient Assisted Living (AAL) for the Aging Society*. The project involved a collaboration of local public health and social care providers, system suppliers, and intermediary research organizations and university researchers. As one of the university partners in the project, we had responsibility for work packages concerned with user engagement and its evaluation (see Chapter 7).

We also draw on other smaller projects and our most recent research with colleagues at the University of Wollongong (funded by an Australian Research Council Discovery Project). This is examining the vexed issue of the introduction of shareable electronic health records in Australia and the UK. This includes a retrospective study of an early prototype of an SEHR developed in the North-East of England (see Chapter 4).

Given the diversity of projects involved, participants in the research came from a wide range of service commissioning and delivery roles. However, we should note that primary research with the 'end-user' was not the sole or even main concern of the research we conducted. Rather we had a deliberate focus on service providers themselves as the key 'users'. This was in part due to the interests of project sponsors in improving service delivery but it was mainly due to the primary focus of our research being on finding ways to facilitate innovation within the service delivery process and associated networks and partnerships. This was something that could not be explored by a concern with just the end-users working alone.

Accordingly, at the hub of the networks we became part of was typically a local government authority or municipality, usually supported in their digital government projects by technology vendors who had been commissioned to develop systems. Much of our work was therefore conducted with local public managers, project officers, project managers, professional practitioners and workers (including health and social workers), partnership development workers, and so on, along with technical specialists working for the information systems suppliers and other intermediaries with whom public agencies were collaborating.

Research Design and Methods

In conventional academic terms we engaged in applied rather than basic research. The projects, more often than not, involved the generation of deliverables (including guidelines and frameworks, demonstrators, prototypes, toolkits, and/or information architecture and service models)—see for an example Vaughan *et al.* (2006). These were either for use within organizations by public managers and professionals engaged in the commissioning, design, and delivery of services, or acted as the basis for a co-production dialogue with project participants over such issues. The opportunity for research was normally provided by new policy requirements for services to be delivered in a multi-agency collaboration of some kind. The research was therefore akin to what has been termed the 'Mode 2' production of knowledge (Gibbons *et al.*, 1994). In Schön's (1983) parlance, our endeavours were topographically located in the 'swampy lowlands' of practice.

Accordingly, the research design and methods reflected the fact that the 'leg work' involved was both grounded in 'real-life' problems and the 'lived experience' of front-line public service delivery and was part of attempts to produce service innovation through the design, deployment, and use of new digital technologies. As a result, at various points, we took active positions as 'action researchers', 'in' and 'for' projects, i.e. working with participants towards practical outcomes and new understanding (Reason and Bradbury, 2001, 2008; O'Leary 2004; Coghlan, 2011). In this context, the action research we conducted invariably involved finding ways to support the development of a more effective and better informed dialogue between the different communities of practice that were invariably brought together in the pursuit of these novel collaborative arrangements.

Our approach here is best understood in terms of the idea of 'bricolage' (Badham and Ehn, 2000). That is, we did not seek legitimacy for our endeavours exclusively in terms of any 'scientific' basis in relation to either our methods or expertise. Rather, our claim to any effectiveness rested as much, if not more, on an ability to understand the social and political dynamics of the projects that we sought to intervene in. We sought to do this, in particular, by being willing and able to respond in *ad hoc* and context-specific ways to given circumstances as they unfolded. Our interventions were, therefore, both attempts to 'tinker' with ongoing projects in order to 'get things done' and efforts in working out 'what to do' on the basis of our academically derived analytical frames and methods (Badham and Ehn, 2000: 79). In other words, we sought to make do with what was at hand, and build our capability through practical experience whilst developing both practical and theoretical knowledge from these efforts (Badham and Ehn, 2000). At all times we sought to do this by becoming accepted as legitimate 'native' members of project teams (McLoughlin, 2010).

Our action research approach was complemented by taking a more conventional distanced academic position in doing a study 'of' the projects using ethnographically informed qualitative research methods (an approach we first developed and began to refine in the AMASE project—see McLoughlin, 2010). We tried to find ways to use these data by assisting project participants in developing ability to share and communicate via 'big and rich pictures' (Checkland and Scholes, 1990). In some of the projects we were able to deploy a visualization tool that provided a means by which ethnographic data from studies of the practices of users and the domain of use could be represented back to project participants, including technical developers. The visualizations or 'projections' were typically in the style of animated multi-screen power point presentations and were intentionally based on the naturalistic language of users. Our experience was that the 'projections' could constitute effective 'boundary objects' that facilitated dialogues, within and between different stakeholder groups, and be a key tool in cultivating co-productive debate and discussion. A key feature was that they were: intended to be recognizable by users as relevant and realistic in their worlds; provide a basis for them to explore non-technical as well as technological conditions and issues; and provide a starting point for them to adopt and appropriate through a process of internalizing and sharing. Ultimately, these representations had the potential to inform detailed requirements and technical specifications or, as in the OLDES case, to produce a 'reference architecture' which in future projects could provide a framework from which such specifications might be developed (see Chapter 7).

The study of *Children's Service Directories* (see Chapter 4) provides a typical insight into the overall approach we evolved combining action research and ethnographically informed methods. In this study we adopted a two-stage research design, comprising exploratory investigation using a variety of qualitative methods, followed by action research with participants in facilitated workshops—a process we also subjected on this occasion to ethnographic study to assist our own reflection and evaluation. In the exploratory phase, data were collected by a combination of desk research, interviewing, and non-participant observation of meetings and events. The second phase consisted of three carefully planned and facilitated workshops. During the workshops preliminary findings from the exploratory phase were presented to the professionals and representatives of the service providing agencies with a stake in the development and use of the directories. Vignettes, stories, and scenarios informed by the exploratory research were also used to stimulate feedback and discussion.

Each workshop was designed for a different set of stakeholders involved in directory production. Participants in the first workshop were voluntary sector service managers. The second was for service commissioners. The third workshop brought together individuals from the statutory and voluntary sectors with an interest in directories. In each workshop participants were encouraged to experience, explore, and respond to the stimulus material. The workshop facilitators animated informed and creative discussions about current situations and future possibilities by inviting participants to share their responses to this material, and also to draw upon their own experiences (Jenkings and Wilson, 2007). Discussions were recorded and analysed after each workshop, and the materials adapted and refined for later workshops as a consequence of each discussion. Analysis was an ongoing process, with discrete data from the exploratory research being analysed 'by hand' to generate categories and themes, which were further refined and developed through frequent meetings with the research team and between the research team and other stakeholders in the workshops.

References

6, P. (2004) *E-Governance: Styles of Political Judgement in the Information Age* (Basingstoke: Palgrave Macmillan).

—— (2006) 'Joined-up Government in the West beyond Britain: A Provisional Assessment', in V. Bogdanor (ed.), *Joined-up Government* (Oxford: Oxford University Press), 43–106.

—— Bellamy, C., Raab, C., Warren, A., and Heeney, C. (2007) 'Institutional Shaping of Inter-Agency Working: Managing Tensions between Collaborative Working and Client Confidentiality', *Journal of Public Administration Research and Theory*, 17(3): 405–34.

—— Leat, D., Seltzer, K., and Stoker, G. (2002) *Towards Holistic Governance: The New Reform Agenda* (Basingstoke: Palgrave Macmillan).

—— Raab, C. D., and Bellamy, C., (2005) Joined-up Government & Privacy in the United Kingdom: Managing Tensions between Data Protection and Social Policy. Part 1, *Public Administration* 83(1): 111–33.

Abiteboul, S., Hull, R., and Vianu, V. (1995) *Foundations of Databases* (Boston: Addison-Wesley).

Accenture (2007) *Leadership in Customer Service: Delivering the Promise* (Government Executive Series; London: Accenture Consulting).

Age, The (2008) 'Further Delays for Melbourne's New Public Transport Ticketing System', 25 Mar.

—— (2010) 'My, How the Myki hath Fallen', 22 May.

AGIMO (2004) *Future Challenges for e-Government*, 2 vols (Canberra: AGIMO).

—— (2006) *2006 e-Government Strategy, Responsive Government: A New Service Agenda* (Canberra: AGIMO).

—— (2008) *National Smartcard Framework* (Canberra: AGIMO).

—— (2011) *Interacting with Government: Australians' Use and Satisfaction with e-Government Services* (Canberra: AGIMO).

Agre, P. E. (1996) 'Towards a Critical Technical Practice: Lessons Learnt in Attempts to Reform AI', in G. C. Bowker *et al.* (eds), *Bridging the Great Divide: Social Science, Technical Networks and Co-operative Work* (Mahwah, NJ: Lawrence Erlbaum Associates).

Alderman, N., Ivory, C. J., McLoughlin, I. P., and Vaughan, R. (2013) *Managing Complex Projects: Networks, Knowledge and Innovation* (London: Routledge).

Alford, J. (2002) 'Why do Public-Sector Clients Coproduce? Toward a Contingency Theory', *Administration and Society*, 34(1): 32–56.

References

—— (2007) *Engaging Public Sector Clients: From Service Delivery to Co-Production* (Basingstoke: Palgrave Macmillan).

—— and Hughes, O. E. (2008) 'Public Value Pragmatism as the Next Phase of Public Management', *American Review of Public Administration*, 38(2): 30–148.

Anderson, R. (2007) 'Government Security Failure'. Blog at http://www. lightbluetouchpaper.org/ (accessed Nov. 2007).

—— Brown, I., Dowty, T., Inglesant, P., and Heath, W. (2009) *Database State* (York: Joseph Rowntree Trust).

Armitage, G. D., Suter, E., Oelke, N. D., and Adair, C. E. (2009) 'Health Systems Integration: State of the Evidence', *International Journal of Integrated Care*, 9(17): 2–11.

Australian National Audit Office (2009) *The Australian Taxation Office's Implementation of the Change Program: A Strategic Overview* (Canberra: Australian National Audit Office).

Australian Senate (2011) *Personally Controlled Electronic Records Bill 2011, Community Affairs Legislation Committee* (Canberra: Commonwealth of Australia).

—— (2012) *Personally Controlled Electronic Health Records Bill 2011*, Senate Standing Committee on Community Affairs, Parliament of Australia, 19 March.

Australian Productivity Commission (2011) *Caring for Older Australians*, Final Inquiry Report, 53 (Canberra: APC, June).

Badham, R. (2003) 'Introduction: New Technology and the Implementation Process', *International Journal of Human Factors in Manufacturing*, 3(1): 3–13.

—— (2005) 'Technology and the Transformation of Work', in S. Ackroyd, R. Batt, P. Thompson, and P. Tolbert (eds), *The Oxford Handbook of Work and Organization* (Oxford: Oxford University Press), 115–37.

—— and Ehn, P. (2000) 'Tinkering with Technology: Human Factors, Work Redesign, and Professionals in Workplace Innovation', *Human Factors and Ergonomics in Manufacturing*, 10(1): 61–82.

Baines, S., Gannon-Leary, P. M., and Wilson, R. G. (2005) 'Practitioner Buy-in and Resistance to e-Enabled Information Sharing across Agencies: The Case of an e-Government Project to Join up Local Services in England', in M. Funabashi, and A. Grzech (eds), *Challenges of Expanding Internet, e-Commerce, e-Business and e-Government* (New York: Springer), 297–312.

—— Wilson, R., and Walsh, S. (2010) 'Seeing the Full Picture? Technologically Enabled Multi-Agency Working in Health and Social Care', *New Technology, Work and Employment*, 25(1): 19–33.

Banks, P. (2002) *Partnerships Under Pressure* (London: King's Fund).

Barlass, T. (2012) 'Patients Reject e-Health', *Sydney Morning Herald* (12 Aug.) <http://www.smh.com.au/it-pro/government-it/patients-reject-ehealth-20120811-24179.html>, (accessed Aug. 2012).

Barley, S. (1986) 'Technology as an Occasion for Structuring: Evidence from the Observations of CT Scanners and the Social Order of Radiology Departments', *Administrative Science Quarterly*, 31: 78–108.

Bason, C., *Leading Public Sector Innovation: Co-creating for a Better Society* (Bristol: The Policy Press).

Bateson, G. (1972) *Steps to and Ecology of the Mind* (Chicago: Chicago University Press).

Bellamy, C., 6, P., and Raab, C. (2005) 'Joined-up Government and Privacy in the United Kingdom: Managing Tensions between Data Protection and Social Policy, Part 2', *Public Administration*, 83(2): 393–415.

—— and Taylor, J. A. (1998) *Governing in the Information Age* (Milton Keynes: Open University Press).

—— 6, P., Raab, C., Warren, A., and Heeney, C., (2008) 'Information-Sharing and Confidentiality in Social Policy: Regulating Multi-Agency Working'. *Public Administration*, 86(3): 737–59.

Benkler, Yochai (2006) *The Wealth of Networks: How Social Production Transforms Market and Freedom* (New Haven: Yale University Press).

Blaschke, C., Freddolino, P., and Mullen, E. (2009) 'Aging and Technology: A Review of the Research Literature', *British Journal of Social Work*, 39: 641–56.

Bloomfield, Brian P., and Hayes, Niall (2009) Power and Organizational Transformation through Technology: Hybrids of Electronic Government', *Organization Studies*, 30(5) (May): 461–87.

Blythe, M. A., Monk, A. F., and Doughty, K. (2005) 'Socially Dependable Design: The Challenge of Aging Populations for HCI', *Interacting with Computers*, 17: 627–89.

Bødker K., Kensing, F., and Simonsen, J. (2004) *Participatory IT Design: Designing for Business and Workplace Realities* (Cambridge, Mass.: MIT Press).

Bogdanor, V. (2005) 'Introduction', in V. Bogdanor (ed.), *Joined-up Government* (Oxford: Oxford University Press), 1–18.

Boreham, P., Hall, R., Thompson, P., and Parker, R. (2008) *New Technology at Work* (London: Routledge).

Boudreau, M. C., and Robey, D. (2005) 'Enacting Integrated Information Technology: A Human Agency Perspective', *Organization Science*, 16(1): 3–18.

Bovaird, T. (2007) 'Beyond Engagement and Participation: User and Community Co-production of Public Services', *Public Administration Review*, 67(5): 846–60.

Bovens, M., and Zouridis, S. (2002) 'From Street-Level to System-Level Bureaucracies: How Information and Communication Technology is Transforming Administrative Discretion and Constitutional Control', *Public Administration Review* 62(2): 174–84.

Bowker, G., and Star, S. L. (2002) *Sorting Things Out: Classification and its Consequences* (Cambridge, Mass.: MIT Press).

Boyle, D., and Harris, M. (2009) *The Challenge of Co-Production: How Equal Partnerships between Professionals and the Public are Crucial to Improving Public Services* (London: NESTA).

Brennan, S. (2005) *The NHS IT Project: 'The Biggest Computer Programme in the World Ever'* (Oxford: Radcliffe Publishing).

—— (2007) 'The Biggest Computer Programme in the World Ever! How's it Going?', *Journal of Information Technology*, 22: 202–11.

Brooks, R. (2007) 'System Failure! A Private Eye Special Report', *Private Eye*, 1179: 17–24.

References

Brown, J. S., and Duguid, P. (2000) *The Social Life of Information* (Boston: HBR Press).

Buchanan, D. A., Addicott, R., and Fitzgerald, L. (2007) 'Nobody in Charge: Distributed Change Agency in Health Care', *Human Relations*, 60(7): 1065–90.

Busuoli, M., Gallelli, T., Haluzík, M., Fabián, V., Novák, D., and Štěpánková, O. (2007) 'Entertainment and Ambient: A New OLDES' View', *Lecture Notes in Computer Science*, 4556/2007: 511–19.

Cabinet Office (2000*a*) *E-Government: A Strategic Framework for Public Services in the Information Age* (London: Cabinet Office).

—— (2000*b*) *Successful IT: Modernizing Government in Action* (London: Cabinet Office).

—— (2005) *Transformational Government: Enabled by Technology* (London: Cabinet Office).

—— (2006) *Transformation Government: Implementation Plan* (London: Cabinet Office).

—— (2010) *Building the Big Society* (London: Cabinet Office).

—— (2012) *Government Digital Strategy* (London: Cabinet Office).

Chadwick, A., and May, C. (2003) 'Interaction between States and Citizens in the Age of the Internet: "E-Government" in the United States, Britain, and the European Union', *Governance: An International Journal of Policy, Administration and Institutions*, 16(2): 271–300.

Chapman, C. S., and Kihn, L.-A. (2009) 'Information System Integration, Enabling Control and Performance', *Accounting, Organizations and Society*, 34: 151–69.

Checkland, P., and Scholes, J. (1990) *Soft Systems Methodology in Action* (Chichester: Wiley).

Chen, D., Doumeingts, D., and ois Vernadat, F. (2008) 'Architectures for Enterprise Integration and Interoperability: Past, Present and Future', *Computers in Industry*, 59: 647–59.

Childs, D., Chang, H., and Grayson, A. (2009) 'President-Elect Obama Urges Electronic Medical Records in Five Years', ABC News, Medical Unit, 9 Jan. <http://abcnews.go.com/Health/President44/story?id=6606536&page=1#. UBa2U6l0WnA> (accessed July 2012).

Christensen, C. M., and Raynor, M. E. (2003) *The Innovator's Solution* (Boston: Harvard University Press).

—— Grossman, J. H., and Whang, J. (2009) *The Innovator's Prescription: A Disruptive Solution for Health Care* (New York: McGraw Hill).

Ciborra, C., and Associates (2001) *From Control to Drift: The Dynamics of Corporate Information Infrastructures* (Oxford: Oxford University Press).

Clark, J., McLoughlin, I. P., Rose, H., and King, R. (1988) *The Process of Technological Change* (Cambridge: Cambridge University Press).

Clarke, J., and Newman, J. (2005) 'What's in a Name? New Labour's Citizen-Consumers and the Remaking of Public Services', paper for the CRESC conference, Culture and Social Change: Disciplinary Exchanges, Manchester, 11–13 July.

Clennel, A. (2007) '$64m Tcard Fiasco over', *Sydney Morning Herald*, 11 Sept.

Cochrane, A. (2004) 'Modernisation, Managerialism and the Culture Wars: Reshaping the Local Welfare State in England', *Local Government Studies*, 30(4): 481–96.

Codagnone, C., and Osimo, D. (2010) 'Beyond i2010: E-Government Current Challenges and Future Scenarios,' in P. G. Nixon, V. N. Koutrakou, and R. Rawal (eds), *Understanding e-Government in Europe: Issues and Challenges* (London: Routledge), 38–58.

Coghlan, D. (2011) 'Action Research: Exploring Perspectives on a Philosophy of Practical Knowing', *Academy of Management Annals*, 5(1): 53–87.

Collins, T. (2007) 'HMRC's Missing Child Benefit CDs: What went Wrong and Lessons for NPfIT and ID Cards', *Computer Weekly*, <http://www.computerweekly.com/blogs/tony_collins/2007/11/hmrcs-missing-child-benefit-cd-1.html> (accessed Nov. 2007).

Colmer, S. (2007) *Technology to Support the Aging Global Population 2007–2027* (Newcastle upon Tyne: Centre of Excellence of Life Sciences, University of Newcastle).

Commission of the European Communities (2001) *eGovernment Indicators for Benchmarking eEurope: Europe's Information Society* (Brussels: European Commission).

—— (2004) *E-Health: Making Healthcare Better for European Citizens. An Action Plan for a European e-Health Area* (Brussels: European Commission).

—— (2005) *Confronting Demographic Change: A New Solidarity between the Generations* (Brussels: European Commission).

—— (2006) *The Demographic Future of Europe: From Challenge to Opportunity* (Brussels: European Commission).

—— (2007) *Information Society and Health: Linking European Policies* (Brussels: European Commission).

Comode, G., and Krishanmurthy, B. (2008) 'Key Differences between Web 1.0 and Web 2.0', *First Monday*, 13(6) June.

Cook, H. (2012) 'Police Handed Data on Myki Users', *The Age*, 18 Sept.

Cornford, J. R., and Pollock, N. (2002) 'Working through the Work of Making Work Mobile', in K. Webster and F. Robins (eds), *The Virtual University? Knowledge, Markets and Management* (Oxford: Oxford University Press), 87–104.

—— Wessels, B., Richardson, R., Gillespie, A., McLoughlin, I. P., Kohannejad, J., Belt, V., and Martin, M. J. (2003) *Local e-Government: Process Evaluation of the Implementation of Electronic Local Government in England* (London: Office of the Deputy Prime Minister).

Cortada, J. W. (2008) *The Digital Hand, iii. How Computers Changed the Work of the American Public Sector Industries* (Oxford: Oxford University Press).

Cross, M. (2007) 'Benefits of £12bn Programme in NHS are "Unclear" MPs Say', *British Medical Journal*, 334(7598), 21 Apr., 815.

Currie, W., and Guah, M. W. (2007) 'Conflicting Institutional Logics: A National Programme for IT in the Organizational Field of Healthcare', *Journal of Information Technology*, 22: 235–47.

Davies, A. (2003) 'Integrated Solutions: The Changing Business of Systems Integration', in A. Davies and M. Hobday (eds), *The Business of Systems Integration* (Oxford: Oxford University Press), 333–68.

Davies, M. (2004) 'Taking Smartcards Forward in Local Government', unpublished paper, London Connect.

Davis, R., Aumgartner, J. C., Francia, P. L., and Morris, J. S. (2009) 'The Internet in U.S. Election Campaigns', in A. Chadwick and N. P. Howard (eds), *The Routledge Handbook of Internet Politics* (London: Routledge).

Deloitte (2008) 'Draft National E Health Strategy', Canberra: National e-Health and Information Principal Committee, Deloitte, Sept.

—— (2011) *Fed Cloud: The Future of Federal Work* (A Gov Lab Idea; Washington, DC: Deloitte Development).

Department of Education and Skills (2003) *Every Child Matters* (London: HMSO).

Department of Health (1998) *Information for Health: An Information Strategy for the Modern NHS 1998–2005* (London: Department of Health).

—— (2000) *The NHS Plan: A Plan for Investment, a Plan for Reform* (London: The Stationery Office).

—— (2001) *Building the Information Core: Implementing the NHS Plan* (London: Department for Health).

—— (2002) *Delivering 21st Century IT Support for the NHS: National Strategic Programme* (London: Department of Health).

—— (2004) *The NHS Improvement Plan: Putting People at the Heart of Public Services* (London: Department of Health).

—— (2008) *The NHS Informatics Review Report* (London: The Stationery Office).

—— (2009) *The NHS Informatics Review Report* (London: The Stationery Office).

—— (2011) *Whole System Demonstrator Project: Headline Findings* (London: Department of Health).

Deutsch, E., Duftschmid, G., and Dorda, W. (2010) 'Critical Areas of National Electronic Health Record Programs: Is our Focus Correct?', *International Journal of Medical Informatics*, 79(3): 211–22.

Dewsbury, G., Taylor, B., and Edge, M. (2002) 'Designing Dependable Assistive Technology Systems for Vulnerable People', *Health Informatics Journal*, 8(2): 104–10.

Dunleavy, P. (2010) *The Future of Joined-up Public Services* (2020 Public Services Trust//ESRC; London: Public Services Trust).

—— and Margetts, H. (2010) 'The Second Wave of Digital Era Governance', paper presented at American Political Science Association Conference, 4 Sept, available at <http://eprints.lse.ac.uk/27684> (accessed Aug. 2011).

—— Margetts, H., Bastow, S., and Tinkler, J. (2005) 'New Public Management is Dead: Long Live Digital Era Governance', *Journal of Public Administration Research and Theory*, 16(3): 467–94.

—— and (2006) *Digital Era Governance: IT Corporations, the State, and e-Government* (Oxford: Oxford University Press).

—— and (2008) 'Australian e-Government in Comparative Perspective', *Australian Journal of Political Science*, 43(1): 13–26.

Dunn, J. E. (2012) 'Oyster Card Accounts Regularly Accessed by Police, Transport for London Admits', *Computer World*, 12 Feb.

Easen, P., Atkins, M., and Dyson, A. (2000) 'Inter-Professional Collaboration and Conceptualisations of Practice', *Children and Society*, 14(5): 355–67.

Eason, K. (2007) 'Local Socio-Technical System Development in the NHS National Programme for Information Technology', *Journal of Information Technology*, 22: 257–64.

Economist, The (2008), 'A Special Report on Technology and Government', 386(8567).

Eggers, W. D., and Goldsmith, S. (2008) *Government by Network: The New Public Management Imperative* (Boston: Deloitte Research/Ash Institute, Harvard University).

Ellingsen, G., and Monteiro, E. (2006) 'Seamless Integration: Standardization across Multiple Settings', *Computer Supported Cooperative Work*, 15(5–6): 443–66.

FAME (2004) *Towards a 'Generic Framework' for Information Sharing between Public Agencies* (Newcastle upon Tyne: Centre for Social and Business Informatics), available at <www.fame-uk.org>.

Fayard, Anne-Laure, and Weeks, J. (2007) 'Photocopiers and Watercoolers', *Organisation Studies*, 28(5): 605–34.

Foley, P., and Alfonso, X. (2009) 'E-Government and the Transformation Agenda', *Public Administration*, 87(2): 371–96.

Foresight (2000) *Healthcare and Ageing Population Panels* (London: Foresight).

Fountain, Jane (2001) *Building the Virtual State* (Boston: Harvard University Press).

—— (2009) 'Bureaucratic Reform and e-Government in the United States: An Institutional Perspective', in A. Chadwick and N. P. Howard (eds), *Routledge Handbook of Internet Politics* (London: Routledge), 99–115.

Frederickson, H. G. (2005) 'Whatever Happened to Public Administration? Governance, Governance Everywhere', in E. Ferlie, L. E. Lynn, and C. Pollitt (eds), *The Oxford Handbook of Public Management* (Oxford: Oxford University Press), 282–304.

Friedman, A. L., and Cornford, D. S. (1987) *Computer System Development: History Organization and Implementation* (New York: John Wiley).

Gannon-Leary, P. M., Baines, S., and Wilson, R. G. (2006) 'Collaboration and Partnership: A Review and Reflections on a National Project to Join up Local Services in England', *Journal of Interprofessional Care*, 20(6): 665–74.

Garrety, K., McLoughlin, I. P., and Wilson, R. (2013) 'Planning and Managing Complex Inter-organizational IT Projects: Lessons from the Health Care Sector', *Australian Journal of Public Management* (forthcoming).

Garud, R., Jain, S., and Tuertscher, P. (2008) 'Incomplete by Design and Designing for Incompleteness', *Organization Studies*, 29(3): 351–71.

Gauld, R., and Goldfinch, S. (2006) *Dangerous Enthusiasms: E-Government, Computer Failure and Information System Development* (Otago, New Zealand: University of Otago Press).

Gershon, P. (2004) *Releasing Resources to the Front Line* (London: HM Treasury).

—— (2008) *Review of the Australian Government's Use of Information and Communication Technology* (Canberra: Australian Government Information and Management Office).

Gibbons, M., Limoges, C., Nowotny, H., Schwartzman, S., Scott, P., and Trow, M. (1994) *The New Production of Knowledge: The Dynamics of Science and Research in Contemporary Societies* (London: Sage).

Glasby, J. (2005) 'The Integration Dilemma: How Deep and How Broad to Go?', *Journal of Integrated Care*, 13(5): 27–30.

—— (2007) *Understanding Health and Social Care* (Bristol: Policy Press).

—— and Dickinson, H. (2008) *Partnership Working in Health and Social Care* (Bristol: Polity Press).

—— and Peck, E. (2006) *We have to Stop Meeting Like This: The Governance of Inter-Agency Partnerships* (Leeds: Integrated Care Network).

Glendinning, C. (2003) 'Breaking Down Barriers: Integrating Health and Care Services for Older People in England', *Health Policy*, 65: 139–51.

Goddard, J., and Cornford, J (2001), 'Space, Place and the Virtual University: The Virtual University is the University Made More Concrete', in H. J. van der Molen (ed.), *Virtual University? Educational Environments of the Future* (London: Portland Press), 131–44.

Goodhue, D. L., Wybo, M. D., and Kirsch, L. J. (1992) 'The Impact of Data Integration on the Costs and Benefits of Information Systems', *Management Information Systems Quarterly*, 16(3): 293–311.

Gore, A. J. (1993) *From Red Tape to Results: Creating a Government that Works Better and Costs Less* (New York: Penguin Books).

Gottschalk, P. (2009) 'Maturity Levels for Interoperability in Digital Government', *Government Information Quarterly*, 26: 75–81.

Grand Designs (2009) *The Complete Series One: Brighton—The Co-operative Build* (London: Channel 4 Direct, DVD).

Granovetter, M. (1973) 'The Strength of Weak Ties', *American Sociological Review*, 78, 1360–80.

Gray, A. (2004) 'Governing Medicine: An Introduction', in A. Gray and S. Harrison (eds), *Governing Medicine: Theory and Practice* (Maidenhead: Open University Press), 1–7.

Green, A., Maguire, M., and Canny, A. (2001) *Keeping Track: Mapping and Tracking Vulnerable Young People* (Bristol: Policy Press).

Greenhalgh, T., Stramer, K., Bratan, T., Byrne, E., Russell, J., Mohammad, Y., Wood, G., and Hinder, S. (2008) *Summary Care Record Early Adopter Programme: An Independent Evaluation by University College, London* (London: UCL).

—— Potts, H. W. W., Wong, G., Bark, P., and Swinglehurst, D. (2009) 'Tensions and Paradoxes in Electronic Patient Record Research: A Systematic Literature Review Using the Meta-narrative Method', *Milbank Quarterly*, 87(4): 729–88.

—— Russell, J., Ashcroft, R. E., and Parsons, W. (2011) 'Why National eHealth Programs Need Dead Philosophers', *Milbank Quarterly*, 89: 533–63.

—— Stramer, K., Bratan, T., Byrne, E., Russell, J., and Potts, H. W.W. (2010) 'Adoption and Non-Adoption of a Shared Electronic Summary Record in England: A Mixed-Method Case Study', *British Medical Journal*, 340.

Guardian (2007) 'Substantial Operational Failure, then a Frantic Search', 21 Nov.

Gulledge, T. (2006) 'What is Integration?', *Industrial Management and Data Systems,* 106(1): 5–20.

Hackl, W. O., Hoerbst, A., and Ammenwerth, E. (2011) '"Why the Hell do we Need Electronic Health Records?" EHR Acceptance among Physicians in Private Practice in Austria: A Qualitative Study', *Methods of Information in Medicine,* 1, 53–61.

Halford, S., Lotherington, A. L., Obstfelder, A., and Dyb, K. (2008) 'Getting the Whole Picture? New Information and Communication Technologies in Healthcare Work and Organization', *Information, Communication and Society,* 13(3): 442–65.

Hambleton, S. (2011) 'Dangers of De-medicalising the PCEHR', *Australian Doctor,* 21 Sept. <http://www.australiandoctor.com.au/opinions/guest-editorial/dangers-of-de-medicalising-the-pcehr> (accessed July 2012).

Hanseth, O., Monteiro, E., and Hatling, M. (1996) 'Developing Information Infrastructures: The Tension between Standardization and Flexibility', *Science, Technology and Human Values,* 21(4): 407–26.

Hanson, J., Osipovic, D., and Percival, J. (2009) 'Making Sense of Sensors: Older People's and Professional Caregivers' Attitudes towards Telecare', in B. Loader, M. Hardey, and L. Keeble (eds), *Digital Welfare for the Third Age: Health and Social Care Informatics for Older People* (Abingdon: Routledge), 91–113.

Hardey, M., Loader, B., and Keeble, L. (2008) 'Introduction', in B. Loader, M. Hardey, and L. Keeble (eds), *Digital Welfare for the Third Age: Health and Social Care Informatics for Older People* (Abingdon: Routledge), 1–14.

Harris, M. (2011) 'Network Governance and the Politics of Organisational Resistance in UK Healthcare: The National Programme for Information Technology', in S. Clegg, M. Harris, and H. Hopfl (eds), *Managing Modernity: Beyond Bureaucracy?* (Oxford: Oxford University Press), 105–29.

—— Clegg, S., and Hopfl, H. (eds) (2011) 'Managing Modernity: Beyond Bureaucracy?', in S. Clegg, M. Harris, and H. Hopfl (eds), *Managing Modernity: Beyond Bureaucracy* (Oxford: Oxford University Press), 1–10.

Harrison, S. (2002) 'New Labour, Modernization and the Medical Labour Process', *Journal of Social Policy,* 31(3): 465–85.

Hartley, J. (2005) 'Innovation in Governance and Public Services: Past and Present', *Public Money and Management,* 25(1): 27–34.

—— (2008) 'The Innovation Landscape the Public Service Organizations', in J. Hartley, C. Donaldson, C. Skelcher, and M. Wallace (eds), *Managing to Improve Public Services* (Cambridge: Cambridge University Press), 197–216.

Hartswood, M., Procter, R., Slack, R., Vob, A., Buscher, M., Rouncefield, M., and Rouchy, P. (2002) 'Co-realization: Towards a Principled Synthesis of Ethnomethodology and Participatory Design', *Scandinavian Journal of Information System,* 14(2): 9–30.

Hasselbring, W. (2000) 'Information Systems Integration', *Communications of the ACM,* 43(6): 33–8.

Haynes, P. (2003) *Managing Complexity in the Public Services* (Maidenhead: Open University Press).

Hebson, G., Grimshaw, D., and Marchington, M. (2003) 'PPPs and the Changing Public Sector Ethos: Case-Study Evidence from the Health and Local Authority Sectors', *Work, Employment and Society*, 17(3): 481–501.

Heeks, R. (2005) 'eGovernment as a Carrier of Context', *Journal of Public Policy*, 25(1): 51–74.

—— (2006) *Implementing and Managing eGovernment: An International Text* (London: Routledge).

Henwood, F., and Hart, A. (2003) 'Articulating Gender in the Context of ICTs in Health Care: The Case of Electronic Patient Records in the Maternity Services', *Critical Social Policy*, 23(2): 249–67.

Hill, P. (2009) 'Count the Cost or Tell the Story? The Issues and Challenges in Developing Information Standards across the Social Care Sector', in P. Cunningham and P. Cunningham (eds), *e-Challenges: e-2009 Conference Proceedings* (London: HMC International), 1–8.

HM Government (2010) *Building the National Care Service* (London: The Stationery Office).

Hoffman, S., and Podgurski, A. (2009) 'E-Health Hazards: Provider Liability and Electronic Health Record Systems', *Berkeley Technology Law Journal*, 22(1): 1524–82.

Hood, C. C. (2005) 'The Idea of Joined-up Government: In Historical Perspective', in V. Bogdanor (ed.), *Joined-up Government* (Oxford: Oxford University Press), 19–42.

—— and Margetts, H. Z. (2007) *The Tools of Government in the Digital Age* (Basingstoke: Palgrave Macmillan).

House of Commons, Health Committee (2007) *The Electronic Patient Record* (Sixth Report of Session 2006–07; London: The Stationery Office).

House of Commons, Justice Committee (2008) 'Protection of Private Data', *First Report of Session 2007–2008* (London: The Stationery Office).

House of Commons, Public Accounts Committee (2007) *The National Programme for IT in the NHS* (London: Stationery Office, 11 Apr.).

—— (2009) *The National Programme for IT in the NHS: Progress since 2006* (London: Stationery Office, 14 Jan.).

—— (2011) *The National Programme for IT in the NHS: An Update on the Delivery of the Detailed Care Records System* (London: The Stationery Office, 3 Aug.).

Howarth, B., and Ledwidge, J. (2011) *A Faster Future: Broadband and What it Means for Business, Society and You* (Sydney: Five Senses Education).

Hudson, B. (2005) 'Information Sharing and Children's Services Reform in England: Can Legislation Change Practice?', *Journal of Interprofessional Care*, 19(6): 537–46.

Hudson, J. (2002) 'Digitizing the Structures of Government: The UK's Information Age Government Agenda', *Policy and Politics*, 30(4): 515–31.

Hughes, O. E. (2008) *Public Management and Administration: An Introduction* (3rd edn, London: Palgrave).

Hutchby, I. (2001) 'Technologies, Texts and Affordances', *Sociology*, 35(2): 441–56.

Inglis, S. I., Clark, R. A., McAlister, F. A., Ball, J., Lewinter, C., Cullington, D., Stewart, S., and Cleland, J. G. F. (2010) 'Structured Telephone Support or Tele-monitoring Programmes for Patients with Chronic Heart Failure', *Cochrane Database of Systematic Reviews*, 8.

Institute of Medicine (2009) *Health and Human Sciences in the 21st Century: Charting a New Course for a Healthier America* (New York: National Academies Press).

Jenkings, K. N., and Wilson, R. G. (2007) 'The Challenge of Electronic Health Records (EHRs) Design and Implementation: Responses of Health Workers to Drawing a "Big and Rich Picture" of a Future EHR Programme Using Animated Tools', *Informatics in Primary Care*, 15(2): 93–101.

Johnson, A. (2007) 'Putting People First', speech given at the launch of the Social Care Reform Concordat, 10 Dec., <http://www.dh.gov.uk/en/News/Speeches/DH_081194> (accessed Aug. 2009).

Johnson, B. (2007) '"We should Assume the Worst": What to Do if you are one of 7 Million Families Involved', *Guardian*, 21 Nov.

Johnson, S. (2010) 'ATO Explains IT "bungle"', *The Australian*, 23 Apr.

Jolly, R. (2012) *The e-Health Revolution: Easier Said than Done* (Parliamentary Library Research Paper, 3, 2011–12; Canberra: Parliament of Australia, Nov.).

Kensing, F., and Blomberg, J. (1998) 'Participatory Design: Issues and Concerns', *Computer Supported Co-operative Work*, 7: 167–85.

Kerfoot, D., and Korczynski, M. (2005) 'Gender and Service: New Directions for the Study of "Front-Line" Service Work', *Gender, Work and Organisation*, 12(5): 387–99.

Kings College London and the University of Reading (2004) *At Home with AT: Introducing Assistive Technologies into the Existing Homes of Older People* (London: Institute of Gerontology, Kings College).

Kinsella, K., and Wan He (2009) *An Ageing World: 2008* (US Census Bureau International Population Reports P95/09-1; Washington, DC: US Government Printing Office).

Klijn, E. H. (2002) 'Governing Networks and the Hollow State: Contracting out, Process Management or a Combination of the Two?', *Public Management Review*, 4(2): 149–65.

Kling, R., Crawford, H., Rosenbaum, H., Sawyer, S., and Weisband, S. (2000) *Learning from Social Informatics: Information and Communication Technologies in Human Contexts* (Bloomington, Ind.: Center for Social Informatics, Indiana University).

Kodner, D., and Spreeuwenberg, C. (2002) 'Integrated Care: Meaning, Logic, Applications, and Implications: A Discussion Paper', *International Journal of Integrated Care*, 2: 1–8.

Kraemer, K., and King, J. L. (2006) 'Information Technology and Administrative Reform: Will the Time After e-Government be Different?', *International Journal of e-Government Research*, 2(1): 1–20.

Laming, L. (2003) *The Victoria Climbié Inquiry: Report of an Inquiry by Lord Laming* (London: HMSO).

Lau, E. (2005) *E-Government for Better Government* (Paris: OECD).

Law, A., and Mooney, G. (2007) 'Strenuous Welfarism', in G. Mooney and A. Law (eds), *New Labour/Hard Labour? Restructuring and Resistance inside the Welfare Industry* (Bristol: Policy Press), 23–51.

Layne, K., and Lee, J. (2001) 'Developing Fully Functional e-Government: A Four Stage Model', *Government Information Quarterly*, 18: 122–36.

Lee, Z., and Lee, J. (2000) 'An ERP Implementation Case Study from a Knowledge Transfer Perspective', *Journal of Information Technology*, 15: 281–8.

Lefevre, H. (1991) *The Production of Space* (Oxford: Oxford University Press).

Leibert, A. (2004) 'The National Smartcard Project: A Great Start...' *e-Gov Monitor Weekly*, 13 Sept. <http://www.egovmonitor.com/features/alco.html> (accessed Jan. 2008).

Leutz, W. N. (1999) 'Five Laws for Integrating Medical and Social Services: Lesson from the United States and the United Kingdom', *Milbank Quarterly*, 77(1): 77–110.

—— (2005) 'Reflections on Integrating Medical and Social Care: Five Laws Revisited', *Journal of Integrated Care*, 13(5): 3–11.

Lewis, I. (2006) Speech given at the commission for social care inspector's annual conference, 29 June, Available at: <http://www.dh.gov.uk/en/News/Speeches/Speecheslist/DH_4137064> (accessed July 2009).

Li, F. (ed.) (2007) *Social Implications and Challenges of e-Business* (London: Information Science Reference).

Ling, T. (2002) 'Delivering Joined-up Government in the UK: Dimensions, Issues and Problems', *Public Administration*, 80(4): 615–42.

Lips, A. M. B. (2008) Keynote Address to the 4th International Conference on e-Government, RMIT University, Melbourne, Australia, 23–4 October.

—— and Schuppan, T. (2009) 'Transforming e-Government Knowledge through Public Management Research', *Public Management Review*, 11(6): 739–49.

—— Taylor, J. A., and Organ, J. (2009*a*) 'Managing Citizen Identity in e-Government Service Relationships in the UK', *Public Management Review*, 11(6): 833–56.

—— and (2009*b*) 'Identity Management, Administrative Sorting and Citizenship in New Modes of Government', *Information, Communication and Society*, 12(5): 715–34.

Lipsky, M. (1980) *Street Level Bureaucracy: Dilemmas of the Individual in Public Services* (New York: Russell Sage Foundation).

—— (2010) *Street Level Bureaucracy: Dilemmas of the Individual in Public Services*, expanded edn (New York: Russell Sage Foundation).

Lupton, C., North, N., and Kahn, P. (2001) *Working Together or Pulling Apart? The National Health Service and Child Protection Networks* (Bristol: Polity Press).

Lyons, D. (2007) *Place-Shaping: A Shared Ambition for the Future of Local Government* (London: The Stationery Office).

—— and Stone, D (2008) 'President 2.0', *Newsweek*, 21 Nov.

McIvor, R., McHugh, M., and Cadden, C. (2004) 'The Potential of Internet Technologies: Insights from the Public Sector', *New Technology, Work and Employment*, 19(1): 63–80.

McLoughlin, I. P. (1999) *Creative Technological Change: The Shaping of Technology and Organization* (London: Routledge).

—— (2009) 'Technological and Organizational Change in UK Local Public Services', in C. G. Reddick (ed.), *Strategies for Local e-Government Adoption and Implementation* (Hershey, Pa.: IGI Global), 121–35.

—— (2010) 'Imaginary Friends? The Role of Organizational Ethnography in the Social Shaping of Technology', paper presented at 26th EGOS Colloquium, Lisbon, Portugal.

—— and Badham, R. (2005) 'Political Process Perspectives on Organization and Technological Change', *Human Relations*, 58(7): 827–43.

—— and Clark, J. (1994) *Technological Change at Work* (2nd rev. edn, Buckingham: Open University Press).

—— and Cornford, J. (2006) 'Transformational Change in the Local State? Enacting e-Government in English Local Authorities', *Journal of Management and Organisation*, 12(3): 195–208.

—— et al. (2004) *Final Report of the Advanced Multi-Agency Service Environments (AMASE) Project* (Newcastle upon Tyne: Newcastle Centre for Social and Business Informatics, University of Newcastle upon Tyne).

—— Maniatopoulos, G., Wilson, R., and Martin, M. (2009) 'Hope to Die Before you Get Old? Techno-centric versus User-Centred Approaches in Developing Virtual Services for Older People', *Public Management Review*, 11(6): 857–80.

Maniatopoulos, G., McLoughlin, I. P., Wilson, R. G., and Martin, M. J. (2009) 'Developing Virtual Healthcare Systems in Complex Multi-Agency Service Settings: The OLDES Project', *Electronic Journal of e-Government*, 7(2): 163–70.

Margetts, H. (2006) 'E-Government in Britain: A Decade on', *Parliamentary Affairs*, 59(2): 250–65.

Martin, M. J. (2006) 'E-Government Evolution: Technical and Organizational Trajectories', Centre for Social and Business Informatics, University of Newcastle upon Tyne, unpublished paper.

—— (2007) 'Representing Identity and Relationships in Information Systems: Research Note', *International Journal of Business Science and Applied Management*, 2(1): 48–51.

—— (2010) 'ERDIP Revisited', Centre for Social and Business Informatics, University of Newcastle upon Tyne, unpublished paper, available at <http://www.ncl.ac.uk/kite/assets/downloads/DDEHR.pdf>.

—— (2011) 'The Architectural Discourse of Organizational Systems: Addressing Issues of Expressiveness and Rigor in the Specification of the Socio-technical', Centre for Social and Business Informatics, University of Newcastle upon Tyne, unpublished paper.

—— (2013) 'Information economies for social care: copy and paste or learning from ecommerce?', *Public Money and Management*, 33(3): 167–8.

Martin, M. J., Bell, S., and Wilson, R. G. (2009) 'A Social Informatics Intervention: Theory, Method and Practice', Centre for Social and Business Informatics, University of Newcastle upon Tyne, unpublished paper.

May, C., Finch, T. L., Cornford, J., Exley, C., Gately, C., Kirk, S., Jenkings, K. N., Osbourne, J., Robinson, A. L., Rogers, A., Wilson, R., and Mair, F. S. (2011) 'Integrating Telecare for Chronic Disease Management in the Community: What Needs to be Done?', *BMC Health Services Research*, 11(1): 131.

—— Mort, M., Mair, F., and Williams, T. (2001) 'Factors Affecting the Adoption of Telehealthcare in the United Kingdom: The Policy Context and the Problem of Evidence', *Health Informatics Journal*, 7(3–4): 131–4.

Mayer-Schonbergger, V., and Lazer, D. (2007) 'From Electronic Government to Information Government', in V. Mayer-Schonbergger and D. Lazer (eds), *From Electronic Government to Information Government* (Cambridge, Mass.: MIT Press).

Maynard-Moody, S., and Musheno, M. (2003) *Cops, Teachers and Counselors: Stories from the Front Line of Public Service* (Chicago: University of Michigan Press).

Milligan, C., Roberts, C., and Mort, M. (2011) 'Telecare and Older People: Who Cares Where?', *Social Science and Medicine*, 72: 347–54.

Mitlin, D. (2008) 'With and beyond the State: Co-production as a Route to Political Influence, Power and Transformation for Grassroots Organizations', *Environment and Urbanization*, 20(2): 339–60.

Monteiro, E., Pollock, N., Hanseth, O., and Williams, R. (2012) 'From Artefacts to Infrastructures', *Computer Supported Cooperative Work* (June).

Moore, M., and Hartley, J. (2008) 'Innovations in Governance', *Public Management Review*, 10(1): 3–20.

More, D. (2011) 'The AMA and Others are Stiffening its Opposition to the PCEHR: Minister Roxon should be Really Worried', blog post, 27 Sept., available at <http://aushealthit.blogspot.com/2011/09/ama-and-others-are-s tiffening-its.html> (accessed Oct. 2011).

Mort, M., Finch, T., and May, C. (2009) 'Making and Unmaking Telepatients: Identity and Governance in New Health Technologies', *Science, Technology and Human Values*, 34(1): 9–33.

—— May, C., and Williams, T. (2003) 'Remote Doctors and Absent Patients: Acting at a Distance in Telemedicine', *Science Technology Human Values*, 28(2) (Apr.): 274–95.

Mráz, M., Roubíček, T., Haluzíková, D., Bošanská, L., Novák, D., Vratislav, F., Štepánková, O., and Haluzík, M. (2008) 'OLDES: A Novel Concept Supporting Elderly People at Homes by a Combination of Entertainment and Health Care Platforms', paper at the 12th World Multi-Conference on Systemics, Cybernetics and Informatics (WMSCI 2008), Florida.

Mulgan, G. (2006) 'Social Innovation: What is it, Why it Matters, How it can be Accelerated', Young Foundation <www.youngfoundation.org.uk> (accessed Jan. 2012).

—— and Albury, D. (2003) *Innovation in the Public Sector* (London: Strategy Unit, Cabinet Office).

Murakami-Wood, D., Ball, K., Lyon, D., Norris, C., and Raab, C. (2006) *A Report on the Surveillance Society for the Information Commissioner by the Surveillance Studies Network*, Full Report, Sept., available at <http://www.ico. gov.uk/upload/documents/library/data_protection/practical_application/ surveillance_society_full_report_2006.pdf>.

Murphy, Lawrence, Parness, Paul, Mitchell, Daniel L., Hallett, Rebecca, Cayley, Paula, and Seagram, Samantha (2009) 'Client Satisfaction and Outcome Comparisons of Online and Face-to-Face Counselling Methods', *British Journal of Social Work*, 39: 627–40.

NAO (2008) *The National Programme for IT in the NHS: Progress since 2006* (London: The Stationery Office, 12 May).

—— (2011) *The National Programme for IT in the NHS: An Update on the Delivery of Detailed Care Records Systems* (London: The Stationery Office, 17 May).

Needham, C. (2008) 'Realizing the Potential of Co-production: Negotiating Improvements in Public Services', *Social Policy and Society*, 7(2): 221–31.

—— and Carr, S. (2009) *Co-production: An Emerging Evidence Base for Adult Social Care Transformation* (London: NESTA).

Negroponte, N. (1970) *The Architecture Machine: Towards a More Human Environment* (Cambridge, Mass.: MIT Press).

NEHRT (2000) *A Health Information Network for Australia* (Canberra: Commonwealth of Australia).

Nettleton, S., and Burrows, R. (2003) 'E-Scaped Medicine? Information, Reflexivity and Health', *Critical Social Policy*, 23(2): 165–85.

NHIMAC (1999) *Health On-Line* (Canberra: NHIMAC).

NHS (2010) *Liberating the NHS: An Information Revolution* (London: Department of Health, Oct. 2010).

Nicolini, D. (2007) 'Stretching out and Expanding Work Practices in Time and Space: The Case of Telemedicine', *Human Relations*, 60(6): 889–920.

Novak, D., Stepankova, O., Mraz, M., and Haluzik, M. (2008) 'OLDES: Improved Welfare for Diabetic Patients', 3rd International Conference on Quality and Efficiency in Healthcare, Prague.

OECD (2003) *The e-Government Imperative* (OECD e-Government Studies; Paris: OECD).

—— (2009) *Rethinking e-Government Services: User-Centered Approaches* (OECD e-government studies: Paris: OECD).

Office of the Deputy Prime Minister (2002) *The National Strategy for Local e-Government* (London: ODPM).

O'Leary, Z. (2004) *The Essential Guide to Doing Research* (London: Sage).

Oliver, Lynn E., and Sanders, L. (2004) 'Introduction', in Lynn E. Oliver and L. Sanders (eds), *E-Government Reconsidered: Renewal of Governance for the Knowledge Age* (Regina, Saskatchewan: University of Regina), pp. i–xiv.

O'Neill, R. (2009) 'The Transformative Impact of e-Government on Public Governance in New Zealand', *Public Management Review*, 11(6): 751–70.

Organ, J. (2003) 'The Co-ordination of e-Government in Historical Context', *Public Policy and Administration*, 18(2): 21–36.

Orlikowski, W. J. (1992) 'The Duality of Technology: Rethinking the Concept of Technology in Organizations', *Organization Science*, 3(3): 398–427.

—— (2000) 'Using Technology and Constituting Structures: A Practice Lens for Studying Technology in Organizations', *Organization Science*, 11(4): 404–28.

—— (2007) 'Sociomaterial Practices: Exploring Technology at Work', *Organizational Studies*, 28(9): 1435–48.

—— (2010) 'The Sociomateriality of Organizational Life: Considering Technology in Management Research', *Cambridge Journal of Economics*, 34(1): 125–41.

—— and Scott, S. V. (2008) 'Chapter 10: Sociomateriality: Challenging the Separation of Technology, Work and Organization', *Academy of Management Annals*, 2(1): 433–74.

Ostrom, E. (1996) 'Crossing the Great Divide: Coproduction, Synergy and Development', *World Development*, 24(6): 1073–87.

—— and Baugh, W. H. (1973) *Community Organization and the Provision of Police Services* (Beverly Hills, Calif.: Sage).

Oudshoorn, N. (2008) 'Diagnosis at a Distance: The Invisible Work of Patients and Healthcare Professionals in Cardiac Telemonitoring Technology', *Sociology of Health and Illness*, 30(2): 272–88.

—— and Pinch, T. (2003) 'Users and Non-Users as Active Agents in the De-stabilization of Technologies', in N. Oudshoorn and T. Pinch (eds), *How Users Matter: The Co-construction of Users and Technology* (Boston: MIT Press), 1–25.

Parker, S., and Parker, S. (eds) (2007) *Unlocking Innovation: Why Citizens Hold the Key to Public Service Reform* (London: Demos).

Parry, L., and Thomson, L. (1993) *Effective Sheltered Housing: A Handbook* (London: Longman).

Peck, E., and 6, P. (2006) *Beyond Delivery: Policy Implementation as Sense-Making and Settlement* (London: Palgrave Macmillan).

Peckover, S., White, S., and Hall, C. (2008) 'Making and Managing Electronic Children: E-Assessment in Child Welfare', *Information, Communication and Society*, 11(3): 375–94.

Peltu, M., Eason, K., and Clegg, S. (2008) 'How a Sociotechnical Approach can Help NPfIT Deliver Better NHS Patient Care', unpublished paper available at <http://lubswww2/COSLAC/index.php?id=54> and <http://www.bcs.org/server.php?show=nav.9932>.

Percival, J., Hanson, J., and Osipovič, D. (2009) 'Perspectives on Telecare: Implications for Autonomy, Support and Social Inclusion', in B. D. Loader, M. Hardey, and L. Keeble (eds), *Third Age Welfare: Health and Social Care Informatics for Older People* (London: Routledge), 49–62.

Pestoff, V., and Brandsen, T. (2007) *Co-production: The Third Sector and the Delivery of Public Services* (London: Routledge).

Pierce, C. S. (1998) *The Essential Writings* (2nd edn, New York: Prometheus).

Pithouse, A., Hall, C., Peckover, S., and White, S. (2009) 'A Tale of Two CAFs: The Impact of the Electronic Common Assessment Framework', *British Journal of Social Work*, 39: 599–612.

Pollitt, C. (2003) *The Essential Public Manager* (Maidenhead: Open University Press).

Pollock, N. (1984) 'Realising e-Government: Shifting and Deferring Ambiguity in the Procurement of a Software Package', unpublished paper, Centre for Social and Business Information, University of Newcastle upon Tyne.

—— (2004) *Messy Technologies: Or Where Capacities Cannot be Read Off* (Newcastle upon Tyne: Newcastle Centre for Social and Business Informatics, University of Newcastle upon Tyne).

—— and Cornford, J. (2005) 'ERP Systems and the University as a "Unique" Organisation', *Information Technology and People*, 17(1): 31–52.

Ponsard, C., Martin, M., Walsh, S., Baines, S., Rousseaux, S., Rinaldi, G., and Tamburriello, F. (2008) 'OLDES: Designing a Low-Cost, Easy-to-Use e-Care System Together with the Stakeholders', in K. Miesenberger, K. Joachim, W. L. Zagler, and A. I. Karshmer (eds), *Computers Helping People with Special Needs*, 11th International Conference 9–11 July, Linz, Austria, *Lecture Notes in Computer Science*, 5105/2008: 1285–92.

Powell, J. (2009) 'Networked Carers: Digital Exclusion or Digital Empowerment', in B. Loader, M. Hardey, and L. Keeble (eds), *Digital Welfare for the Third Age: Health and Social Care Informatics for Older People* (Abingdon: Routledge), 76–88.

Poynter, K. (2008) *A Review of Information Security at HMRC: Final Report* (London: HM Treasury, June).

Prencipe, A. (2003) 'Corporate Strategy and Systems Integration Capabilities: Managing Networks in Complex System Industries', in A. Davies, A. Prencipe, and M. Hobday (eds), *The Business of System Integration* (Oxford: Oxford University Press), 114–32.

Publicnet Briefing (2009) 'Care Costs: Councils Explore High Tech Solutions', available at <http://www.publicnet.co.uk/news/2009/10/20/care-costs-counc ils-explore-high-tech-solutions> (accessed Aug. 2010).

Purves, I. (2002) 'Concepts in Health Informatics', in L. Simpson and P. Robinson (eds), *E-Clinical Governance: A Guide for Primary Care* (Abingdon: Radcliffe Medical Press).

PwC (2013) *A Review of the Potential Benefits for Health and Social Care from the Better Use of Informational Technology* (London: Department of Health).

Randell, B. (2007) 'A Computer Scientist's Reactions to NPfIT', *Journal of Information Technology*, 22(3): 222–34.

Reason, P., and Bradbury, H. (2001) *Handbook of Action Research: Participative Enquiry and Practice* (London: Sage)

—— and (2008) *Handbook of Action Research: Participative Enquiry and Practice* (2nd edn, London: Sage).

Reed, J., Cook, G., Childs, S., and McCormack, B. (2005) 'A Literature Review to Explore Integrated Care for Older People', *International Journal of Integrated Care*, 5: 1–8.

Richter, P., and Cornford J. (2007) 'Customer Focus in UK e-Government: Or, Putting the Politics back into e-Government', *International Journal of Business Science and Applied Management*, 2(1): 34–46.

—— and (2008) 'Customer Relationship Management and Citizenship: Technologies and Identities in Public Services', *Social Policy and Society,* 7(2): 211–20.

—— and McLoughlin, I. P. (2004) 'The e-Citizen as Talk, as Text and as Technology: CRM and e-Government', *Electronic Journal of e-Government,* 2(3), 207–18.

—— and Wilson, R. (2013) '"It's the Tip of the Iceberg": The Hidden Tensions between Theory, Policy and Practice in the Management of Freedom of Information in English Local Government bodies. Evidence from a Regional Study', *Public Money and Management,* 33(3): 177–85.

Rinaldi, G., Martin, M., and Gaddi, A. (2011) 'Establishing an Infrastructure for Telecare: Combining the Socio-technical and the Clinical', *Handbook of Digital Homecare Communications in Medical and Care Compunetics,* 3: 43–66.

Robinson, M., and Cottrell, D. (2005) 'Health Professionals in Multi-Disciplinary and Multi-Agency Teams: Changing Professional Practice', *Journal of Interprofessional Care,* 19(6): 547–60.

Röhracher, H. (ed.) (2005) *User Involvement in Innovation Processes: Strategies and Limitations from a Socio-technical Perspective* (Munich: Profil-Verlag).

Roxon, N. (2011) 'Release of Draft eHealth Legislation', press release (Canberra: Department of Health and Ageing), <http://www.health.gov.au/internet/ministers/publishing.nsf/Content/mr-yr11-nr-nr195.htm> (accessed Oct. 2011).

Schön, D. A. (1983) *The Reflective Practitioner* (Aldershot: Avebury).

Sheikh, A., Cornford, T., Barber, N., Avery, A., Takian, A., Lichtner, V., Petrakaki D., Crowe, S., Marsden, K., Robertson, A., Morrison, Z., Klecun, E., Prescott, R., Quinn, C., Jani, Y., Ficociello, M., Voutsina, K., Paton, J., Fernando, B., Jacklin, A., and Cresswell, K. (2011) 'Implementation and Adoption of Nationwide Electronic Health Records in Secondary Care in England: Final Qualitative Results from Prospective National Evaluation in "Early Adopter" Hospitals', *British Medical Journal,* 343: d6054, publ. online, 17 Oct.

Silcock, R. (2001) 'What is e-Government?', *Parliamentary Affairs,* 54(1): 88–101.

Slay, J. (2011) *Personal Budgets and Beyond: What Co-production can Offer Personalisation* (London: NESTA).

Star, S. L., and Ruhdler, K. (1996) 'Steps toward an Ecology of Infrastructure: Design and Access for Large Information Spaces', *Information Systems Research,* 7: 111–33.

Stam, K., Stanton, J., and Guzman, R. (2004) 'Employee Resistance to Digital Information and Information Technology Change in a Social Service Agency: A Membership Category Approach', *Journal of Digital Information,* 5(4): 10–20.

Stevenson, A., Bardsley, M., Billings, J., Dixon, J., Doll, H., Hirani, S., Cartwright, M., Rixon, L., Knapp, M., Henderson, C., Rogers, A., Fitzpatrick, R., Hendy, J., and Newman, S. (2012) 'Effect of Telehealth on Use of Secondary Care and Mortality: Findings from the Whole System Demonstrator Cluster Randomised Trial', *British Medical Journal,* 345: e4622.

Stewart, J., and Williams, R. (2005) 'The Wrong Trousers? Beyond the Design Fallacy. Social Learning and the User', in H. Röhracher (ed.), *User Involvement in Innovation Processes: Strategies and Limitations from a Socio-technical Perspective* (Munich: Profil-Verlag).

Stillman, L., Herselman, M., Marais, M., Boshomane, M. P., Plantinga, P., and Walton, S. (2010) 'Digital Doorway: Social-Technical Innovation for High-Needs Communities', unpublished paper.

Stroetmann, K., Artmann, J., Stroetmann, V. N., Protti, D., Dumortier, J., Giest, S., Walossek, U., and Whitehouse, D. (2011) *European Countries on their Journey towards National eHealth Infrastructures: Evidence on Progress and Recommendations for Cooperative Actions*, Final European Progress Report, European Commission. <http://www.e-health-com.eu/fileadmin/user_upload/dateien/Downloads/eHealthStrategies_Final_Report.pdf>.

Sugden, R., Wilson, R. G., and Cornford, J. R. (2008) 'Reconfiguring the Health Supplier Market: Changing Relationships in the Primary Care Supplier Market in England', *Health Informatics Journal*, 14(2): 113–24.

Sullivan, H., and Skelcher, C. (2002) *Working across Boundaries: Collaboration in Public Services* (New York: Palgrave Macmillan).

Suter, E., Oelke, N., Adair, C., and Armitage, G. (2009) 'Ten Key Principles for Successful Health Systems Integration', *Healthcare Quarterly*, 13: 16–23.

Systems Thinking for Girls (2013) '3 Reasons Why Human by Default is Better than Digital by Default', Blog, 18 April, available at http://systemsthinkingforgirls.com/2013/04/18/3-reasons-why-human-by-default-is-better-than-digital-by-default/ (consulted May, 2013).

Taylor, J. A., Lips, A. M. B., and Organ, J. (2007) 'Information-Intensive Government and the Layering and Sorting of Citizenship', *Public Money and Management*, 7(2): 161–4.

Teicher, J., and Dow, N. (2002) 'E-Government in Australia: Promise and Progress', *Information Polity*, 7: 231–46.

Trist, E. L., and Barnforth, K. (1951) 'Social and Psychological Consequences of Longwall Coal Mining', *Human Relations*, 4(3): 3–38.

United Nations (2008) *E-Government Survey 2008: From e-Government to Connected Governance* (New York: United Nations).

—— (2010) *E-Government Survey 2010: Leveraging e-Government at a Time of Financial and Economic Crisis* (New York: United Nations).

—— (2012) *E-Government Survey 2012: E-Government for the People* (New York: United Nations).

Varney, David (2006) *Service Transformation: A Better Service for Citizens and Businesses, a Better Deal for the Taxpayer* (London: HM Treasury).

Vaughan, R., Bell, S., Cornford, J., McLoughlin, I. P., Martin, M., and Wilson, R. (2003) 'Information Systems Development in Public Sector Organizations: Working with Stakeholders to Make Sense of What Information Systems might Do', paper presented at European Group on Organizational Studies Annual Colloquium, Copenhagen, July.

—— Martin, M. J., Wilson, R. G., Gannon-Leary, P. M., Baines, S., Walsh, S., Carr, J., and Cornford, J. R. (2006) *FAME Generic Framework Guidance and*

Readiness Assessment Toolkit, On-line Patent (London: Office of the Deputy Prime Minister), available at <http://www.fame-uk.org>.

Walker, P. (2001) *Tell No Secrets, Tell No Lies* (Birmingham: NHS Information Authority).

Walsh, S., Wilson, R., Baines, S., and Martin, M. (2012) '"You're Just Treating us as Informants!" Roles, Responsibilities and Relationships in the Production of Children's Services Directories', *Local Government Studies*, 38(6): 1–20.

Wanless, D. (2002) *Securing our Future Health: Taking a Long-Term View* (London: HM Treasury).

Ward, C. (n.d.) 'Walter Segal: Community Architect' available at: <http://www.segalselfbuild.co.uk/news/waltersegalbycol.html> (accessed July 2012).

Webster, A. (2009) 'Information and Communication Technologies and Health Care: User-Centered Devices and Patient Work', in B. Loader, M. Hardey, and L. Keeble (eds), *Digital Welfare for the Third Age: Health and Social Care Informatics for Older People* (Abingdon: Routledge), 63–75.

Wessels, B., and Bagnall, V. (2002) *Information and the Joining up of Services: The Case of an Information Guide for Parents of Disabled Children* (Bristol: Policy Press).

—— Walsh, S., and Adam, E. (2008) 'Mediating Voices: Community Participation in the Design of e-Enabled Community Care Services', *Information Society*, 24: 30–9.

West, D. M. (2005) *Digital Government: Technology and Public Sector Performance* (Princeton: Princeton University Press).

Whitaker, G. (1980) 'Co-production: Citizen Participation in Service Delivery', *Public Administration Review*, 40: 240–6.

White, S., Wastell, D., Broadhurst, K., and Hall, C. (2010) 'When Policy Overleaps itself: The "Tragic Tale" of the Integrated Children's System', *Critical Social Policy*, 30(3): 405–29.

Whitney, G., and Keith, S. (2006) 'Active Ageing through Universal Design', *Gereontech Journal*, 5(3): 125–8.

WHO (2002) *Active Ageing a Policy Framework* (Geneva: WHO).

Wigfall, V., and Moss, P. (2001) *More than the Sum of its Parts? A Study of a Multi-Agency Child Care Network* (London: National Children's Bureau).

Williams, R., and Pollock, N. (2008) *Software and Organizations: The Biography of Enterprise-Wide Systems or How SAP Conquered the World* (London: Routledge).

—— Stewart, J., and Slack, R. (2005) *Social Learning in Technological Innovation: Experimenting with Information and Communication Technologies* (Cheltenham: Edward Elgar).

Wilson, R. G. (2012) 'Joining-up or Joining-up the Joining-up? Integration and Over-Integration in Health and Social Care', doctoral statement, University of Newcastle upon Tyne.

—— and Baines, S. (2009) 'Are there Limits to the Integration of Care for Older People?', in B. D. Loader, M. Hardey, and L. Keeble (eds), *Third Age Welfare: Health and Social Care Informatics for Older People* (London: Routledge), 17–27.

—— Cornford, J. R., and Martin, M. J. (2007a) '"Trying to Do a Jigsaw without the Picture on the Box": Understanding the Challenges of Care Integration in the Context of Single Assessment for Older People in England', *International Journal of Integrated Care*, 7: 1–11.

—— and Martin M. J. (2012) 'Innovation and Information in Public/Third Sector Partnerships for Older People's Services: Case Studies from England and Italy', in S. Osborne (ed.), *Handbook of Public Service Innovation* (London: Routledge).

—— Martin, M. J., and Vaughan, R. (2004) 'A Case Study of Governance in Public Sector Virtual Organisations: The Emergence of Children's Trusts', in L. Camarinba-Matos (eds), *Virtual Enterprises and Collaborative Networks* (New York: Kluwer Academic), 541–50.

—— Cornford, J. R., Baines, S., and Mawson, J. (2011a) 'Information for Localism? Policy Sensemaking for Local Governance', *Public Money and Management*, 31(4): 295–300.

—— Martin, M. J., Walsh, S., and Richter, P. (2011b) 'Re-mixing the Digital Economies of Care in the Voluntary and Community Sector (VCS): Governing Identity and Information Sharing in the Mixed Economy of Care for Children and Young People', *Social Policy and Society*, 10(3): 379–91.

—— Walsh, S., and Vaughan, R. (2007b) 'Developing an Electronic Social Care Record: A Tale from the Tyne', *Informatics in Primary Care*, 15(4): 239–44.

Wintour, P., (2007) 'Privacy Watchdog Calls for Power to Carry Out Spot Checks', *Guardian*, 21 Nov.

Woolgar, S. (2002) 'Five Rules of Virtuality', in S. Woolgar (ed.), *Virtual Society? Technology, Cyberbole, Reality* (Oxford: Oxford University Press), 1–22.

Yang, K. (2003) 'Neo-institutionalism and e-Government: Beyond Jane Fountain', *Social Science Computer Review*, 21(4): 432–42.

Zammuto, R. F., Griffith, T. L., Majchrzak, A., Dougherty, D. J., and Faraj, S. (2007) 'Information Technology and the Changing Fabric of Organization', *Organization Science*, 18(5): 749–62.

Zuboff, S. (1988) *In the Age of the Smart Machine* (Cambridge, Mass.: Harvard University Press).

Name Index

Name Index

Fountain, J. 7, 9, 13–14, 21–3, 35, 40–3, 45, 54–5, 99, 113, 118, 131, 162, 164–5
Frederickson, H. G. 96
Friedman, A. L. and Cornford, D. S. 66

Gannon-Leary, P. M. et al. 121
Garrety, K. et al. 81, 84
Gauld, R. and Goldfinch, S. 9, 53
Gershon, P. 20, 25
Gibbons, M. et al. 173
Glasby, J. 52, 59–60
Glasby, J. and Dickinson, H. 58
Glasby, J. and Peck, E. 60
Glendinning, C. 58
Goddard, J. and Cornford, J. 56
Goodhue, D. L. et al 56–7
Gore, A. J. 6, 22
Gottschalk, P. 67
Granovetter, M. 69
Gray, A. 96
Green, A. et al. 73, 75
Greenhalgh, T. et al. 81, 84, 87–8
Gulledge, T. 56–7

Hackl, W. O. et al. 81
Halford, S. et al. 136
Hambleton, S. 84
Hanseth, O. et al. 63
Hanson, J. et al. 139, 141
Hardey, M. et al. 136, 138–9
Harris, M. 84
Harris, M. et al. 7, 53–4
Harrison, S. 116
Hartley, J. 9, 27–9
Hartswood, M. et al. 141–2
Hasselbring, W. 57
Haynes, P. 116
Heath, D. 94
Hebson, G. et al. 116
Heeks, R. 7, 35–7, 53
Henwood, F. and Hart, A. 116
Hoffman, S. and Podgursky, A. 23
Hood, C. C. 72
Hood, C. C. and Margetts, H. Z. 8
Howarth, B. and Ledwidge, J. 137
Hudson, J. 20, 58, 75
Hughes, O. E. 6, 24, 53–4
Hutchby, I. 46–7

Inglis, S. J. et al. 136

Jenkings, K. N. and Wilson, R. G. 88–91, 175
Johnson, A. 71

Johnson, B. 96
Johnson, S. 25
Jolly, R. 86

Kensing, F. and Bloomberg, J. 48
Kerfoot, D. and Korczynski, M. 114
Kinsella, K. and Wan, He 134
Klijn, E. H. 15
Kling, R. 8
Kling, R. et al. 8, 33
Kodner, D. and Spreeuwenberg, C. 58
Kraemer, K. and King, J. L. 13, 54–5

Laming, Lord 74
Lau, E. 19
Law, A. and Mooney, G. 116
Layne, K. and Lee, J. 16–17
Lee, Z. and Lee, J. 56
Lefevre, H. 10, 143, 163
Leibert, A. 99
Leigh, E. 83
Leonardie, P. M. and Barley, S. R. 44
Leutz, W. N. 58
Lewis, I. 71
Li, F. 9
Ling, T. 71
Lips, A. M. B. 6–7, 30
Lips, A. M. B. and Schuppan, T. 14, 31
Lips, A. M. B. et al. 93–5, 99
Lipsky, M. 113–14
Lloyd George, D. 79
Lukensmeyer, C. J. and Torres, L. H. 7
Lupton, C. et al. 73
Lyons, D. 20
Lyons, D. and Stone, D. 23

Margetts, H. 2–3, 7–8, 20–1, 26–7, 30, 162
Martin, M. J. 88, 90, 157, 170 1 n1
Martin, M. J. et al. 157
May, C. et al. 136
Mayer-Schonbergger, V. and Lazer, D. 18
Maynard-Moody, S. and Musheno, M. 114
Mbeki, President of South Africa 37
McIvor, R. et al. 72–3, 117
McLoughlin, I. P. 8–9, 33, 37, 40, 174
McLoughlin, I. P. and Badham, R. 8
McLoughlin, I. P. and Clark, J. 8
McLoughlin, I. P. and Cornford, J. 120–1
McLoughlin, I. P. et al. 143
Milligan, C. et al. 135
Mitlin, D. 132
Montiero, E. et al. 63, 67
Moore, M. and Hartley, J. 27, 30
More, D. 85
Mort, M. et al. 136, 139, 141

General Index

virtuality
  children's services and 73
  virtual agency 35, 50,
    53–5
  virtual health care 140–1
  virtual state 6–7, 13, 50
  virtual team 123

see also children's services, voluntary
  and community sector; digital
  government

Web 2.0 Government 6, 162
web portal 135
websites 27